SEP - 7 2002

The
Dilemmas
of Care

The
Dilemmas
of Care:
Social and Nursing Adaptions
to the Deformed, the Disabled
and the Aged

Ronald Philip Preston

ELSEVIER · NEW YORK
New York · Oxford

Exclusive Distribution
throughout the World by
Greenwood Press, Westport,
Ct. U.S.A.

Elsevier North Holland, Inc.
52 Vanderbilt Avenue, New York, New York 10017

Distributors outside the United States and Canada:
Thomond Books
(A Division of Elsevier/North-Holland Scientific Publishers, Ltd.)
P.O. Box 85
Limerick, Ireland

Library of Congress Cataloging in Publication Data

Preston, Ronald Philip.
    The dilemmas of care: social and nursing adaptations to the deformed, the
    disabled and the aged.
    1. Nursing—Psychological aspects. 2. Humanism. 3. Hospitals—
    Sociological aspects. 4. Abnormalities, Human—Psychological
    aspects. 5. Philosophical anthropology. 6. Ambiguity. 7. Ambivalence.
    I. Title. [DNLM: 1.Long term care—Chronic disease—Nursing.
    2. Handicapped. 3. Philosophy, Nursing. 4. Attitude to health. WY152
    P939d]
RT86.P68   610.73′01′9   79-20414
ISBN 0-444-99068-2

Desk Editor   Louise Schreiber
Design   Edmée Froment
Art Assistant   José Garcia
Production Manager   Joanne Jay
Compositor   J.M. Post Graphics, Corp.
Printer   Haddon Craftsmen

Manufactured in the United States of America

I dedicate this book to Jennie and J. Wallace McDonald, my beautiful grandparents, whose mutual tenderness, devotion and courage before their own mortality sustained me in this work, and whose radiance yet brightens my life.

Contents

Acknowledgments

I wish to acknowledge Raymond S. Duff, Kai T. Erikson and Jerome K. Myers, all from Yale, whose encouragement and advice were vital to this project in all its stages.

I also wish to acknowledge all the many wonderful people with whom I worked in the hospital.

The
Dilemmas
of Care

HUMAN AMBIGUITY
AND THE GREGOR EFFECT

I

The Dilemma
of Ambiguous Man

In Franz Kafka's *The Metamorphosis*, Gregor Samsa awakens one morning to find that in appearance he has become a giant cockroach. Not entirely a roach, he retains human size, intelligence and his inner personality; yet, since his remaining attributes are those of a roach, he is not quite a man either. Gregor has become an acutely ambiguous man.

Gregor's former self had been a serious, industrious young man. A traveling salesman, he was the sole support of his family which consisted of his parents, a sister, and himself. He was the family's chief decision maker and a kindly big brother. His parents respected and depended on him. His sister loved him. Above all, Gregor considered himself indispensable to his family's economic well-being, and bore his responsibility gravely.

Upon realizing his plight, Gregor's first impulse is to follow his human routine to fulfill his social obligations, but he is quickly disabused of this notion. He can barely rock his armored body out of bed. Stupendous effort is required to stand upright to open the bedroom door. A truly human voice cannot be managed at all, and his appearance so horrifies people that normal human interaction is impossible.

Within a few hours of his change, Gregor substantially compromises his former identity. No longer is he a traveling salesman, the sole provider of his

1

family, an active family member or a citizen. He tries to spare his family by adjusting to his new status. Remaining in his room, Gregor hides from sight whenever anyone enters. However, some hold is maintained on his former pride and prerogatives. He cleans himself regularly, concerns himself with his family's welfare such as he can, and dreaming of freedom, peers from his window. Gregor expects to be fed and to have his room cleaned regularly.

As time wears on, Gregor grows more dispirited. He acts more like a roach and less like a man. His confinement and physique bar him from all human activity. The urge to crawl on the walls and hang from the ceiling becomes overwhelming. His family ignores him increasingly. Dust, fluff and hair cling to and trail from his body. He refuses to eat.

Ultimately, Gregor is soundly rejected by his family, and subsequently, he dies. Having waxed insensitive to his wretched appearance and to his family's welfare, he crawls into the drawing room to hear his sister who is playing the violin for the benefit of three boarders. Upon espying Gregor, the boarders become curious and then incensed. The family is mortified. His sister, his favorite, slams the door on him—after which Gregor drags himself back into his room to die.

Gregor's tale is a sorry one, but his is not the only tale in the story. The persons who cope with and care for Gregor live their own travail that ends not in sorrow but in relief.

From the onset of his affliction, Gregor cannot mingle with the general public. His position in the outer society is immediately forfeit. This situation, together with Gregor's presence, burden his family suddenly and crushingly. They must endure his appearance, compensate for his economic absence, seclude him from outsiders and suffer their grief at his fate and their own.

Initially, though they are ambivalent, the family treats Gregor with some consideration. They are repulsed by his appearance. They imprison him in his room to be spared the sight of him. Yet, they also maintain him as best they can. Gregor is fed regularly, his room is cleaned daily, and his furniture is removed so that he may have unrestricted movement. The family hopes for his rejuvenation.

The hope fades, the reality oppresses, and the family's perception of Gregor changes. Alternately, the family shrinks from and is angered with his presence. Financial matters are worked out; Gregor is no longer counted on for moral and financial support.

The family busies itself with diversions so that it is spared 5
attending to the son or reflecting on his ambiguity. Ultimately,
Gregor's care is foisted onto a charwoman who neither fears
Gregor nor sees his humanity.

At first, Gregor's family thinks of him as a son, partially
because his metamorphosis was so traumatic, but the roach does
not look like their son; neither does it act like their son. The
family has no rationale to account for the change and no formula
to set things right. As a result, the family gradually ceases to
think of the man-roach as their man-son. During the transition,
the relatives pass through a stage in which they attribute to the
man-roach responsibility for the son's fate and for its consequences for them. This period of hate marks a process of affective
separation. This reaction makes the man-roach more despondent.
Consequently, he behaves less like a normative person. This
shift away from human presentation enables the family to
strengthen its rejection. By dying and thus removing himself
further from manhood, and ultimately from sight, the son provides the final impetus for the family's resolution. The family
concludes that the roach was never their son.

What is a tragic ending for the son is a happy ending for the
family. The relatives have solved their problem and have turned
to optimistic musing concerning the daughter's future. Yet, the
problem was not resolved until its source was beyond perception,—dead and gone.

The Metamorphosis is fictional and bizarre, yet in essence its
scenario is real and common. In many repects, Gregor's fate is
shared by all persons who suffer gross and irremedial deformity;
but also this fate is an eventually for a multitude of men, those
who face their mortality in real and rote degeneration.

Is this story of a beloved grandfather so different from Gregor's?
Grandfather is rushed to the hospital with congestive heart
failure. The greater family is alerted, and there is a deluge of
cards and visits. After a normalizing dose of modern medicine,
grandpa comes along nicely, and holds court for his children and
grandchildren. He is both attentive and nimble minded, learning
all the nurses' names and regaling them with quips and stories.
Charmed, the nursing staff delights in his presence, and does
him little favors.

A week later grandfather suffers what seems to be a small
stroke which befuddles his brain. Conversion with him becomes
something of a strain. The progeny, but for certain grandchildren,
dutifully and sorrowfully continue to visit. Sometimes the vigil

6 is silent. The harried physician, always a gray presence, never seems available to answer the family's urgent questions. Grandpa does not seem to be getting the attentive care from the nursing staff that he received when he was "fun," and this development concerns some of the children. But, grandfather rallies again, and though racked and tottery, is discharged to go home with one of his daughters.

At home he is not the man he once was. He is unstable, cranky and demanding. He exhausts his daughter and irritates his son-in-law. She angers, and then feels remorse. She strives to treat grandpa respectfully, but finds herself treating him as a child which he deeply resents. Grandfather grows despondent. His unreliability makes having guests difficult, and in general reduces the social lives of his daughter and her spouse.

One morning his daughter finds that Dad has had another "spell." Again grandfather is hospitalized. This time the cards and visits are less numerous. There is talk that perhaps it is time for the old man "to go." Visitors become more fidgety than sorrowful. Grandpa is messing his bed and is unable to feed himself. Nurses and staff call him by his first name, talk at him loudly and deliberately and chat amiably with one another as they roll him this way and that to wash him and to make his bed. Some relatives begin to nag the nurses. Others schedule their visits so that they can feed grandpa. Grandfather begins to show some improvement, then stabilizes. It is time for discharge once again. Daughter has tearfully decided that she cannot take him again. So, he is sent to a convalescent home.

By this time almost all of the relatives are strongly ambivalent about grandpa. They are tired of the situation. They are annoyed at him. They feel sorry for him. Seeing him "this way" has become an increasingly burdensome responsibility. Yet, one member of the family remains resolute. His sister is convinced that his condition is due to a dearth of professional care. She is livid that he has not been provided with private duty nurses. She is certain that the proper medical specialist would cure her brother. In the nursing home, the sister visits grandpa every day, but the children "schedulize" their visits to twice a week, once a week, once every two weeks or not at all. For most, the visits are dues. Their eyes are averted from the conditions in the "home."

A month later, the relatives awaken to learn that the "home" has hospitalized grandpa. Now there is open consensus, but for the sister, that the old man's passing would be a blessing.

Woodenly, those who come stand around the swollen, heaving
form, his eyes clouded and mouth agape. Some hold his hand,
and talk to him loudly—deliberately. His eyes shift, his mouth
moves, nothing intelligible comes. Then the visitors find themselves talking with grandfather's roommate and his visitors. This
conversation grows convivial. The visit ends. Only the sister
cries at the funeral. It is a blessing.

The foregoing accounts of Gregor and the grandfather hardly
explicate the subtle yet powerful influence human abnormality
has upon people. Broadly, the consequences of deformity and
incapacity have always been known and bemoaned in story and
song. Contemporarily, the incomplete man has been scrutinized
socialogically and psychologically. His plight and adjustments
have been chronicled and dissected. Books and articles are readily
found concerning persons blind, deaf, insane, paralyzed, hemo-
philiac or otherwise physically stigmatized. Yet, another class of
consequences has not been examined so rigorously. This class is
the impact of human abnormality upon normative witnesses.
Gregor had an effect on those persons who beheld him, who
cared for and coped with him. An exploration of this effect, the
Gregor Effect, shall be the theme of this book.

To explain the significance that unwhole deformed or incapacitated men hold for mankind, I will discuss theoretically the
nature of man as it related to human frailty and mortality. I begin
by paraphrasing and expanding the relevant ideas of Ernest
Becker as they were developed in his latest two books: *The
Denial of Death* and *Escape From Evil*.

Ernest Becker:
Heroic Transcendence

According to Ernest Becker, man is a fearing animal, obsessed with his own vulnerability and mortality. He is an anomalous hybrid: part mind and part body. This mind allows man to see what no other animal can see: all living organisms die; all living organisms are in constant peril. " Man has a symbolic identity which brings him sharply out of nature."[1] He would be a godlike, ethereal being, yet his body anchors him to a mortal reality. Thus, man is anxious, and his fears of calamity and annihilation are potent movers.

Becker disagrees (as I do) with what he terms the "healthy minded" view of man—that men are not inherently anxious, that they do not naturally fear death or debility, that anxiety is inculcated into men by a repressive, twisting upbringing. This view holds that proper therapy or nurturance will rid men of needless inhibitions, and that then they will exhibit their innate equanimity and courage. Transcendental meditation, yoga or Zen Buddhism will tune one in to oneself and to the universe. The "primal scream" will purge primordial fears and resent-

[1]Ernest Becker, *The Denial of Death*, New York: Macmillian Free Press, 1973, p. 26.

2

ments. Psychotherapy will work it out. Life can be had with a beatific grin. "Bunk!" cries Becker. The ultimate mysteries of life and death hang over men every minute. The need for adjustment to a mercurial world is ever present. Insecurity is real and ultimately irremediable. All animals are anxious, and so is man. Indeed, he is more anxious for his capacity to perceive. So it is that men are primarily moved by the ongoing—existential— realities of human existence: the requisites of survival, an awareness of mortality and the problematic nature of a universe that is capricious and infinitely complex.

Having minds capable of idiosyncratic development, men are the most individuated of animals. Each man has his own face, his own personality. As individuals, men are universally narcissistic. As Freud maintained: "We are hopelessly absorbed with ourselves." Men are primarily concerned with their own survival, their own mortality, and their own adjustment to the world. In a vast and seemingly indifferent universe, men want to be individually significant, to be a head above the crowd. Yet, terror at uncertainty and mortality consigns men to immerse themselves in a social existence that offers security at a cost of all but minimal individuality. Equanimity comes at the expense of both myopia and illusion.

Men cope with their vulnerability and mortality by denying them. The first requisite of this denial is repression. In relation to man the universe is overwhelming; to witness its horrifying scope is to recognize the meager position that men hold in it. It is to realize the transience of human life. Also to give full vent to human imagination would undermine delicate denial systems. Thus, men suffer from the "Jonah Syndrome"—so named after the Biblical character who evaded God's commands because he thought himself inadequate. Men evade the true intensity of life; they do not live up to their potential; they simply lack the strength to bear the superlative.

> In these days then we understand that if the child were to give in to the overpowering character of reality and experience he would not be able to act with the kind of equanimity we need in our non-instinctive world. So one of the first things a child has to do is to learn to 'abandon ecstasy,' to do without awe, to leave fear and trembling behind.[2]

Men turn from the real world to a diminished world, to what

2*The Denial of Death*, p. 55.

10 Becker calls a 'second' world, a symbolic world of human fabrication, one which is manageable and in which death is disguised, explained or banished. This 'second' world shrinks the perceived world to a social stage upon which are acted fantasies of power, significance and permanance. Men are too feeble to feel strong in themselves. They would deny their 'creatureliness,' but in order to do this, they must transcend themselves by identifying with a humanity that is more durable than that found within. Thus, men face outward to society and its culture. They cling to symbols, to knowledge, to edifices.

> The hope and belief is that the things that man creates in society are of lasting worth and meaning, that they outlive or outshine death and decay, that man and his products count.[3]

Becker claims that all societies are mythical systems of immortality. They are theological as are all men. In this sense, Becker stands Durkheim on his head. Durkheim maintained that the prime function of religion is to affirm common sentiments, and to confirm social sodality; whereas Becker maintains that common sentiments and social sodality are used for religious purpose: to gird men in the face of their individual ultimate concerns of life and death.

> Every society thus is a 'religion' whether it thinks so or not: Soviet 'religion' and Maoist 'religion' are as truly religious as are scientific and consumer religion, no matter how they try to disguise themselves by omitting religious and spiritual ideas from their lives.[4]

Unlike other animals, men do not instinctively know what to do or how to perceive. They must learn their orientations via their symbolizing, rationalizing minds. These lessons in living are substantially social. The child is raised by men. In his knowing and in his certainty, each individual stands on the shoulders of generations. Through culture, each man learns how to act before the awesomeness of the physical world. So it is that man fills his statuses and plays his roles and thereby lives from day to day. But certainty in daily affairs does not dispel the uncertainty of human existence, for as men are aware of their vulnerability and mortality, so they crave an affirmation of life and identity.

[3]*The Denial of Death*, p. 5.
[4]*The Denial of Death*, p. 7.

This affirmation is heroism: a strutting—an unflinching action and stance before the frailty and mortality of man. Heroism is a universal need and is almost entirely choreographed by society:

> The fact is that this is what society is and always has been: a symbolic action system, a structure of statuses and roles, customs and rules of behavior, designed to serve as a vehicle of earthly heroism.[5]

Heroism comes in many forms. Courage in the face of death is probably the most pristine variety, but there are oblique heroisms as well. Garnering social honor and power augments the individual, providing him with symbolic manna to combat insignificance and death. Money is another form of social potency that men interpret to be personal power. There is the quiet heroism of living responsibly and assuredly in terms of one's social identity. Living up to social ideals is an heroic attempt to manifest that which is of enduring significance in a society. Heroic stature comes in partaking of and defending theological rationales and rituals. Building lasting institutions or concrete monuments is to make one's mark in the world and to act with strength.

The creative man makes his work his private immortality system. He does not play the standard heroic roles. He does not recreate that which symbolically affirms a society's greatness and immortality. The creative man provides his own significant and enduring production, but to this he clings as tenaciously as any standard hero would cling to his ideal, and ultimately what is the creative act but a gift to society, a bid for recognition and honor by the artist.

All heroisms entail the association of the individual with that which is deemed enduringly important. Would-be heroes think: "I may die but by my action, my nation, family, religion, party will live." "I may die but through my actions goodness will prevail; men will be inspired by my writing, music, scientific discoveries." "I may die but the building I helped to construct will endure." Perhaps, though, many men are so transfixed by their heroic transcendence that they hardly are conscious of their own transiency and insignificance. They see only the immortal ideal in their mortal heroism.

There is greater and lesser heroism. Most of the greater heroism

<hr>

[5]*The Denial of Death*, p. 4.

is staged naturally enough by "heroes" who are cheered by a multitude which vicariously partakes of the heroic affirmation of a common mythology. Heroes are thus most lauded when they buttress central societal ideals of goodness, strength or glory by epitomizing them. Generally, unimaginative heroes are mostly in demand. Creative heroes may find themselves lynched figuratively or literally if they undermine a system that nourishes the confidence of many. Of course, if the creative hero's transgression seemingly augments a society's mythology and is adopted into the culture, then this creative hero is dubbed "pathfinder" and to him goes the greatest plaudits; for as much as men fear individuality, they would all be individuals, and thus a man who succeeds in his individuation within society is a prime inspiration.

Becker distrusts heroism in any form. He sees heroic denial as a lie. "All is vanity." Men do die. All their works perish. The universe is too overwhelming for human powers of comprehension. Becker dislikes heroic transcendence for its fantastic qualities, but also for the evil and the narrowness that it engenders.

Men wish association with a self-transcending drama—a dramatization of greatness and power. Such enhancement requires victory. Sometimes a victory is staged against the elements as a successful voyage or technological discovery, but most often the victory is won on a social field. Men augment themselves at the expense of others. The proponents of one religion or one nation prevail at the expense of another religion or nation. Competition and conflict are fostered by a human craving for significance. In moderation the contest might be productive, but the intensity of the insecurity leads frequently to excesses that are evil and ugly. Men swell themselves by diminishing others, a process that is painted large in wars and small in petty cruelties and bickering. Power is gleaned from destruction and also from grotesque building or accumulation. Men hoard and deny to other men both parity and sustenance. Men also ravage nature with wanton displays of technological power. Mortal panic tends men to the heinous and the hideous.

Power fantasies form one side of the denial coin; the flip side is repression or "fetishization" as Becker terms it, which also has negative effects. The individual armors himself with his character—that personal combination and interpretation of roles and statuses, that self-image that defines what he is, what he sees and what he does. By tending to business and by living his social self as society determines it, the individual is spared the uncertainty that a true assay of the world would inspire. He does not think of his own death or of the disruptions that might befall him at any time. He does not wonder at the mysteries of the universe. He "fetishizes," biting off only what he can chew in terms of experience. Thus, for Becker, "character" becomes a prison, baring men from exploration and discovery, rendering men bigoted and narrow. Men become what Kierkegaard calls Philistines, intermediate men who keep their minds on small problems as society maps them out.

According to Becker most men are Philistines in their daily lives, but Philistines who desire greatness, albeit a safe greatness in the form of a transcending power with which they can merge themselves. In their active lives most Philistines opt for small-scale claims to significance. Without reflection, they plunge into their social parts and execute them religiously. Generally, they augment their positions via a spectator transcendence. From the sidelines they root for their heroes, their team, their nation, and then bask in reflected glory. However, dormant Philistines are liable to become active fanatics: chauvinists, patriots, religionaries. Whether dormant or active, they shy from imagination and from setting their own courses; their compulsive servility demeans mankind.

For Becker all men are neurotic in that they constrict their experience and their action:

> The individual has to protect himself against the world, and he can do this only as any other animal would: by narrowing down the world, shutting off experience, developing an obliviousness both to the terrors of the world and to his own anxieties.[6]

Men who are clinically neurotic are men who cannot live as Philistines, and yet who cannot create their own augmenting illusions. Clinical neurotics see social life as empty play. Not benefiting from cultural solutions, neurotics are weighed down with anxiety and cannot act with any resolution.

Like clinical neurotics, creative men cannot abide by society's illusions of power and permanence, but unlike neurotics, creative men are talented, and use their imaginations to engender their own illusions. Becker distinguishes the common hero from the artistic hero in this way:

[6]*The Denial of Death*, p. 177.

14   The whole thing boils down to this paradox: if you are going to be a hero then you must give a gift. If you are an average man you give your heroic gift to the society in which you live, and you give the gift that society specifies in advance. If you are an artist you fashion a peculiarly personal gift, the justification of your own heroic identify, which means that it is always aimed at least partly over the heads of your fellow man.[7]

To be oriented, men must fashion or adopt an illusion and view the world in its terms. Without illusion, infinitude would crowd man into madness, for he would have no handle on a perilous and incomprehensible existence. If, however, men are blinded by their illusions, they become brutes—unreflective automatons—likely to wreak horror in their clawing for significance, in their priggish adherence to their "way."

Man is caught in a bind. He needs heroism yet heroism is ultimately fantastic and dangerous. Becker shows no path out of the dilemma. Men must live and yet men will die. Becker suggests only that men live as openly as they can. In reference to Rank's thought, Becker writes:

> Only in this way says Rank, only by surrendering to the bigness of nature on the highest, least fetishized level, can man conquer death.[8]

The more that men can approximate the agape of self-surrender before the full awesomeness of existence, the more honest and broad they will be—the less likely they will brutilize themselves and their environment. Yet, Becker admits that terror must forestall the multitude in any attempt at open vision. "Full humanness means full fear and trembling, at least some of the waking day."[9] Not many men can tolerate the insecurity.

Becker's Relevance

The foregoing cataloging of Becker's ideas can do no more than adumbrate his efforts, yet I trust the shadow is apt. Becker himself does not claim much credit for originality. Repeatedly, he asseverates that his work is no more than a synthesis of ideas and discoveries developed primarily by Rank and Freud. Like his

[7]*The Denial of Death*, p. 173.
[8]*The Denial of Death*, p. 174.
[9]*The Denial of Death*, p. 59.

mentors, Becker is a skeptic. He would avoid delusion at all costs. He clearly distrusts all notions of glory and heroism. He dwells on the darker manifestations of human aspiration rather than on the more sublime. If statesmanship, music or painting were mentioned, I did not notice. Becker wades through the underside: through cowardice, greed, bellicosity, pomposity. His discussions of creativity are entirely abstract. His discussions of evil are all too graphic. His descriptions of existence are meant to shock and to exorcise any ethereal misconceptions.

> Existence, for all organismic life, is a constant struggle to feed—a struggle to incorporate whatever other organisms can fit into their mouths and press down their gullets without choking. Seen in these stark terms, life on this planet is a gory spectacle, a science fiction nightmare in which digestive tracts fitted with teeth at one end are tearing away at whatever flesh they can reach, and at the other end are piling up the fuming waste excrement as they move along in search of more flesh.[10]

Becker's work is a polemic against Pollyannish views of man and society. Becker would warn us of the vitriol that may flow from an illusion grown to salve a veiled, yet desparate, anxiety at our mortal state. Believing in the vise grip of "mythical systems of transcendence," he could not be expected to assail them with plunger tipped arrows.

However, the pessimism of his tone and the ardor of his argument do not detract from lucidity of his conception with which I agree:

1. Men are moved by a fear of death and calamity, by an anxiety at an incomprehensible, capricious universe, and by desires for meaning, immortality, and personal significance.
2. Men flee from uncertainty and dread by repressing their experience of the world and of themselves, by constricting it to manageable proportions.
3. The experience that men allow themselves is substantially social: culturally defined and populated with men. Conscious thoughts rarely linger on anything that has no social significance. Some men who even find society intimidating reduce (fetishize) their meaningful world even further to their own imaginations and personal spaces. These men dwell on

---

[10]Ernest Becker, *Escape from Evil*, New York: The Free Press, 1975, p. 1.

"things" and seemingly idiosyncratic "games," but the scores for these "private" preoccupations are derived from social programming, the quirks of upbringing.

4. Men transpose their existential quest to a social stage. To fortify themselves before their fate, men seek transcendent power. This manna always has some social connection. The tacit, overt or supposed support of other men buttresses the individual's sense of security and significance. Thus, men seek social power, honor, acceptance and approval.

5. Cultures and societies are mythical systems of transcendence. They provide the heroic scenario. They supply the individual with illusion, with ideologies and rituals by which he can cloak himself with power and significance by identifying with the prestige, the permanence and the power of corporation, clan, profession, nation or religion. The ideologies place the individual significantly within a meaningful existence. The rituals affirm the ideologies and the individual; rituals are an exercise of power, and are thus life giving.

6. Heroic transcendence assuages man's situation, but it cannot dispel his uncertainty; reality is ultimately too obtrusive. Men remain anxious.

The backdrop of death reduces all human works to insignificance, renders human existence absurd and men minutiae, as the existentialists well knew. Without transcendence there can be no enduring meaning to the corporeal. The great religions have long taunted the foolishness of temporal transcendence, of men who worship mammon: social honor and power, physical beauty and capacities, for these will pass away as if they had never been, dissipate as the dew. Our eventuality as dust is the ultimate stir to humility. And the great religions themselves, in that they are close to human living, they are steeped in social regulation: morals and mores, a social transcendence as any other; in that these religions scan the cosmos, they are intangible to mundane men and conjecture for the great multiude who are "Doubting Thomases" caught on the brink unable to make the "leap of faith." I doubt that any man actually makes a "leap of faith," an escape to certainty. Saints doubt, suffer and pray for their faith. It seems that what men want to know most, they cannot know. They can hope and dream. What certainty men have is earned by constant effort.

Becker never makes explicit just how men become aware of the precariousness of their moral state. He does imply that consciouness and intelligence are integral to the awareness. Yet, human mortality and its ramifications are not intuitively obvious, neither are they abstract "truths." The threatening reality is manifest in real men. Men learn of their vulnerability and mortality from the examples of other men who are injured, sick, old, dying or dead.

In explaining human existence, and denying and transcending mortality and insignificance, men must cope with human exemplars of human frailty. The haunting faces of death are flesh. Any resolution must entail some posture toward the decrepit, the incapacitated, the deformed.

Though Becker does not address himself to phenomena directly associated with abnormal men, his conception holds definite implications concerning the treatment of abnormal men and concerning their relationships with normative mankind. If Becker is right, one would expect to see certain things in reference to manifestations of human vulnerability and mortality.

1. If men must deny their mortality, they must generally shun the men who demonstrate it. Abnormal men would thus be kept from the pathways of normal social living; they would be sequestered in some special place.
2. If men would rationalize their mortality, they must explain abnormal men. There would have to be notions relating the meaning of abnormal men, the reasons for their abnormality, and perhaps the means for the afflicted to escape from their calamity and mortality.
3. If, to find meaning, men must transpose (restrict) their existential quest to a social arena, then they must deny the graphic physical manifestation of mortality in abnormal men, and dwell on them as social beings with social problems.
4. If society supplies the illusions by which men deny mortality and its implications, then society must explain abnormal men and provide the ideological and ritual means for coping with them.
5. As the ultimate in heroism is courage and effectiveness before the maw of death, so heroic power must be perceived in coping competently and directly with abnormal men who embody the dragon of mortality.
6. In that abnormal men can think and act like men, being men, they will tend to adhere to the societal myths concerning themselves and their conditions. They can be expected generally to help stage society's denial of their plight.
7. As men can never entirely adjust to mortality, so they can never entirely adjust to the human exemplars of mortality.

18   With refinements and qualifications these seven assumptions
are borne out by my hospital study (which I will discuss latter);
they do not, however, cover all aspects of heroic adaptations to
the men who demonstrate human mortality. For such an understanding, Becker's view must be expanded, and the dynamics of
human orientation must be conceptualized.

Becker caricatures heroism to stress the potential for evil
entailed in the dependence of an insecure mankind upon social
illusion. The partiality of Becker's polemic pushes it beyond
realistic sobriety to unwarranted pessimism. Becker implies that
men are social only because fear drives them to comforting social
illusion; he implies that heroism is spurious activism born of
this illusion.

Such implications are erroneous. Men are essentially social;
they do not resort to society from fear. As Becker himself notes,
all individuals aspire through society, through cultural expression, the creative geniuses as well as the Philistines. Truly
idiosyncratic living is unthinkable.

The illusion of which Becker speaks is a product of the same
process that generates realism or utility. Men rationalize and
adapt by categorizing and symbolizing. Man's categories and
symbols define his reality; their relationship to an objective
reality is more and less true; their relationship to the man's
needs is more and less apt. Because existence is complex and
confusing, men and societies must struggle for what genuine
adaptation and understanding they achieve. Because this exist-
ance is ultimately inexplicable and man is mortal, empirical
understanding cannot be sufficient for a tolerably comfortable
orientation; thus, men and societies must dream and, in part,
interpret these dreams to be reality.

Artifice is essential to heroism, but so is aspiration, and
aspiration is the catalyst for all utility. Heroism that buffers
reality also provides men with interpretation and support to
confront their existence. Only through the hope that heroism
fosters can men aspire to adaptation and survival. Only through
an heroic confrontation with the ultimate questions can men
live wisely.

Heroism entails the good and the bad, the strength and the
weakness, the magnanimity and the meanness—that mix that
men usually attribute to men. Yet, heroisms and individual
interpretations of heroisms are not equal in their reflections of
human character. They are not equally fantastic—realistic or
wise. They are skewed toward the best and the worst in man.

Institutionalized heroisms represent the judgement and the character of society. Heroic acts, as individual efforts, derive from
individuals' judgement and strength.

A wise heroism accommodates the human state. To live, men
must strive and strut, but they must also accept an inexplicable
and inexorable fate. The great religions accommodate this dual
reality by coupling pomp with atonement. The Roman Catholic
Church is a prime example. It has splendid cathedrals and ornate
ceremonies, but it also has rituals of self-mortification. A proper
balance of aspiration and humility yields a proper combination
of hope, realism and catharsis.

Heroism can be passive as well as active since heroism can
reflect humility as well as aspiration. "Humble" and "aspirational" heroisms complement each other and yield a "heroic balance"
when properly combined. "Heroic balance" produces a wise
adaptation; whereas an excess of one or the other heroism leads
to foolishness or evil. An "aspirational hero" aspires to move the
world to his own ends. To be an "aspirational hero" exclusively
is to be guilty of the classical sin of hubris. Odysseus and
Oedipus were such heroes. Through personal acumen and
strength, they aspired to mold their own fates, but their pretension highlighted their impotence and the tragic dimension of
human existence. The other heroic mode is that of the "humble
hero," a man who accepts and accommodates fate. Humility in
pursuit of an ideal is heroic because substantial resignation to
fate on faith is arduous, but also exhiliarating in that idealized
humility suggests union with a superhuman entity or force. An
excess of this form of heroism leads to irresponsibility and
stagnation. Horrors that might be alleviated are permitted, because all is up to fate or God. An "aspirational hero" can be
humble in his aspiration and a "humble hero" can be aspiring in
his humility, but, in that, one form manipulates while the other
accommodates, a proper combination of these heroisms is the
most satisfactory means of coping with human mortality. Thus,
the wise man works for "heroic balance" and the well-developed
institution supports it.

"Heroic balance" implies wisdom because a "proper" combination requires both a heroic ideology that correctly characterizes
the existential predicament of man—and awareness and practi-
cality from the individual. To act in a balanced fashion, a man
must realistically assess his situation; thus, his philosophy
cannot be too cursory—ethereal or stilted—and he cannot be
mindlessly absorbed in the illusion that shores his adjustment.

20 Consequently, balance and wisdom come with trail and some uncertainty.

Monomania and fanaticism are incompatible with "heroic balance" since obession with a finite ideal leads to excesses. As a conception, an ideal represents imperfectly an infinitely complex reality. As an ultimate aspiration, an ideal supplants and thus subverts its own end—good living. As a plan for perfect living, an ideal is unobtainable since the world follows no human script. A man who seeks the wisdom of heroic balance must possess a subtle belief, for neither the world nor living is simple. He must cling to the Biblical notion that there is a time and a place for everything. An institution that supports heroic balance must itself be subtle for the simple passion incited by cults serves a spurious truth and a transient euphoria.

To achieve heroic balance it is not necessary that every heroic act promote some rarefied version of man. Societies and individuals have immediate needs dictated by temporal realities. Unfortunately, some of the very "evils" that Becker decries are virtues in certain contexts. Thus, a nation encircled by bellicose neighbors might do well to be bellicose itself. Hunting does not have similar significance for a small, isolated tribe and a large, crowded industrial society.

The ultimate test of heroism is whether it abets good living for a society. Does the heroism foster a salubrious environment? Does it inculcate functional attitudes and skills? The answers are similar and disparate as men are ever the same and yet culturally and circumstantially different.

Not every thrill a man seeks should have cosmic significance. Men need diversions and the respite of fantasy. Sainthood is not an end for all men, but a vocation to be society's conscience. No society can afford too many saints, since sainthood is a full-time job. A man is not damned or demeaned if he entertains such petty heroisms as skiing or social climbing, as long as he is not obsessed with them and keeps a quieter, more profound self capable of keeping his living in perspective. Similarly, a society should tolerate meretricious institutions, but it must preserve the institutions that sustain a profound perspective.

The maintenance of heroic balance is a prime function of religion, for heroic balance is ultimately morality. The great religions have spawned numerous fanatics, but these religions have also been the bulwark of heroic balance since their view man has been the most profound, and their institutions have done the most to maintain perspective among the peoples of the earth. In recent times, secular ideologies such as Nazism, Leninism and Maoism have been presented as alternatives, but these are shallow by contrast.

The great religions are founded on works of literature frought with parables and sagas. The essence of human existence and morality can be defined only literarily because this essence is emergent and thus impalpable. The literary vagueness of religious doctrine guides, but it does not determine action.

Ultimately, heroic balance is achieved through individual moral struggles. It cannot be had by formula. The truly moral are hard thinkers who accommodate principles with hard but shifting reality. They are melancholy men whose clearer perception forces an awareness of the tragic state of man. A blissful pulpiteer is a cultist.

The exemplars of human mortality: the disabled, the deformed, the dying and the dead confront mankind with its most poignant questions, questions that men cannot answer definitively. Yet, the poignancy of these questions requires men to seek answers if men are to feel secure. The only answers possible are unsubstantiable, the stuff of heroic illusion, and thus the postures toward the unwhole fostered by these answers are heroic. There is no recourse but an avoidance of the questions and an animalistic rejection of the unwhole. Heroic illusion is fact fortified with desire. In that this desire intelligently reflects human needs, the heroism will be moral or socially functional.

A society's treatment of its unwhole is a litmus for its moral development, since this treatment is indicative of the society's definition of man and view of human living. A society's sense of "the good" can lead to the murder, incarceration, torture or banishment of living deformed or debilitated men—or to efforts to accept them.

Becker would see the former as evil heroic pretension; he would see the latter as 'good' and therefore as unheroic or minimally heroic. But Becker errs in making such distinctions. There is no sense of evil without a sense of good, and there is no definition of good without some heroic conception of man and human living. "The good" for Becker seems to be formless, cosmic experiencing as if experience ever meant anything without conception and perception that presuppose structure and, therefore, presumptions which are substantially social.

In the real world, the best posture toward unwhole men is not a mindless experiencing of them, but a developed heroic balance. Such can be sustained in society only by developed moral

22 institutions. For his own optimal benefit and for his society's, a man needs careful guidance in when to accept the unwhole as men and when to reject them, when to alter them or try and when to accept them as they are, when to confront them and when to shy from then, and how to do all of these. There would be no basis for such decisions without presumptions and wishful thinking. That bogey, heroic illusion, provides the only basis for moral action and, in this case, the only basis for a moral adjustment to deformed, debilitated, dying and dead men.

Heroic transcendence is the only intelligent response to the ultimate questions of human identity and purpose. Moreover, this transcendence is a natural product of the way men think and socialize. Becker explains the great folly to which the heroic process is prone. He hardly acknowledges the necessity of this process so much does he distrust it; yet, heroic transcendence is structurally inherent and functionally imperative. It cannot be avoided but it can be morally developed.

I shall not discuss here a moral development of heroic postures toward unwhole men, but I shall wait to the end of the book when I can be specific. The ideas that I have outlined in my "expansion of Becker" cannot be clear without an understanding of the Gregor Effect, which cannot itself be defined without considering the process of human orientation, the significance of unwhole men and both individual and institutional adaptations to these men.

Orientation

Uncertainty and Orientation

The uncertainty of human identity reified by uncertain men is but a part of the general uncertainty that plagues mankind. Men cope with this special, central doubt much as they cope with all uncertainty. The means of orientation are standard, and thus a general consideration of them is in order.

Uncertainty is always present in human experience. Our experience is our reality, and what knowledge and certitude we possess depend on the regularity, continuity and clarity of our experience; yet, herein lies no perfect regularity, no certainty that apparent consistency is inviolate, and no patent intelligibility. Dasein is a beguiling chromatic splashing. Existence is kaleidoscopic, fluid and infinitely complex. To make sense of it, our minds segment and categorize. Approximations are perceived as identities. Parts are taken for wholes. Symbols stand in for the symbolized. Life is predicated on crude regularities that can fail or confound by appearing in diverse combinations which have diverse implications.

Yet, in that men live, they believe, they assume, they have faith in knowledge of world and self. Otherwise, they would be psychically

3

24 paralyzed. Doubt is uncomfortable, but absolute doubt allows no basis for thought or action. Innumerable assumptions govern the thought and the behavior of the individual in daily life. This is faith in a mundane sense, a faith which must be nurtured by all people.

Orientation is the operational certainty which man mines from a protean actuality. Since confusion is the bane of meaningful, painless experience, orientation is the mind's ultimatum, the sine qua non of all other vital actions. Before he can react, man must evaluate his experience. The definitiveness of his reaction depends on the certainty and the clarity of his evaluation. To this end, all but the most tenuous possess an "orientation drive" that can be likened to an "I" that stands aside from the sum of mental and sensory experience and compels an understanding. This work may be interaction between an adaptive mind and a mutable milieu, or intra-action within the mind, or both. The objective–subjective mix of orientation will never be known; yet it seems that experience consists of mind and world, and that man works for his certainty with an inner self and a separate outer existence.

People labor ceaselessly to be oriented in a immediate navigational sense, and also in a larger, structural, "outlook" sense. Through each day, people must navigate their ways. Guiding a car is an immediate, ongoing exercise in orientation; a car is steered and coaxed in accordance with its performance, the driver's purpose and the developments on the road. To react to others appropriately, the individual must tend to each who is encountered. To remain oriented, the individual must be continuously orienting, reading each situation, processing observations, and acting. As each situation arises, the individual wants to know how to react to it—with the desire for continuity and sense in reactions. Some accommodation is required between the individual's views of reality and self, and each action, so that there is some basis for further navigational decisions and for felt security before the vagaries and unknowns of existence. The individual wants living to reflect a definite identity. Thus, while the individual works to negotiate each situation, he or she works to define and to affirm basic postures and a self-image.

To be oriented, man thinks and learns. He constructs perceptual patterns that codify the more abiding or recurrent aspects of his sensory experience. An experiential panorama is cut into figurations which are bound together conceptually by selected relationships. The infinite, fluid complexity of the world is refined into typifications that reify and simplify the two temporal dimensions of reality into constellations of given moments and formulas of process—cause and effect. Knowledge is typification of things and events. The defining properties of a lemon comprise its typification: the color, the odor, the shape, the size, the texture and the contents. An event is typified by such qualifications as time, place, purpose, actors, costume and ritual. The individual orients himself to a given experience by reading typifications manifest in it, that is, looking for an event such as a greeting, a church service or a business transaction.

The individual does not expect the world to conform to explicit idealizations. Experience is never perfectly continuous or repetitive. Since no object or event can be identical to any other, there must be some breadth to the qualifications that define the world. Every qualification in a typification entails some normal range of variation. There are large lemons and small lemons, but generally no mature lemon is the size of a pea or a watermelon. Generally, one expects a mature lemon to be some shade of yellow. No real lemon conforms to an explicit ideal; all real lemons have unique though similar color, odor, shape, size and texture. No event, regardless how ritualized, is exactly like another; yet there are limits to what constitutes a given type of event. Weddings differ from funerals, and both differ from storms, sailing or bookbinding.

People read their lives to be oriented, but orientation is not just a matter of learning patterns and citing them in one's experience. Human purpose is a factor, but also the nature of outer experience itself is a factor. The world does not divide up neatly into things and events. There is much room for ambiguity in perception. Part of this potential arises from the limitations of perspective; part of it arises from the multifariousness of perception; and part of it derives from the obstreperousness of reality to human demands.

Since the individual is based in the body, he is in a position to perceive only so much at one time. Generally, he cannot see more than half the surface of an object. He sees the face of a man but not the back of his head. He cannot see the interior of a whole lemon. He cannot hear all the conversations in a crowded ballroom. He cannot taste what is not in his mouth, nor touch what is beyond his reach. Thus, one senses rarely all the elements of a typification. However, since a man trusts in the integrity of numerous perceptual patterns, he infers the whole from the part noted. He surveys the color and contours of a lemon and perceives a lemon. The existence of its juicy interior is inferred. Through binoculars, a man sees music stands and instruments manipulated by musicians, and infers that music is being played. A man presumes that the automobile he sees speeding down the highway is propelled by an engine, though he in no way perceives that engine with his five senses.

In inferring the whole from the part there is a question of limits. How much or what aspects of a pattern must be sensed for a man to be reasonably sure that the whole pattern exists? For every typification there will be limiting cases in which a person does not "see" enough to be certain that a particular pattern is manifest. This sort of ambiguity is dependent upon the availability of alternate definitions for the given data. In the distance, a man sees a yellow object, but he cannot determine whether the object is a lemon, a ball or an Easter egg. The situation is ambiguous. If the only small yellow objects a man knew were lemons, he could reasonably expect such an object to be a lemon, unless the context ruled it out. If the man knew of another object which differed from a lemon only in the color of its juice, he might not only have to approach the yellow object, he might have to slice it open in order to feel sure of its identity.

Ambiguity due to insufficient evidence is not a major concern to an individual unless he has some special reason to know the identity of an ambiguous phenomenon. If a small yellow object is not an incongruous element in the person's frame of reference (it is not stuck in a snowdrift in uninhabited Antarctica!), he may ignore the ambiguous object altogether especially if he feels secure that cursory probing would resolve the mystery.

Manifest Ambiguity

Inherently more troublesome than ambiguity that arises from a dearth of data is ambiguity that arises from the perception of an incongruous element. Because the individual infers wholes from parts, the elements or qualifications of a pattern tend to hang together as an entity. If, in terms of a given pattern, an element does not fall within a specified range of normal variation, and there is no alternate ideal type to account for the diversion, then this element is incongruent and a source of manifest ambiguity. If one finds a lemon the size of a grapefruit, and knows of no other lemonlike fruit that is that size, then one has found an ambiguous lemon, something which both seems to be a lemon and seems to be not a lemon. It is almost certain that the discovery of the grapefruit-size lemon would cause more interest and consternation than the perception of a small yellow object in the distance, because in the former case the ambiguity is manifest. No mere investigation will resolve manifest ambiguity.

Manifest ambiguity arises from more than blatant incongruities. Manifest ambiguity commonly comes from an element that borders on meeting and not meeting a qualification. The boundaries that delimit the characteristics of a pattern, an entity, are not lines which definitely divide the certainty that a phenomenon meets a qualification from the certainty that it does not. The boundaries are bands of ambiguity. It is not at all certain how large a lemon must be before eyes behold a freak, or how much larger it must be before eyes do not behold a lemon at all.

Manifest ambiguity pertains to events as well as to objects. Boisterous cackling would likely be a blatantly incongruous element in a funeral service and would likely distress the mourners. A sport coat that is perhaps too bright for a funeral service might be a borderline incongruous element and would likely discomfort the mourners, but less so than laughter. In both cases a note of ambiguity is added to an occasion.

Since perceptual patterns are commonly more multifarious than conceptual patterns, one may be unconscious of many of the qualifications that are used to interpret a scene; yet, manifest ambiguity is often felt wherever it appears. Whenever one thinks of a phenomenon, conceptions will generally form only a schematic and selective reflection of perception of the same phenomenon. However, an otherwise unconscious perceptual qualification can become glaringly obvious when it is manifestly violated. When a man thinks of a lemon, he may not consider the special texture of the lemon's skin; yet, an encounter with a smooth or jagged lemon would jar the man into an awareness of texture. Manifest ambiguity does not have to make one aware of the relevant qualification to disturb him. When a perceptual pattern is improper, a man may not know the source of the manifest ambiguity; he may just have a vague feeling that something is out of place. There may be something in another's manner that belies the sincerity he professes.

Manifest ambiguity is intrusive. Seeing people with watermelon-size heads is a far more powerful experience than hearing that such people exist. It is easier not to think of an ambiguous phenomenon than it is not to perceive it when it is manifest in sensory experience. In the face of an ambiguous manifestation, it may be to no avail that a man had convinced himself that this particular deviance is inconsequential. To aid his orientation, a man may bunch phenomena together by a simplistic definition that covers them all, and yet, this method may not stop the man from perceiving an ambiguous disparateness among the phenomena. A man may console himself that if it walks like a duck, has webbed feet like a duck and quacks like a duck, it must be a duck; yet, if he encountered such a creature and it talked, the ambiguity would shine through. A man may console himself that all Homo sapiens are human like himself, and yet he may have trouble perceiving a man of a different race to be a human.

Conditions can lessen the obtrusiveness of manifest ambiguity, and there are means to attenuate its impact. These buffers will be discussed.

Human Requirements and Man-made Order

Man would confront much less manifest ambiguity than he does if he were not an active being who requires of his world. Nature does present man with incongruities without his assistance. The Westerners who first encountered flying fish confronted such an incongruity. However, most manifest ambiguity does not arise from lapses in what man sees a natural order; most manifest ambiguity arises from incongruities in the personal and social order that serves human purposes and that man attempts to superimpose on nature through physical labor.

Man acts; he meddles in his world, seeking to maintain and to obtain conditions essential for his survival and certainty. Not only are man's actions a factor in his external experience, his efforts in the world are vital to his orientation. By itself, the rest of nature would not sustain man. Man is substantially responsible for securing a milieu that supports or at least allows inner orientation—identity. Man works to put his experience in an order that serves his purposes. Being a social animal, man frequently works for social purposes as well. But, the world is recalcitrant, and society is confounded and complex. Thus, manmade order is problematic. There is much occasion for manifest ambiguity that can be either *natural* or *social*.

Nature tirelessly threatens man-made order and will ultimately tarnish and then destroy any human fabrication. Man builds cars, homes, gardens, and so forth. Rust rots his cars. Hurricanes assail his homes. Weeds grow in his gardens. Mortality is the end of all. Ambiguity opens and creeps into the crevices of man's edifaces. To compensate for this *natural* manifest ambiguity,

man must be as tenacious as nature—cleaning, refurbishing,
rebuilding, reordering.

Men are social animals. The demands of life and limb are largely met socially. The more rationalized the division of labor and the more advanced the technology, the more shielded men are from sheer nature by social manifestation and the more men's realities are defined in social terms. But even in the most rudimentary societies, individual orientation depends upon social coordination. Social coordination depends on communication.

Communication comes through symbolic actions, trappings and settings. Through speech, countenance, body language and recordings, men negotiate relations among themselves and co-ordinate their activities. Clothing and grooming express an oc-casion and the self-conception of the man. Buildings, areas and furnishings establish frames of reference in that they are reserved for limited ranges of activity.

The intricacy and the precariousness of social ordering as well as the complexity of communication itself provide ample poten-tial for manifest ambiguity in communication, for *social* mani-fest ambiguity. Men can be at cross purposes; incongruities can be compounded in a social scene by the multiple purposes of participants. Men can work on misinformation. They can delib-erately strive to mislead each other. They can honestly misread a situation. For all these reasons, the signs that signal a social context can be or seem confounded. In innumerable ways, deeds, men and settings can seem improper in terms of one's interpre-tation of a scene.

People cannot fully fabricate the order they require in their world. They can lay out cities, plan rituals and wash their clothes. They cannot restrict humankind clearly to comparable, comprehensible entities. Regardless of human effort, the world provides men who are so disparate that they defy attempts at comprehensive definition that would be meaningful to normative men. There are the mindless, the blind, the insane, the paralyzed, the stunted, the deformed, the dead, the rotting. Somehow, the more normative men must deal with these manifestly ambiguous men, if the former are to build for themselves any certainty or security.

Dirt, Stigma and Manifest Ambiguity

Manifest ambiguity and man-made order are central theoretical concerns to the structural anthropologists Levi-Strauss, Edmund Leach and Mary Douglas. These theorists propose that there is

30 a human propensity to manifest mental patterns and to maintain the boundaries of such manifestations. To stem confusion and to establish order, men choreograph and segregate appearances and actions into clusters and combinations relative to given contexts. Behavior manifest an inner vision of reality, a vision that cannot persist without such manifestation. Thought, action and perception are integrally combined. In his mind, in his world, man divides the sacred from the profane, the private from the public, the cold from the hot and the raw from the cooked.

Morals, mores, religions, philosophies, technologies and styles are conceptions that become real only when action paints them into the world. They are reified; then the perception of them perpetuates the inspiration that fostered them. The world does not provide the props for cultural reality; people must and do. Their imagery of grandeur is made real; it is mortared into castles, cathedrals and skyscrapers. Men's sense of propriety is drawn in clothing, architecture, and in the way in which these men group and segregate their activities. People, seeking orientation, look out upon a world rife in the guiding symbolism of their society.

Initially, the manifestation of human vision requires construction, but from then on, it requires maintenance. According to Mary Douglas, concerns for cleanliness derive from a desire for clear limits and perceptual order. She notes that dirt is a relative designation or opprobrium that is attributed to anything deemed an inappropriate and confounding element within a given context. Dirt is stigma, the source of manifest ambiguity. Dirt muddies perceptual limits and draws disgust for the ambiguity it entails. Dirt is that which mars the order that men would impose on nature. Anything can be clean or dirty. Earth in the ground is dirt on a floor. Shoes on a floor are dirt on a dining table. Hair on a head is dirt on a champagne glass. Even space can be dirt; a missing tooth is dirt. The absence of a proper greeting is dirt.

It is the ambiguity that is poignant, not the dirt in itself. Dirt is an incongruity; it is stigma in that it spoils an identity. Stigma mars the fit of an interpretation. The degree of perceived ambiguity is related to the degree of stigmatization but not directly. There are a number of factors that influence the relationship; yet even when these are qualized, the variation of manifest ambiguity relative to perceived stigmatization resembles a normal curve rather than a straight line. A phenomenon can be more and less stigmatized in terms of a *given definition*; a

phenomenon can be so stigmatized that there is hardly evidence
that the definition pertains. If only the bones remain, the turkey
has ceased to exist for most men. In terms of a turkey, a
featherless turkey would be far less stigmatized than a skeleton
one, yet the featherless bird would likely be more ambiguous
than the bones. Perceived ambiguity is the ambivalent perception
of "this and not this," yet generally the mix contains more of
one than the other. The apex of the curvilinear relationship
between ambiguity and stigma represents the demarcation between the perception of an entity with incongruent elements and
the perception of something else with elements of that entity.
Prior to this point, waxing stigmatization increases the ambiguity
of the entity; after this point, the manifest ambiguity wanes as
the certainty grows that the thing is not the entity. If everyone
is laughing, the funeral is acutely ambiguous. If everyone is
laughing and the coffin is empty, chances are that a funeral is
not transpiring.

The impact of a stigma (the ambiguity it generates) is influ-
enced by the individual's immediate frame of reference, and is
dependent upon his whole system of order. Each man has his
own sense of reality. No man has a place for everything or just
one place for anything. Orientation is a relationship between a
man's inner realm and his outer world. The purposes of his inner
realm guide a man's vision. Man does not endeavor to order
rigidly everything in his world as he does not endeavor to see
everything at once,—to perceive all potential patterns. He sees
what he considers significant and focuses on what he considers
most significant at any one time.

Focus sways the preception of ambiguity. If a man's attention
is directed elsewhere, he is less likely to perceive flaws that
otherwise would be evident to him. If a man is preoccupied with
conversation, he may not note blemishes in decor. If he is
preoccupied with decor, he may not notice quirks in a
conversation.

Any one phenomenon can be defined in innumerable ways
since it can be defined relative to innumerable frames of reference. What is flawed by one standard may not be by another
standard. In England there is a race whose object is to dent and
muck the cars as much as possible; within this context, the most
dented and mucked car will not be perceived to be the "dirtiest"
one. According to the prevailing interests of the man, a phenomenon can be judged by typifications which are more or less strict
and more or less multifarious. The qualities that herald a prize

lemon are more exacting than those qualities that define a lemon as food which are more exacting than those qualities that define a lemon as a yellow object.

Counteracting substantially the perceptual winnowing of immediate interpretation and purpose is a constant concern for certain configurations which are more central to a man's orientation than are others. Violations of his more significant constructs are more likely to draw a man's attention than are violations of his less significant constructs. Some sensitive concerns are peculiar to the individual; others are more or less common; still others are universal. If man has concentrated (transposed) his quest for order into a fetishism, he will be particularly sensitive to the object of his obsession. Short of fixation, there are things that are of particular moment for an individual; for sentimental reasons, a certain waltz may always attract a man's attention. Some sensitivity is occupational (role connected). A dentist is likely to be especially aware of teeth. There are sensitivities that are broadly cultural. An hysterical man at a church service would likely intrude upon the awareness of the entire congregation. Ultimately, anything that grossly disrupts the world will likely distrub most men. If gravity were to go, most men would take note. The universal need for a meaningful and secure identity will compel attention toward anything that the individual deems threatening to this ultimate concern.

Not all deviations from the normal range of an ideal are enigmatic. Some deviations are common enough to be named, explained and defined via their own "dirty" typifications. There are lemons and there are moldy lemons, rotten lemons and wizened lemons. There are men and there are blind men, Mongoloid idiots, senile men and amputees. For every typification that determines expectation within a given situation, there can be any number of "dirty" typifications. For every normal manifestation, there can be any number of deviant manifestations.

A change of purpose or context can alter expectation so that a heretofore "dirty" (abnormal) typification becomes itself a norm orbited by its own "dirty" typifications. The tables can be turned. If one is studying lemon molds, the defiantly moldless lemon in a collection of moldy lemons is the dirty one. When a person is in a home for the deaf, he anticipates deaf men; here hearing is incongruous.

However there are limits to the relativity of typifications. When an ideal is an ideal in the common sense of the word, it persists as a standard. The configurations that are more central to a man's orientation are these "ideals." The true ideal always operates although its influence can be mitigated by circumstantial expectation. A true man is one with all the components in "proper" proportions and in "proper" working order. Thus, even in a home for the deaf, the deaf remain ambiguous men though less poignantly so for being within a context where deafness is normal.

When an ambiguous manifestation is definitely mirrored by a "dirty" typification, there is some question concerning the basis of this manifestation's impact. Does the manifestation's essence or its ambiguity move a man? Are men moved by certain characteristics attributed to blindness or by the uncertainty inherent in blindness? They are moved by both. Blindness has been typfied and associations have grown concerning it. An individual may hold more or less elaborate expectations concerning the significance of blindness. These expectations influence his reactions to the condition. However, blind men are ambiguous men; they imperfectly meet the ideal criteria of their kind. They are abnormal manifestations that challenge the fragile reality fabrications of men and suggest the uncertain state of their existence. Often, this underlying uncertainty colors the definite expectations. Fantastic prejudices are often associated with ambiguous things. Preternatural evil has been attributed to deformed men, delapidated houses, wrecked ships and criminals. Such mundane things as dead birds can be seen easily as evil omens.

Ambiguity is more fearsome than definite expectation. To see the greater terror of uncertainty one need only consider monsters. Monsters do not symbolize concrete expectations. Monsters are palpable combinations of the incongruous. If death is their theme, as so often it is, they do not lie pallid and still in the ground but walk about manifesting a most ambiguous death. Disorder is the ultimate nemesis of man.

Unless they are conjuries born of apprehension, "dirty" typifications do reduce the uncertainty of the manifestly ambiguous. Manifest ambiguity is most gripping when it is inexplicable or unexpected. In that the world and man have something of an adversary relationship, men are not surprised that there are flaws in the order they attempt to enforce, nor are they surprised by many of the particular flaws. Defining an abnormality and explaining it are two of a number of methods by which manifest ambiguity is attenuated and experience is thereby cleansed.

34   Generally, men work to cleanse their experience. Men do, however, possess some propensity to seek dirt, to confront it, and sometimes, perversely, to wallow in it, as a demonstration of independence and power. (I shall discuss this phenomenon soon.) Most of the time, men will combat dirt with an effort commensurate with its felt poignancy. The means are variously conceptual, behavioral and perceptual. The means used in adjustment to ambiguous men will be discussed, also. For now, to give a sense of the process, I shall list a number of common ploys against ambiguous perceptions: a man may rationalize a bridge between his definition and the incongruent elements. He may alter his definition so that the dirt is taken into account. He may physically avoid the ambiguous manifestation. He may perceptually avoid manifest ambiguity by concentrating on diversionary interests. He may work to remove the ambiguous specimen. He may fix an ambiguous specimen so that it is no longer or is less ambiguous. He may seek out an ambiguous manifestation and laugh at it to release tension and to persuade himself of its inconsequence. He may seek out an ambiguous manifestation so that he may grow inured to it. He may use some combination of the above means. He may rationalize and avoid. He may partially avoid, partially confront, partially divert his attention, and all the while have grown somewhat indurated to the situation.

Before an especially poignant ambiguity, any combination of the above means is possible, however contradictory the components may seem, because in the face of acute manifest ambiguity, no one means can suffice, and a man may shift from one to another. When a function is essential yet formidable, men are less prone to be particular about the means they use to effect it; they will even countenance inconsistencies. When ambiguity hurts, men will counter it frenetically with anything and everything at hand. Before the ultimate concerns, a diverse array of methods is used in a compulsive drive for security and meaning, yet these means must fall short of their goal.

Manifest ambiguity can defy solution. Certain ideals are symbolically charged for the individual; they are keystones for an array of assumptions concerning world and self. For orientation's sake, a man endeavors to preserve these typifications though the world defies them and bends not to human will. The significance of central ideals lessens a person's capacity to ignore, to redefine, to camouflage, or to grow insensitive to any manifestation that conflicts with these ideals; if then one cannot "normalize" the

manifestation, the ambiguity endures. Mortality is the prime
arena where nature does not give way and man cannot give way.
Human orientation presupposes the integrity of human identity.
Thus, although manifest human ambiguity can be palliated, it
persists.

Ambiguity, Ambivalence and Power

Man battles disorder but he does not necessarily loath it.
Manifest ambiguity inspires ambivalence. It both repels and
attracts. It repels because it is disorder. It attracts because it is
a job and at times a mystery. Life is a process of orientation.
Man-made order is just that; it is made, and once it is made, it
must be maintained or remade. This building and maintenance
are steady efforts in terms of mind and body. The progress of the
process is a concern of man in and for itself. Men find comfort
in resolving as well as in resolution. They seek the means as
well as the end of the orientation process. Men seek to resolve
and they seek order. Some men lean more one way, and some
more the other; in other words, some men are predisposed toward
order and others toward the challenge to order. But all men crave
some order and some contest. Consequently, manifest ambiguity
repels as disorder and attracts as contention.

Power feeds security in an uncertain world. In forestalling or
resolving disorder men garner a sense of power. The challenge
need not be spectacular. Some sense of mastery flows from
competent routine before mundane exigencies. Little mystery
stems from most of the imperfections that mar man-enforced
order. There are ready explanations for these flaws that yield to
remedial routine. Work defrays both natural and social ambiguity. Labor is tiring, but there is comfort for man in the humming
of his engines and in a demonstration of his competence. Idleness
is impotence and misery.

Yet, ultimately, mundane routine cannot suffice to preserve an
individual's sanctuary. Nothing can. Man is everywhere insecure.
Thus, there is lure for heroic, dramatic demonstration of competence. More power comes with greater challenge and thus with
greater discomfort and often with greater danger. The harrowing
routines of policemen, firemen, physicians and combat soldiers
both exhiliarate and exhaust. These men must both welcome
and fear the objects of their professions. However, the true dragon
is mortality—that cancer of many guises, which lurks and parades, defies explanation and remedy, and threatens to dismember

36 the man and to dissemble his world. Going beyond routine, to solve a puzzle or mystery or to joust quixotically with mortality is to taste euphoria.

The ultimate hero has ever been the fighter—the man who swells himself through death-defying contest. He is the sole survivor of many battles, his preeminence proved by a sea of corpses. He has climbed the most precipitous, most frigid, most blustery mountains. He has rocketed his car down rain-drenched streets. He has plunged into infernos. He has chosen to amplify himself with cunning and courage, to drown out anxiety with his own din, to assault fate rather than to live in quiet desperation.

The siren song of ambiquity in mortality mixes peril with power. This duality is exemplified in the concept of taboo. Taboos are combinations of men and not-men, human and non-human, natural and supernatural; thus they represent the boundaries between these. Taboos reify ambiguities central to man's ultimate concerns. Tabooed objects are dangerous, untouchable, filthy and unmentionable, but concomitantly they are sacred and powerful. They are surrounded by a threat of severe punishment, but they are also beneficently magical.

Significance
of Ambiguous Man

Identity, Society and Ambiguous Man

Central to human orientation is human identity because man lives through himself. A spectrum of selfish and selfless impulses derives from the processes of self-definition. The outer world is seen in relation to oneself and one's requirements, and service to the world is predicated on identification with it. Constructing, nourishing and preserving a serviceable identity is a human preoccupation. Internal order and stability have priority: without them the outer world cannot be considered effectively.

Yet there is no stasis for the self. The individual changes inexorably, and within any interval he is as multifarious and intangible as the rest of his world. The individual's social identity is ever problematic; social support for it must be perpetually won anew. Social identity is perennially at the mercy of social conditions beyond the individual's control. As a mortal being, man is heir to a life span and liable to a phantasmagoria of transmogrifications. He comes apparently from nothing, waxes into adulthood, degenerates into decrepitude and rots into oblivion. Any of his senses, any part of his body or any aspect of his motility

4

38 can be fortuitously lost or distorted. He can become insane or feebleminded. Man is protean and vulnerable.

That individuals derive their identities from society is a major tenant of social theory. The child constructs his identity through a play of action and reaction to peers and adults. He interprets reactions to himself, acts accordingly, interprets the reactions, acts accordingly, and so on. In this way, character is developed. In time, adult roles are learned by which a man navigates in a world of other men, and statuses are acquired by which a man is positioned within a social order. A man's renderings of his roles and statuses comprise his social identity, which is generally what social theorists consider identity to be. Social identity both defines the man as an individual, and binds him to his society. A coherent social identity is essential to orientation. It tells a man, in terms of society, what he is and might be, how worthy he is and what he should do.

The development and the preservation of specific forms of men are the core of man-made order. Man is his own chief project. Yet, although the existence of man depends on his efforts, the animal, "man," is no mere manikin for social dressing. Men do not create themselves from nothing, and thus man-made or social identity does not subsume man.

"Man" is the raw material from which the social actor is worked. The primordial being has an identity of his own, a "natural" identity. The nature of man—his mortality, body, mind, life cycle, vulnerabilities, exigencies, powers and propensities—generates a human experience that transcends social programming. Perceptions of pleasure and pain, the rush of realization, the pall of confusion, the colors, the contours and the motions of the animal precede social interpretations.

Knowing the "man," and how to handle him is a transcendent factor in orientation. This knowledge is largely derived from social identity which channels natural propensities, provides the means to slake needs and interprets much of "natural" experience. Yet, social constructs cannot ultimately couch the transience and the plasticity of man. The question and the threat of mortality remain. Nature encroaches on the integrity of individual identity. Beneath cultural stolidity, shift the quicksilver sands of humanity; ironically it is society that impresses the individual with this reality.

Man learns his natural identity through self-awareness but also through society. Not only are other men negotiators and behaviorist inculcators of roles and statuses, but as beings, they

are also exemplars of human identity and mimes of the individual. Man presumes that his perception of other men is some
reflection of what he himself is as a man. Experience of society
is fraught with models of humanness in variegated array. Other
men exhibit to the individual something of what he was and
will be, of what he might have been and might be. Without other
men, the individual would not know the range of calamities that
can befall a human body; nor would he realize the generative-
degenerative fate of all men. Other men clarify his personality;
yet they also threaten its integrity since the manifest profusion
of humanity portrays an uncertain human identity.

There is no self-evident definition of man; neither is there an
explicit description. Men are neither tightly regular nor consistent. Idealized visions of man manifested in art, in champions, in
beauty queens and in movie stars are mocked by the multitude
that does not conform to these "idealized" ideals. Generally,
men discern mankind by somewhat broader, although by no
means broad, ideal types that from man to man tend to be similar
but never identical. These ideal types entail ranges of normal
variation, and these are also flouted by "men." Any typification
of "man" must encompass dissimilar beings and entail limits
that "men" will challenge by meeting these limits incompletely
or imperfectly. However "men" are designated, no man is identical to another man, and no man himself remains constant over
time. An individual man is protean, emerging from protoplasm
and mutating incessantly until he or his vestiges meld with the
earth. Within a zone he is a man, whereas before and after it
there is the promise and the vestiges of a man. Yet, whatever
signs are designated to mark the zone, and whatever similarities
are determined to comprise a man, there will be beings who are
ambiguously both human and nonhuman in terms of these signs
and similarities.

To the eyes of the individual there are always ambiguous men.
These men are *manifestly* ambiguous; they display some char-
acteristic that is incongruent with the individual's perceptual
typification of man. Does "man" have a head; then a headless
man would be an ambiguous man. Does he respond to other
men; does he walk, see, think, talk; is he two-legged, two-eyed;
there are manlike creatures deficient in each of these criteria and
in combinations of them. Do arms and heads have a certain
appearance; what of men with withered arms and tumid heads?
Wherever the individual may "draw the line," there will be
beings who will mock his definition, even if the typification is

so broad as to be meaningless, even if bones are likened to breathing beings. Men blend into nonmen.

Assumptions Concerning Man

Any categorial supposition concerning man includes an implicit definition of man. Above, man has been depicted as seeking orientation, concerned with his own identity and seeing other men as some representation of himself. This delineation does not include men who do not have the potential to act, think or socialize. Sleeping men are excluded, as are dead, comatose, premature and severely retarded men. The criteria are narrow in comparison to what generally, conceptually marks men. However, "orienting" man is the protagonist, as seen here, and although he has his ambiguous specimens, in this discussion, the actor shall be given, and the ambiguity shall be a figment of his perception.

The Impact of Face-to-Face Encounter

The existence and nature of other men must always be somewhat problematic for the individual. What he knows of other men, he knows only through his senses. He infers their identities from what he perceives of them. In direct encounter, other men are heralded by complex sensation; their identities are manifest in intricate combinations of face, touch, odor, motion and sound. The full presentation of a man is highly multifarious, and thus there is large latitude for elliptical and distorted presentations of man.

To perceive a man entails more potential for equivocality than to conceive of him because perceptions are more detailed than conceptions. The individual is substantially unaware of the complex perceptual criteria which for him signals "man." This inattention or ignorance enables a man to sketch "man" conceptually so that ambiguity is minimized. Conceptions are schematic and scanty; they generally ignore qualifications of texture and gesture that would be evident in perception. Conceptual delineations are more certain in application for the same reason. Because conceptual definitions are selective descriptions with few dimensions, they may cast from humanity or embrace as humanity what eyes would retain in uncertainty.

Perceived man is also less variable than conceived man. The perceptual typification of man is exacting. A perceptual encounter with a "man" implies some social interaction; and thus the individual generally expects every man he encounters to be a competent social actor. This expectation applies most comprehensively and implies strictest scrutiny in a one-to-one interaction, but the expectation holds to some degree even if a confrontation is more substantial than inclusion in one's social scenery. "Man in thought" is not bound by this social stricture. Conceptual definitions can and do stem ambiguity through latitudinarianism in encompassing incompetent and "non" actors. It might not matter in terms of legal, humanitarian or religious conceptions of man that some "men" stutter—that they are blind or retarded or one-armed or eight feet tall. These things do matter in perceptual experience.

Operational, perceptual typifications invariably are at odds with broader but simpler conceptual definitions that entail undetailed and unsocial men. This incongruence compounds the ambiguity perceived in a "man" who does not present himself as a viable social actor. A "Right to Life" idea of man, that a living being who has been or might be born of woman is unequivocally human, may comfort the individual while he is spared challenging experiences. Yet, this view can increase the individual's torment when he perceives freaks, when experience apprises him of his narrow perception of man.

No perceptual delineation will be conceptualized here. There is no *one* perceptual typification of man, and each one is ultimately ineffable. Men do hold similar perceptions of man that are quite limited in terms of criteria such as arms, legs, dimensions, capacities and so forth. Yet, to conjecture on the precise similarities is beyond the scope of this discussion and is too tricky. Thus when ambiguity is examined here, it is considered in relation to what is ambiguous in the eyes of the beholder. For purpose of example, specific instances of ambiguity will be proposed that will suggest that the qualifications which signal unambiguous man are strict.

Undoubtedly, differential experience has some differentiating effect on the perception of man. Members of a heterogenous society are likely to be more cosmopolitan in their views than are members of a more homogeneous community. To the eyes of a 10th-century Viking, a black African would likely have been ambiguous, and vice versa. Yet, considering that the similarities of the various ethnic groups far exceed the disparities, the variation in "ideal types" among these groups should not be great.

42   The perceptual criteria for man are strict, but they are also variable relative to several images of man. The individual distinguishes between males and females, children, adults, and the old. Each group has its own image. A mixture of these images is sure to be ambiguous. A baby with a hoary head would be an ambiguous man, as would a man with breasts, or an elderly pregnant lady.

Factors in the Perception of Human Ambiguity

As with all typifications, there are degrees of manifest ambiguity regarding perceptual typifications of man. Perceived ambiguity varies with perceived stigmatization curvilinearly. Ambiguity first gains then dimishes with increasing stigmatization. A corpse is likely to seem more ambiguous than a blind man, but also more ambiguous than a skull. When context is taken into account, a man without a hand is as ambiguous as a hand without a man. The former is almost certainly a man, while the latter is almost certainly not a man.

Some characteristics are more central to one's perception of a man than are others. The individual is more sensitive to flaws in terms of his more central criteria. Thus, the quality of a stigma influences its impact. The face is the most significant aspect of the human form. Consequently, deformities of the face are more stigmatizing than comparable deformities of other parts of the body. Generally, the upper part of the body is more central to human identity than is the lower part. Thus, a mermaid would be less startling than a woman with a fish head. Personality is also closely associated with manhood. Thus, a personality disorder will generally be more damning than a comparable motor disorder.

The individual perceives men in terms of conditioned expectations and present appearances. History colors current perception. Memory or reputation of a normative past exacerbates the confusion of an ambiguous present. A man is reluctant to accept a traumatically altered status for another person, especially if that person had been a "significant other" such as spouse, kin or friend. Memory of a man and to a lesser extent, reputation will tend one to treat the vestiges as a man; but the incongruence between past and present produces a strain that renders such empathy exhausting. In wartime, women have clung to the maggot-ridden corpses of their husbands. However, widows do not embrace their husbands' remains indefinitely without ceas-

ing themselves to be human. Ultimately, one must react to what
one is currently and continuously seeing. History cannot save
the currently ambiguous man, nor the persons who perceive him.
Yet, earlier memory will forever bend perception its way to some
degree.

Social Ambiguity and (Natural) Human Ambiguity

Other men can threaten the individual's human (natural)
identity; they can also threaten his social orientation. Both of
these are challenges to the individual's orientation, but they are
different challenges. Human ambiguity is distinct from social
ambiguity. A man can be humanly ambiguous without being
socially ambiguous. Throughout history, certain types of ambiguous men played definite social roles. Midgets were court fools.
Epileptics were oracles. On the other hand, nonambiguous men
do not necessarily have positive or clear social identities. The
manhood of a gangster is rarely doubted. Ambiguous man is not
"marginal man." There are men who confound the individual's
social expectations or disrupt the social order in which he walks.
They impede his orientation through inappropriate intrusions or
through illegible presentation of their social identities; yet they
are not ambiguous men. The ambiguous man does not plainly
present himself as a man.

Human ambiguity and social ambiguity are readily confounded
for a number of reasons. Both types of ambiguity emanate from
"men" and both challenge the individual's identity. Human
ambiguity can result in social ambiguity, and can be so obtrusive
that it interferes with social events. Human ambiguity causes
social ambiguity when an ambiguous man cannot meet in appearance or behavior the statuses and roles which he attempts or
which context demands of him. A deaf man would be socially
ambiguous as a musician, but not as a tenant in a home for the
deaf. A man who cannot appear as a proper human being can
disrupt social order by drawing attention from the normal exigencies of an occasion; a hydrocephalic child at a wedding will
rival the ceremony for the eyes of the congregants. A man who
cannot act appropriately or consistently can readily derail the
role playing of other men; composure is difficult in the presence
of a delirious man; conversation with a senile man is a strain.
The difficulty of distinquishing human and social ambiguity is
further exacerbated by the reality that social deviants, miscast
and temporarily indisposed men wreak similar havoc.

The surest way to distinguish the socially ambiguous man from the humanly ambiguous man is to consider their impacts, their particular dysfunctions for other men. This consideration requires a view of the difference between the purposes served by social identity and those served by human identity. In general, if a man confounds navigational orientation he is socially ambiguous, and if he confounds the nature of man he is humanly ambiguous.

Reading the social identities of other men is vital for the individual's perception of his social self, and for his capacity to navigate in a world of other men. Socially, men are disparate. They are divided into types, into purposeful permutations or role and status sets. Ultimately, they are divided into unique personalities. To build their social identities, men mime role models, but they also "triangulate" unique identities through differential interactions with different kinds of men. Unique individuals who manifest social types comprise a functional social order that is based upon oppositions and reciprocities as well as mutualities. A man navigates within this social order via a repertoire of patterned expectations associated with his interpretations of his statuses and roles and associated with his typifications of time, place and the social identity presentations of other men.

Reading the natural identity in other men has no navigational utility. The individual's concern with natural identity is primordial. It is a concern for the ultimate meaning of humanity in terms of the cosmos and eternity. A vision of "man" serves to circumscribe the denominators of human existence. It relates to questions of basic human experiences; to primary compulsions, conflicts and paradoxes, and to mortality, and to the transience of body and personality through life.

The Significance of Ambiguous Man

The individual himself is changing and realizes that a precarious continuity seals his appearance and personality. This personal uncertainty charges the significance of persons who transcend the perceived bounds of viable humanity. There is a fear of dissolution and transmogrification, which translates into a fear of ultimate disorientation. Thus, those persons who are on the fringe of the human distribution—the deformed, the unborn, the dead, the decrepit, the insane and the crippled—are preceptual scourges for the center of a gelatinous mankind which seeks

security and certainty. Normative man fears deviants who are
ambiguous men, who are too manlike to be perceptually quar-
antined but too grotesque to be accepted as representations of
man and self.

Yet the fear of ambiguous man is alloyed with fascination.
Being a combination of man and not man, the ambiguous man
reifies the boundary between them. He embodies the mystery of
human identity that is a central concern of men. He is taboolike.
Thus, ambiguous man inspires a painful ambivalence. Concomitantly, the individual is compelled and repelled by visages of
human ambiguity.

The fascination and the fear of nebulous man are evidenced in
numerous portraits that have been traditional expressions of
horror. The terror of morbidity is reified in conjurations of living
dead, in skulking corpses and skeletons, in ghosts and vampires.
Monsters meld human appearance and inhuman demeanor or
inhuman form and human behavior as in "the possessed," witches, extraterrestrial aliens, automatons and anthropomorphized
animals or things. Monsters are physical agglomerations of man
and animal or man and machine. Monsters are scatological men
with gummy appendages. Horror is manifest in the transition
from normative to grotesque in the man who becomes a monster,
the werewolf, the man whose brain is stolen by martians and the
famous scientist who becomes a brain in an aquarium. Contagion
makes monsters of men who revel in the mysteries of ambiguity,
in the obscene, in direct, and in death. Finally, monsters are
caricatures of normative men; they are men with tumid heads,
withered legs and scurfy skin. Monsters are ambiguous men, and
conversely, ambiguous men are monsters, fiends, ghouls, brutes
and miscreants.

The fascination and the fear of human ambiguity is further
evidenced by the public's reaction to it. Men will crowd in upon
gore from an auto accident, but only so far. They will stand
uncertainly as if they are being compelled and repelled. Bystand-
ers may shove through the crowd to "see"—only to become sick.

For power's sake, men may consciously or unconsciously desire
to joust with the manifest mystery of ambiguous men. Man's
play with human ambiguity is like his play with all mystery
stories in which loose ends are flung out so that they may be
tied together, somehow, in the end. Mortality hangs specterlike
on the minds of men. In the form of ambiguous men the great
adversary is found in the open. So, the individual confronts

46   ambiguous men to mitigate their ambiguity and his uncertainty, and in the process, to augment his sense of competence in the world.

To maintain his self-orientation, the individual copes with the uncertainty embodied by ambiguous men. His reaction is a denial. The individual assuages the ambiguity of nebulous men by working to exclude them from or to include them in humanity, or by disdaining or avoiding their significance. His means of denial are variously conceptual, perceptual and behavioral. They are frequently combined in a palliative pastiche against an irrefragable uncertainty.

Adaptation
to Ambiguous Man

The Power of Doing

Human ambiguity piques men with their ultimate concern: the unfathomable mystery of human identity and significance in light of mortality. This towering enigma makes taxing and
tenuous any orientation vis-à-vis ambiguous
men. Because men cannot resolve the mystery,
their orientations to manifest human ambiguity
must be something of a sham. Viewed objectively,
the reality of mortality will scuttle human pretensions every time, and thus men tend not to
keep both eyes on this reality. While battling
mortality, they mezmerize themselves with meretricious power. They dance to their conceptions.

Orientation comes via a concert of conception,
perception and behavior. The conceptual and perceptual components of orientation are self-evident, but as was stated earlier, behavior is also
integral to the process since men must rework
nature to match their visions. The action manifests the thought, and the perception reflects both
thought and accomplishment. The association of
mind and hand is close. Action is man's envoy to
the world.

The proof is in the pudding; the power is in
the doing. Consummation is the proof of efficacy.
But since there is no ultimate efficacy before

5

mortality, there can be no ultimate consummation. Still men must "do" if they would accommodate themselves to ambiguous men. Men must perceive power in action that is less than consummate, action which, if it "does" anything real, defeats mortality by distancing ambiguous men, or sometimes cures or lessens human ambiguity temporarily.

Every system of cosmic interpretation has its rituals. Science has its technologies. Religions have their rites. These rituals are essential to their ideologies. Interpretation cannot stem mortal anxiety, and thus if a man is to believe, his belief must offer substantial comfort. Even promises of positive immortality are not enough. Men desire tangible reassurance when confronted with patent danger and uncertainty.

Those persons who would rend ritual from religion are naive. Where there is religion there is ritual, however apparent or oblique its manifestations. If certain ritual observances are cast from the front door, others will steal in from the back door if religion remains. If men are disabused of ritual practices, their religion will have been slain in the process. Manifest rituals and their supporting rationales are religion itself for perhaps most adherents who are deaf to the filigree philosophies and subtle ceremonies of the religious intelligentsia.

Science's relevant representative is medicine, a belief system also heavily dependent on procedure. Sheer medical evaluation is an empty gesture. If nothing else, tests must be administered. In medical practice it is difficult to do nothing. There is a pervasive presumption among physicians and laymen that medicine entails ministration, and that cure comes from antidote rather than judgment. In treatment there is a placebo effect for patient and physician. Thus, even when the physician has no proven remedy, there is spur for him to do something—to order tests or therapy, however tenuous their medical utility. If faith is to be placed in medicine, some demonstration is required.

The distinction between technology and ritual would be palpable if technology could rehabilitate all ambiguous men or if its use were restricted to demonstrably effective application. Yet, medicine has limited empirical effectiveness, and like all ritual systems, it palliates much of the time. Medicine has no handle on eternity or cosmic transcendence. The security that medicine provides depends on the prospects of temporal amelioration. Thus, practitioners frequently invite hope by practicing medicine even though their effort has minimal real effect. This reality is more apparent today than it was earlier when dramatic cures

were first applied to a plethora of acute maladies since this
success has augmented the population of patients with incurable
chronic maladies.

The distinction between medicine and myth is further attenuated by the fact that the latter is not devoid of empirical
effectiveness. The power of ritual depends on some demonstrable
efficacy. The confidence that ritual inspires is salubrious; so is
the social support it engenders, and perhaps the diet and the
activity it enforces. There are occasions when myth would
distance ambiguous men rather than bind them to humanity.
The means for dividing ambiguous men from men are somewhat
effective as well.

Medicine, mythologies and religions are all ideologies that
interpret human ambiguity. They all generate methods by which
human ambiguity is combated, ameliorated but not defeated. In
each case, the enactment of rituals—rites, procedures, techniques, remedies—in itself nurtures a sense of power to sustain
the ideology in the face of the real shortfall in its capacity to
resolve the ultimate concerns.

Men garner security and meaning from their rituals and beliefs
even though the world does not confirm them. The idea fosters
the ritual that fortifies the idea which fosters the ritual. Belief
and ritual form a reflexive game catalyzed by desire, a combination that generates a show of light so selfcontained, and so
alluring that men believe and act with a certainty unwarranted
in terms of sheer empirical reality. In their fear and need, men
turn to themselves even while they reach out to move their
worlds.

The action inspired by the presence of ambiguous men is not
always ritualistic, and in that it is ritualistic, it is not uniformly
so. The most sublime rituals require settings and expertise that
are not generally available. If a man encounters that for which
he has no protective preconception or foil, or if he is too startled
to summon his defenses, he cannot react ritualistically. An ill-
defined conception such as a phobia, aversion, or philia which
generates a standard but hardly delicate reaction. An untested
rationalization grown in the absence of mannifest human ambiguity and devoid of ritual expiation will likely inspire a confused
reaction to the actual presence of ambiguous men. The most
developed rituals are associated with an esoteric grasp of the
most comprehensive and refined cultural views of man, such as
medicine or religion would provide to physicians and priests.

There is some sense of power in all doing, but the greatest

50 sense of power derives from acting in terms of an evolved ideological-ritual system. Momentary exhilaration surges from "glandular" reaction: a salvo of hate or violence or a sucessful flight from danger, but as a rationalizing animal, man garners a more enduring sense of power due to intelligence. The more definite his rationales and techniques, the surer he feels about them.

The Means of Assuagement

All reactions to ambigous men entail both ambivalence and denial. The ambivalence arises from the mystery of human identity that ambiguous men represent—a mystery that both frightens and fascinates. Men fear ambiguous men's threat to the boundaries of human identity, and yet men are drawn by a promise that if they can subdue the threat of human ambiguity, they can resolve, or at least attenuate human uncertainy. Thus, men take up the means that assuage human ambiguity passively for defense and actively for strength. The challenge of ambiguous men is both feared and coveted.

Men defend and bolster themselves by denying human ambiguity. Thus denial assumes two basic forms: a denial of the ambiguity itself, or an avoidance of it. Toward the first end, men work to separate ambiguous men definitively from mankind, or to bind them definitively to it. The means can be materially consequential or purely expressive. Avoidence can be either physical or perceptual. Men can stay clear of ambiguous men or they can divert their attention from the ambiguity of ambiguous men, thereby diminishing their poignancy.

The following are summary descriptions of the means by which men assuage their perception of manifest human ambiguity:

Impulsive reaction. The least sophisticated reation to ambiguous men is impulsive. This is impromtu reaction to a surprise encounter with manifest human ambiguity. The individual is startled, and thus his reaction manifests an uncertainty and ambivalence so acute as to preclude any denial but flight. The countenance will show astonishment, fear and fascination. The man may shrink from the sight with stiff hesitant movements, or he may similarly draw nearer. Generally, the behavior serves to separate the individual from the ambiguous man since the

former instinctively moves to protect himself in an uncertain 51
situation. Temporarily, a blend of terror and curiosity can transfix
the individual. Ultimately, he is likely to flee.

Prejudiced reaction A reaction is prejudiced when it is governed by a protective preconception that is not integrated with
a developed ideology. Prejudices are folk conceptions, supersti-
tions and distorted fragments or religious rationale. They are
means of separation generally visited upon the more acute
manifestations of human ambiguity—persons with gross deformities or debilities. Prejudiced reaction assumes two forms: in the
first, "taboo reaction," ambivalence is ascendant; in the second,
"aversion reaction," denial is ascendent.

"Taboo reaction" is manifestly similar to "impulsive reaction"
in that both the ambiguous stimulous evokes an abrupt and
ambivalent response characterized by fear and curiosity, repulsion and attraction. Stylization distinguishes "taboo reaction"
from "impulsive reaction." Taboo reaction is choreographed and
is thus a "safe" experience. The ambiguous man is seen as
mysterious, disgusting and powerful but not dangerously so as
long as he is treated according to the prescribed regimen. Here
the ambiguous man becomes a witch or an oracle or more
commonly an idiot in Bedlam or a freak in a side show. If he is
chained or caged he may become an object of ridicule, which is
a means of affective separation arising in this instance from
uncertainty rather than hate. Association with the ambiguous
man as taboo fosters a sense of power; it allows a purgative
expression of uncertainty concerning human identity, it enables
an affirmation of self through contrast. In this last effect, taboo
reaction is a means of separation, though not so strongly as
"aversion reaction."

"Aversion reaction" is also an abrupt response, serving to
protect the individual by distinguishing the ambiguous man from
mankind. Curiosity is transformed into aggression. Hate and fear
dominate "aversion reaction" in rage, horror, attack, flight or
mockery. Expression and action set the ambiguous man apart.
Men will both flee from and turn against the "unclean." Men
may bolt from a man with an "evil" eye or they summarily run
him out. The cripple is hounded and tormented so that the
"normal" can assure themselves that they are different. For the
same reason, the town idiot is mocked. Cruelty marks most
aversion reactions. Terror marks the rest.

52   *Obscenity reaction.* A person's reaction to ambiguous men is obscene when he is obsessively drawn to mingle with them because they are ambiguous and when his behavior is unsupported by ideology and sublime rituals. A man may wallow among ambiguous men to prove his power to withstand their ambiguity and to enhance his identity through contrast with theirs. The individual who is perversely attracted to manifest human ambiguity defends himself in its presence idiosyncratically through scorn, cruelty or private ritual, which can become both rigid and elaborate. If an individual finds many occasions for obscene reaction, he is engaged in a perversion. The compulsive and the private nature of obscenity reaction distinguish it most clearly from both forms of "prejudiced reaction." In obscenity reaction, there is an attempt to quiet the ultimate concerns by "fetishizing" ambiguous men, by reducing the process of ultimate or cosmic orientation to a play of power and stamina in the presence of the embodied mystery of ambiguous men. Ambiguous men become props in a game by which the individual hopes to quiet his uncertainty concerning himself.

Ritual separation. Ritual separation is founded on a developed ideology and is a sublimation of aversion reaction. In its ultimate form, this action severs ambiguous men from mankind conceptually and physically. More often, ritual separation distinguishes and removes ambiguous men less absolutely through labeling, explanation and sequestration.

Death rites are the ultimate form of ritual separation. Funerals are religious rites by which the moribund are ritualistically removed from mankind. This procedure always entails actual removal: interment, incineration or immersion. That men must resort to such eradication testifies to the resiliency of manifest human ambiguity. Medicine, too, entails rites of ultimate separation. Standardized tests are administered to the deceased so that he may be pronounced dead and bereft of the considerations due living patients.

As a hedge against confusion, people define categories of human abnormality. "Dirty typifications" are used to preserve the integrity of human identity. Ideologies distinguish ambiguous men by definitions and explanations—manifested in ritual tests. Men of medicine diagnose; they certify ambiguous men to be suffering from various maladies that set them apart from healthy men. Chapter 13 of Leviticus proclaims signs for ascertaining

leprosy, and procedures by which men are judged "unclean." The
chapter begins:

> And the Lord spake unto Moses and Aaron, saying,
> When a man shall have in the skin of his flesh a rising, a scab or
> a bright spot, and it be in the skin of his flesh like the plague of
> leprosy; then he shall be brought unto Aaron the priest, or unto
> one of his sons the priests:
>
> And the priest shall look on the plague in the skin of the flesh:
> and when the hair in the plague is turned white, and the plague
> in sight be deeper than the skin of his flesh, it is a plague of
> leprosy: and the priest shall look on him, and pronounce him
> unclean.

In Chapter 21 of Leviticus there is the following passage:

> And the Lord spake unto Moses saying,
> Speak unto Aaron saying,
> Whosoever he be of thy seed in their generations that hath any
> blemish, let him not approach to offer the bread of his God. For
> whatsoever man he be that hath a blemish, he shall not
> approach: a blind man, or a lame, or he that had a flat nose, or
> any thing superfluous:
> Or a man that is brokenfooted or brokenhanded. Or crookbackt,
> or a dwarf, or that hath a blemish in his eyes, or be scurvy, or
> scabbed, or hath his stones broken;
> No man that hath a blemish of the seed of Aaron the priest shall
> come nigh to offer the offerings of the Lord made by fire: he hath
> a blemish; he shall not come nigh to offer the bread to his God.

At times, formal banishment or sequestration follows the testing
and the pronouncing. Historically, lepers were forced from the
byways of normative society. Currently, those persons judged
insane are with due process put away in mental hospitals.
Paraplegics are committed to rehabilitation centers. Thus hidden
away these ambiguous men spare the sensitivity of the general
public.

If they remain in view, acutely ambiguous men will remain
upsetting regardless of labels and explanations. Labels, rationales
and tests can ease the impact of transient or minor abnormality,
but they cannot stem the ambiguity of resistant and gross
deformity or debility. This insufficiency causes men's central
concern for a coherent, secure and significant identity. This

desire maintains a normative ideal type as a standard by which all men are judged. Thus, men cannot content themselves by delineating a variety of men.

Humanitarianism or a broadening of perspective. Unlike the foregoing four methods, humanitarianism is a means by which ambiguous men are bound to mankind. In consummate humanitarianism the definition of mankind is broadened so that all but perhaps dead men are included definitively in humanity. Humanitarianism is founded on a conceptual gerrymander. Man is conceived in terms that qualify most ambiguous men unequivocally. Humanitarians locate human essence in the invisible and intangible realm of the spirit. To them, the actual form of the body is not supposed to matter.

In a variation of humanitarianism, all men are conceived as imperfect mortal representations of a divine ideal; in this sense, ambiguous men are thought of as merely more imperfect than normative men. All men are profane in that they are imperfect, but they are also sacred in that they, ambiguous men included, suggest the sacred ideal. The humanitarian values all men for their sacred essence, however dimly it is portrayed.

However, as was affirmed earlier, a latitudinarian conception cannot forestall a perception of manifest ambiguity and offers in itself meager protection against manifest ambiguity. In order to combat reality, humanitarianism must and does entail more than the thought.

Humanitarianism is part of a world outlook, an ideology that is religious or of religious derivation. The rituals that affirm the ideology implicitly affirm humanitarianism. However, humanitarianism can itself involve rituals in the form of prayers and trials. The individual prays that he may not be repulsed by the visages of human ambiguity—indeed, that he may love ambiguous men. Confronting ambiguous men with equanimity and caring for them become a trial, a penance by which faith in a divine, transcendent human identity is attested.

The "do-gooderism" is undoubtedly a difficult method to use effectively. Human concern is drawn to the corporeal and the temporal. It is not easy to deny that the body is consequential to human indentity.

Spiritual transcendence. Like humanitarianism, spiritual transcendence is tied to religion and locates the human essence in the ethereal. Spiritual transcendence differs from humanitarianism in the former is concerned with the dead and the prospect of death, while the latter is concerned with living ambiguous men. Ideologies of spiritual transcendence draw a path between man's temporal state and immortality. The rituals prepare normative mortals for positive immortal identities, and usher the dearly departed into heaven. Thus, funerals are not only rites of temporal separation but also rites of spiritual transcendence.

Spiritual transcendence is a more credible and prevalent method than is humanitarianism. Transcendence is more credible because even though it cannot be empirically verified, it is not belied by the presence of ambiguous men as is humanitarianism. The dead are buried. Transcendence is more prevalent because it is the only prospect for surmounting the grave.

Normalization. Normalization is an effort to reduce the ambiguity of ambiguous men by making them more manlike. Anodynes, surgeries, therapies, incantations or exhortations are used to attack the conceived source of the human ambiguity. The appeal of normalization is that it is a courageous technique of confrontation and assuagement in the here and now. It is meant to have material consequences, and is akin to all effort to accommodate the world to human purpose. In coping with manifest human ambiguity, the rituals of normalization best represent the perceived power of doing since they are enacted not to avoid, conceal or tolerate human ambiguity but to diminish or to eliminate it.

Normalization binds ambiguous men to the bosom of humanity through reform or rehabilitation. Reform is acheived through persuasion in the form of rationales, or negative or positive reinforcement. The reformer presumes the ambiguous man's rational control over his predicament. Since abnormal behavior is most readily seen as willful, reform efforts are usually directed at it. However, when deformities have been thought to result from moral lassitude, unwhole men have been urged to repent and thus to reform. Since men infrequently consider human ambiguity to be self-willed, men do not seek to reform ambiguous men so often as men seek to rehabilitate them.

Rehabilitation is manipulation either of a man's psyche or his soma, either through symbolic nostrums or through physical agencies. The purpose of rehabilitation is to mend or to restore deformed or incapacitated persons, a purpose that seems so laudatory that men generally accept it at face value without probing for deeper significance. Yet, what does the therapist or the rehabilitator do? He diagnoses the abnormality and determines the normalcy toward which he pushes his client. A client-centered approach is but a cover as would become apparent if the client opted for more abnormality. The rehabilitator works to diminish what to him is manifest ambiguity. He works to cleanse his perception of unsettling forms. He exercies his power over the mutability and the mortality of men.

Curing is a heady experience but any discernible normalization of an ambiguous man rewards the Samaritan. He feels his power most keenly when the ambiguous are fully restored, when the bandages are removed to reveal an unmarred visage, or when the cast is removed to unleash unbridled locomotion. However, any move toward normalcy can flush the therapist with his power, especially if he considers the abnormality to be especially resistant. The nose the plastic surgeon constructs may not be flawless, but it is a nose where there was none before. If the blind cannot be made to see, they can be made to behave almost as if they can. They can be taught to be "productive members of society." They can be taught to navigate urban sidewalks; they can be taught to read.

Men who by occupation are rehabilitators or reformers are drawn more to the challenge to order than to order itself regarding the identity of man. They seek out ambiguous men to achieve, to practice and to demonstrate curative powers. Rehabilitators and reformers desire the power more than the cure. If they wanted a tidy view of mankind, they would not seek the company of ambiguous men. Cures are the best evidence of curative power, but they are not essential for the perception of it since men credit other evidence.

In the face of human ambiguity, men generally garner comfort from the sheer process of remedial doing. Activity fosters hope and thus a placebo effect. Men tend to grasp at straws when bereft of ready remedy, trying any would-be antidote—anything that might be effective in their estimation or in the testimony of other men. In societies where Western medicine has been superimposed on native culture, people often shop for relief, turning to their medicine men or folkways when Western medicine proves unsatisfactory and vice-versa; sometimes they hedge their bets by using the methods of all camps. As was suggested earlier, physicians are likely to use dubiously effective techniques rather than do nothing.

Remedies are used against human ambiguity ranging from passing indisposition to gross deformity. Men work to match

their medicine to their complaint. They use what they deem to
be their stronger antidotes against the more resistant and obtrusive ailments. Stronger medicine reflects a more sophisticated scheme of explanation and interpretation. The thought behind a modest anodyne born of folkways may be a simple "cause and effect," such as chewing a weed to relieve a belly-ache. When men would take on severe affliction, they turn to medicine-men for rituals imbued with cult, delivered with pomp and circumstance.

Diversionary focus and actions. The perceptions of ambiguity can be attenuated by attention to other concerns. In the presence of ambiguous men, a man may preoccupy himself with any of the countless dramas remote from manifest ambiguity. He may dwell on petty feuds. He may muse on home and family. He may imagine that he is engaged in a quest for honor and preeminence, competing successfully with foes and competitors. He may transpose the dilemma of ambiguous men to a social plane and fume at their social peccadilloes.

In the presence of more acute human ambiguity, preoccupying thoughts are usually alloyed with preoccupying activity since the perceptual pull of the ambiguity would overwhelm mere musing. Since it is incumbent upon a person to do his job, job-related activity is an excellent diversion. As she maneuvers around his bed, scrubbing away and day dreaming, a housekeeper substantially quells the impact of a contracted and drooling ancient. In general, frenetic activity is a good opiate since it allows little occasion to ponder the manifest ambiguity or to absorb its implications.

Although they are directed at ambiguous men, the more elaborate methods of normalization readily double as diversions, since they require concentrated effort and since they are used against the most painfully acute ambiguity. In the presence of the grotesque, rehabilitators will tend to employ the added protection of diversion by immersing themselves in their ritual work. Normalization can become so ritualized that a displacement of goals may result with men becoming more intent upon the proper administration of a remedy than upon its actual effect. An old adage illustrates this point: the surgery was a complete success but the patient died. Men can seduce themselves with a play of ritual power. The fineness, the institutional trappings, the ornateness or the solemnity of ritual can be taken as demonstration of its import. The "import" of ritual detracts from the

58 impact of ambiguous men. Thus, "making big medicine" can entail diversion and a displacement of goals if the goal is taken to be the recovery of the patient. However, regarding the function of normalization to provide a capacity to cope with manifest human ambiguity, diversion entails no displacement of goals.

Diversion is a universal tactic used against far more than ambiguous men. Daily routine salves the ultimate concerns. Men lighten their lives with mundane affairs which illumine the shadows that would flower in questions and doubts. Men in whom this tendency is pronounced are the men Kierkegaard named Philistines—men who dare not peer beyond the perimeters of lives lived by social formulas.

The **M*A*S*H** *effect and method.* The MASH Effect is named after the movie, *M*A*S*H* which depicts the "goings on" in an army field hospital in Korea during the Korean War. The story is notable for its descriptions of raucous humor and antics. In the midst of carnage and danger, MASH nurses and doctors seem irreverent, rollicking, cavalier and pert. Kinks and tomfoolery hold center stage. Yet, this relentless and frantic comedy is steeled with muted desperation and shadowed with fatigue. Throughout the mayhem, the surgery gets done. The movie renders the impression that the antics are essential to saving lives, that without humor, sanity could not be maintained under such pressure, and serious performance would be impossible.

Stress evokes the MASH Effect, a pastiche of humor and antics which eases stressful situations with diminution, diversion and release. When a "momentous" occasion is inundated with irreverent and irrelevant concerns, laughter and disarray, the occasion is likely to seem less than momentous. The bite is softened in a scene made surreal or jocular. Antics jostle attention from skit to skit. Cloaking itself in feigned madness, the mind stages and partakes of tangles so that it will not linger on doubt and dread. Laughter and frenzy purge.

Most men experience a mild MASH Effect regularly since humor and antics are a common ploy against mundane tensions. *The* MASH Effect portrayed in the movie tends to appear when events press hard and long. One can expect it among combat pilots, firemen, critical-care personnel and even some university students. Prolonged crises, such as war and plagues, are prime breeders of the MASH Effect. During more tranquil times, the MASH Effect is generally job-related since only then an occupation is likely to embroil a man chronically in a highly stressful situation. Such an occupation would be any occupation that entails direct and prolonged association with acutely ambiguous men.

Protracted contact with acutely ambiguous men does not always inspire a fullblown MASH Effect. The quality of the contact is important; contact that entails substantial direct interaction is more taxing than ephemeral contact. Ingrained tendencies toward other defense mechanisms or an atmosphere conducive to other mechanisms will lessen the likelihood of the MASH Effect. Obscenity reaction is an alternative; so is non-adjustment in the form of depression. Standard diversionary thoughts and routine can be made sufficient if one is not interrupted by substantial interaction with ambiguous men. The ethic of humanitarianism or normalization can hang so heavily upon a scene that comic relief and self-indulgence are discouraged. The MASH Effect requires a break of inhibitions.

Yet, when the pressure of manifest human ambiguity builds, the impetus toward the MASH Effect becomes strong. An atmosphere or license helps the emergence; but the MASH Effect can be realized as a delicious but naughty undercurrent to humanitarianism or normalization. It is easier to frolic if others do, but one can frolic, too, by being eccentric, and sometimes eccentricity is necessary for productive endurance.

The movie implies that the MASH Effect is conducive to purposeful performance. Within bounds this claim seems to be true. Under trying circumstances the alternatives to humor are depression, anxiety and tears, all of which are incapacitating. "If I did not laugh, I would have to weep" is a dictum made famous by Abraham Lincoln who maintained that humor kept him going. In that it makes performances possible the MASH Effect is conducive to duty. Yet, if it spills over, the MASH Effect colors a performance. If it grows excessive, levity stifles any serious endeavor.

Humor can mask indiscretion and breakdown. That which is mirthful is not meant to be taken seriously, but playful digressions can be real evasions of duty. Chiding can be covert cruelty. Laughter can be hard with hostility. Mania signals a breakdown of orientation.

Intermittent, mild MASH can ease adaptation to difficult situations. True levity is incompatible with impulsive, prejudiced and obscenity reactions since fear or compulsion sways these. But, mild MASH is a good chaser for the difficult "ideological" techniques of humanitarianism, normalization and, to a lesser

60 extent, spiritual transcendence and ritual separation since all these ritual systems are characterized by a solemnity that can itself become burdensome.

In its more amplified versions the MASH Effect is a last-ditch effort, an oil slick, a smoke screen born of desperation. Its presence signals the shortfall of other methods of alleviation. Hyperactivity is exhausting even when it is only expressive in the form of quips or skits. The MASH Effect cannot be a long-term remedy. If the pressure is relentless, the MASH Effect will ultimately degenerate into an obscenity reaction or into irritability and disorientation that resembles battle fatigue. To avoid such eventualities, the pressure must be reduced by some form of direct avoidance, such as departure from the arena, or a reduction of contact with it. In the case of ambiguous men, withdrawal will relieve pressure; a man can remove himself from ambiguous men or make his contacts with them short and superficial.

Induration. Induration is an unconscious diminution of the impact of manifest human ambiguity. In the face of threatening experience, the mind moves to protect orientation through a selective myopia in which the stigma is perceived but its implications are not felt. The logical and the affective ramifications of the sensation are repressed.

Induration develops gradually as a shield against chronic exposure to human ambiguity. The less acute the ambiguity the swifter the insensitivity comes. Yet, some measure of induration will grow against the most acute ambiguity if a man can tolerate the period of gestation.

Although it can be consciously acquired, induration is not so much a means of assuagement in itself as it is a buffer for active methods of assuagement. Induration is never found in its pristine form—indifference—but is always alloyed with active methods— action being essential to the process of orientation. Impulsive and taboo reactions depend on the ambiguous men being peculiar, and thus induration is not found with these methods. It is found with all the others. Induration can be united with aversion to form cool cruelty. It will enable more pronounced perversity in obscenity reaction. Induration will cause a smooth officiousness when melded with any of the four ideological techniques; ritual separation, humanitarianism, spiritual transcendence or normalization.

Although induration is never a sole means of adjustment, it is an inevitable buffer to extensive exposure to human ambiguity. Under such conditions induration is necessary to the success of diversionary behavior; without induration to loosen the grasp of uncertainty, the avoidance of MASH would be impossible. Induration is essential to the preservation of schematic ideological "solutions" in the face of a debunking multifarious reality. It is necessary to a belief in the utility of ineffectual process.

Like the others, induration is not a consummate accommodation. The selective myopia of the indurate is not absolute. At some level ambiguity must be acknowledged to be culled from conscious experience. Induration is repression, and repression comes with a tiring tension. Thus, in operation, induration fatigues. The more acute the ambiguity and the longer the contact with it, the more fatiguing induration becomes, and the less likely it is to stifle uncertainty. As with MASH, induration will not withstand unabated intimacy with acutely ambiguous men; exhaustion and disorientation will ultimately result.

The Resistance of Manifest Human Ambiguity

In that ambiguous people cannot be cured, their ambiguity can rarely be resolved since the perceptual ideal type of person can be only minimally broadened to include them. The unsettling effect of ambiguous people can be assuaged, but in their presence assuagement is taxing—increasingly so as they are more ambiguous. A limp can be perceptually touched-up more readily than missing legs. However, a minor air-brushing is not always easy. It might be years before an individual grows inured to another man's speech impediment or lack of a finger. Attention tends to be drawn to an ambiguous man's incongruous elements. An individual would focus upon these elements to resolve the paradox of their presence and thus to lessen the uncertainty. Yet, since the ambiguity cannot generally be resolved, its magnetism generally retards an adjustment to it.

Men work to assuage manifest human ambiguity whenever they perceive it. Passing an ambiguous man on a street or seeing him on a subway is a fleeting contact that is easily tolerable unless he is particularly grotesque, and even then he is not likely to create a lasting problem. Facing an ambiguous man more than briefly impels a determined effort at orientation to him. The intensity of the effort corresponds directly with the degree of discomfort. An acute ambiguity will inspire an exhausting renitence. The more adept a man becomes at blunting an ambiguity, the less of a thorn it will be to him. The urgency of further alleviation will be less great. However, at its extremes, human ambiguity is beyond comfortable mitigation and will thus always draw an enervating effort at orientation.

Big effort is needed to cope with a substantial manifest human ambiguity. Since the impetus is compelling and all the means of assuagement are inadequate to the task, men combine them *in toto* or piecemeal. So it is that a man can build tolerance to manifest human ambiguity by haloing himself in a humanitarian outlook, learning rationales and rites of normalization, practicing these rites "ritualistically" as diversion, musing on his growing eminence as a healer as diversion, easing his strain intermittently with MASH, now and again venting a masked hostility toward the ambiguous men, obscenely reveling in his normalcy in contrast to their abnormality and in his capacity to tolerate them—and all the while waxing indurate. Such involved adjustments, even when "mastered," require great effort just for enactment. Thus, an adjustment to acute manifest human ambiguity is consuming even in that it is successful.

Ambiguous men often exact adjustments whose methods are inconsistent in spirit or rationale. One can work to cure an ambiguous man even while one proclaims him to be a human being as any other. One can avoid or resent ambiguous men while one proclaims a humanitarian view. One can delight in the diseases of others, even as one is working to cure them. The function is denial; that remains constant. This function being imperative and difficult will oblige a man to bear the strain of "unholy" alliances. Personalities can have many faces.

Yet, this inconsistency is taxing in itself since pretense must palliate it. The individual desires to be coherent and thus delineates an overt, frontstage posture vis-à-vis human ambiguity. The means he uses that are incongruent with this posture are kept covert in that he is able. The individual rationalizes a congruity between his covert doings and his overt purposes. He endeavors to hide his covert actions from the eyes of others who might unmask them.

In that a man's adjustment to ambiguous men is inadequate, he will be dunned with anxiety in their presence. When a man becomes uncomfortably anxious, he reverts to the more primordial reactions. The objective cool required for the ideological methods wanes. A man is more likely to be nasty and cruel, more likely to abrogate social responsibilities toward ambiguous men, more likely to flee and more likely to practice a frantic or

frenzy or the MASH can come overtly or as overtones or under-
currents to ideological rituals. The shaman may thrill at the pain
his remedies produce. His dogged ritualism may serve as avoidance. A cavelier implementation of rituals is MASH. Excessive
anxiety spells breakdown, Ambiguous men can generate such
anxiety, but are rarely given the chance, since a man will
generally flee before they do.

The Lure of Ambiguous Men: Power and Competence

For a number of reasons, men suffer the onus of ambiguous
men. The golden rule lends some impetus. Men fear abandonment if they should become debilitated, and therefore some men
would not have ambiguous men abandoned. To preserve a sense
of human dignity, men are solicitous of ambiguous men. However, more prevasive than these motives is the special magnetism
or manifest human ambiguity, the lure of mystery and power.

A sense of power attends confrontation with that which
terrifies men. A direct challenge to mortality garners momentary
euphoria. More enduring comfort comes with a capacity to live
amongst horrors. Since ambiguous men reify the uncertainty of
human identity, confrontation with them is felt to be a demonstration of power. Exhiliaration can follow a quick encounter
with ambiguous men. A smugger, more enduring aura of strength
emanates from the ability to tolerate close contact with ambiguous men for extended periods.

Men would bolster their self-certainty by using ambiguous
men as props in plays of ascendency over mortality. Men seek
out ambiguous men to dismiss their faces of doom with a limited
cosmetic and curative potential and with pantomime power, an
array of cant, charades, bluster, humbug and postures. Normalization is an effort to control directly the mutability of man.
Toleration refutes the threat of manifest ambiguity. Rejection
distances men from ambiguous men. Concealment and destruction remove the manifest thorn. The manipulation and the
sufferance of ambiguous men do not nearly resolve the dilemma
of mankind but they do nurture a specious sense that men wield
the power to grasp and to cope with the problems of human
identity and mortality.

Yet, without amulet and panoply to fend off the dark implications of ambiguous men, proximity to them is cold comfort.
Men must toughen their hides and apply strategems to endure

prolonged contact with the acutely ambiguous. The sheer presence of ambiguous men does not provide power; it merely provides occasions for its use. The power comes from the methods of assuagement. Men must develop some competence with these methods if they are to tilt with the uncertainty of ambiguous men.

True competence is an ability to be at ease in close and direct contact with ambiguous men. The capacity is always more specific than general. Men become competent relative to given afflictions. A man who has learned to endure calmly the presence of burn victims may be unable to countenance confrontations with the insane. To be at ease with an affliction, men must have had occasion to familiarize themselves with it and to practice their defenses against it. However, by successfully attenuating the impact of one malady, a man gains a degree of dexterity with the process—a degree commensurate with the arduousness of the conquest. This dexterity will facilitate the man's attainment of further competences should he be exposed to other maladies. Also, a single but encompassing competence can be devised against a number of different afflictions if they are part of a single situation such as a hospital situation wherein patients confront hospital personnel with a variety of ailments.

Competences denote degrees of power commensurate with the challenge of their objects. Calm before a cut finger is not so impressive as calm before a corpse. In general, competence before a more acute ambiguity implies more power since the greater the adversity, the more equanimity before it is taken to be a sign of strength.

The composition of a competence, the methods of assuagement it entails, also affects its "power" because some methods render a greater sense of power than others. Since efforts to diminish manifest human ambiguity would mold reality, they generally denote more mana than efforts merely to endure the ambiguity. The physician's aura of power is greater than the hospital housekeeper's, although both witness human ambiguity at close hand because the physician works on the ambiguity while the housekeeper works around it. Undertakers' prestige rose in America when they became beauticians for corpses.

In the face of human ambiguity, the power than men want most is the power to push ambiguous men firmly into a meaningful and positive identity. They desire this power because they so fear their own departure from normative manhood. Also, redemption is considered a greater manifestation of power than demonstrated.

Ambiguous men can be made men, positively and meaningfully, in two ways: they can be ritualistically included in a divine and transcendent humanity, or they can be physically normalized. Spiritual transcendence deals with death, and thus has no utility regarding living ambiguous men. In coping with dead men, only embalmment and the cosmetic efforts of morticians represent normalization. Some religions through a transcendent humanitarianism attempt to bind living ambiguous men to mankind, but normalization is inherently a more appealing technique to mundane men since its efforts promise to be tangible and immediate.

Professionalization, Institutionalization and Dramatization

The most "powerful" competences are founded on efficacy intended to be extraordinary—a heightened "power" to normalize ambiguous men or to transcend their corporeal state. Such premier competences (hereafter, "competences") cannot be entirely genuine in terms of their "powers" since demonstrable efficacy against mortality is too limited to sustain much confidence before the faces of grossly and resistantly ambiguous men. The sense of efficacy necessary for a "competence" requires illusion, a sense of power socially conjured: borne by professionals, facilitated by institutions and realized by drama.

"Competences" are generally associated with men whose primary occupational concern is the humanizing or the apotheosizing of ambiguous men, and who are professionals in their callings in the sense that their roles are traditionally defined, difficult to master and socially honored. In societies more sizable and complex than tribal villages, men of "competence" tend to be professionals organizationally as well, forming sects that restrict their memberships, train neophytes and maintain, through mystification and politics, a monopoly of their most powerful rituals.

The priests, the shamans and the doctors cultivate, covet and dispense dogmas and active amelioration. These professionals reserve their "competences," but provide their powers to laymen who would be comforted by the professional mantle. The shaman prepares anodynes, the priest incantations and prayers, the doctor surgeries, therapies and medicines that inspire hope for a cure or a transcendence of human ambiguity.

The professionalization of "competences" is virtually inevitable. Being "competent" must be extraordinary since men are generally too aware of their ignorance, anxiety and impotence to credit themselves with great "power" against mortality. They can more readily believe in the "power" of a special few who have developed a smooth act and outfitted themselves with impressive props and trappings. The "competent" want to maximize their "power," in part, so that they can maintain the confidence to be "competent." Practitioners professionalize to maximize their social confirmation, eminence and social power.

The effort and the ability requisite to learn a "competence" prompts is professionalization. Often, real efficacies, such as many medical methods, are intrinsically difficult. "Competences" are difficult, however, regardless of their empirical verifiability. Complexity and exactness render an illusion of power that compensates for a dearth of empirical corroboration. Those persons who would move a spiritual realm are generally at a loss for definitive ramifications of their power. Often, too, the rites of shamans and the technologies of physicians do not cure. Thus, men resort to intricate and precise rituals and rationales. Such strategies are not easily mastered. To acquire a "competence," a man must devote himself to the quest. Also, he must be able to learn the act, and have the stage presence to perform it. Since such ability is not general and the necessary dedication is unlikely outside of an occupational framework, a "competence" must almost be the province and the primary function of a group with restricted membership—a profession.

The economy of power provides another impetus toward the professionalization of "competences." "Competence" requires a strong sense of power, a sense that cannot be built on true efficacy alone since this is too limited. If men are to be "competent," they must buttress their confidence with social prominence and power. This necessary prominence and power can be obtained by a practitioner whose "competence" is sufficiently wanted and honored. A "competence" is a substantial power in itself; it is also a means to political and social power since society both honors and requires "competences." Any effect on the power of or the demand for a "competence" is compounded; what increases them increases the practitioners' access to political and economic power as well; conversely, a decrease in the former leads to a decrease in the latter. For any population and "competence," a certain number of practitioners is necessary to establish the legitimacy of their calling, to advertise it and to provide for prospective clients so that they are not frustrated into looking elsewhere; but above this minimum the availability of a "competence" inversely affects both its "power" and its demand, and thus substantially affects both the "power" and the social standing of the practitioners. Above the necessary minimum, the fewer hands that can legitimately claim a "competence," the more power that will be associated with it. Also, the number of practitioners who divide a constant demand inversely affects the demand for each practitioner since each gets a correspondingly bigger or smaller piece of the action. Thus, men who would possess a "competence" would be advised to form a sect to establish and to restrict membership in this sect and access to the "competence," to both the methods and the titles. In short, they would be advised to form a guild and in this sense, to professionalize.

The "competent" will generally act to restrict their numbers and to do all else that might build their sense of efficacy, and laymen will aid them since the human appetite for sway over mortality is insatiable. Before the maw of mutilation and death, men would puff themselves up like blowfish. As much as they can and dare, they would inflate themselves with "power" real and specious. Alternately, they would cling to pillars of strength. Specialness and other accoutrements of a professional establishment facilitate the mystery and the illusion without which there could be no true "competence," and thus neither blowfish nor pillars.

Charisma can fuel idiosyncratic "competences," but charisma is a knotty method. Individuals can orchestrate their own illusions and pander them for the necessary social support. Such charismatic "competence" is rarely more than medical or spiritual hucksterism. One-man shows are hard pressed to produce an aura of efficacy and even harder pressed to maintain one. Charismatic practitioners must persuade without the benefit of tradition or institutional stages. Indeed, to be tenable at all, these men often feign august traditions and fabricate what institutional trappings and settings they can. Frequently, they are confidence men, sellers of patent medicine or true salvation, whose aim is not true "competence" at all, but money and position exclusively. True charismatic "competence" is a difficult and risky proposition. It is a rare man who by himself can be sufficiently credible to be truly "competent." If a charismatic practitioner obtains

68 grand props and numerous assistants, he can augment his production, but then he is taking the first steps toward professionalization and institutionalization.

As institutions, professions have an aura of authority and probity. A legally constituted and recognized professional society, by its very existence, gives credence to its "competence." Tradition is testimony to veracity since people are usually disinclined to think a sham what has been credited for generations. Certifications or consecration is a sign of extraordinary adequacy. Standards imply that there is a true "competence" to be maintained. Trappings evidence the reality of a "competence."

Being a primary representative of an awesome establishment enables a professional to draw on "power" that he could not convincingly claim on his own recognizance. Not only does association with a greater beyond serve to persuade others, it also serves to persuade the professional himself, for, being a man, his limitations confront and disquiet him. The professional is thus ultimately one with the laymen in that both would comfort themselves by attaching themselves to a greater "power." The professional's contact is more direct and intimate; indeed, he mediates between the source and the layman. The professional represents and dispenses the power of the church or of medicine—and ultimately of God or of science.

The more grandly and firmly the "competent" can institutionalize themselves, the more powerful they will seem. Institutionalization externalizes and thus reifies the professional's source of power. Traditions, documents, monuments, trappings, settings and functional relations with other institutions make a professionals' ideology tangible. The awesomeness of the establishment is taken to reflect the power of the "competence." In that it is functionally integrated with other social institutions, a "competence" profession assumes a social legitimacy. The more integral the profession is to its society and culture, the more "real" it seems.

Men interpret reality in terms of context, and thus in that a professional's setting is supportive, it augments his credibility. Consequently, in that they are able, "competence" professionals backdrop themselves with august, institutional settings, e.g., hospitals, cathedrals and temples and, on smaller occasions, chambers and offices. The symbols of the pertinent ideologies suffuse these scenes, and stand as mute, multifarious and patent testimony to the veracity of the "competences." Bathed in stained glass light, standing, dwarfed, before the mammoth presence of a Gothic cathedral, a man with the desire is likely to feel Almighty God. In similar fashion, the medical milieu substantiates medical ideology. Hospitals proclaim the power of medicine with beehive officiousness and with the meretricious pragmatism of technological paraphernalia.

Another means by which professionals aggrandize their institutions and themselves is to surround themselves with auxiliaries: hierodules, acolytes, attendants, technicians. Auxiliaries are intermediate figures—part professional, part layman. To varying degrees more than laymen, aids are privy to institutional rites and rationales, but they lack the professionals' expertise and certification. Aids augment the professional establishment by increasing its size and elaborateness while enhancing the prestige of their superiors. A great variety of assistants leads to an impressive organizational involution. The assistance of knowing seconds allows more labrinthine rituals. Aids maintain grand settings. They promote the status of professionals by restricting access to them and by serving them.

Auxiliaries abet the professional's illusion of power by cushioning him from reality. They do the dirty work, freeing the professional to dwell on "powerful" ritual performance. The menial, backstage preparations of auxiliaries transform raw reality into an institutional stage, a new "reality" in which the professional's exalted role seems both legitimate and essential. In that the professional does not fabricate his own stage and props, he does not have to confront their artificiality.

The greatest service, in the way of dirty work, that auxiliaries can perform for the professional is to spare him unceremonious or protracted contact with ambiguous men. To apotheosize or to humanize ambiguous men is the blazoned object of "competence," and thus ambiguous men must play a central role in any demonstration of such efficacy. Yet, the failure of many ambiguous men to respond graphically to professional ministrations saps the ethos of professional "competence." In the face of this failure, ceremonial pretension is the saving grace, but this depends on adherence to stately ritual and bearing, and without conditioning, ambiguous men would frequently thwart such affectation. Filth, stench, tatters and raucous behavior can be most indecorous. Even remnants or normative, civilian identity can disrupt the professional trance. Auxiliaries may ease this problem by readying ambiguous men for professional rituals, by tidying and subduing them, by garbing them in institutional raiment and planting them on institutional altars to emphasize

70 their functional identity as central props in rituals of "competence."

If an institution must maintain ambiguous men, its auxiliaries may bear the brunt of this task and exempt the professional from a damning exposure to human ambiguity. Lengthy contact with ambiguous men under the multiple requirements of daily living is bound to press the reality of their state upon their normative caretakers, pressuring their abstract defenses and illusions. Aids enable the professional to limit his contact with ambiguous men to short, ritualistic encounters, assisting him in keeping faith with his professional ethos.

As the optional and the variable presence of auxiliaries illustrates, "competence" institutions can be more and less complex organizationally. The simplest institution consists of a single professional—a shaman who may be assisted or followed by laymen in performances of his grander ceremonies. Professionals and auxiliaries can become increasingly specialized and stratified so that there is no internal limit to the potential complexity of a "competence" institution. This complexity reflects in degree the organizational development in the rest of the society. More rationalized, diversified and stratified societies spawn more rationalized, diversified and stratified "competence" institutions.

Organizational complexity compliments a "competence" in a number of ways. As has been suggested, many hands of many ranks and kinds allow for impressively elaborate rituals, trappings and settings. In themselves, the largeness and the intricateness of an organization show its greatness, and thus its credibility.

An institution consists of many classes of functionaries, becoming a reality, independent of its professional hierophants or any other component group. Each specialty develops an ethos that is somewhat its own. Together, the specialties triangulate and reinforce an institutional ethos that forms the reality within which each group works. No one group can fully identify with an institution that is the product of numerous groups, but this very externality objectifies the institution. A church is more than an emanation of its priests and for this reason, the priests can more readily take their church as evidence of the reality of their "competence." A hospital exists through its physicians, nurses, technicians, secretaries, administrators, maids, cooks, maintenance men and more; its social reality is patent through the living testimony of a diverse multitude.

A division of labor eases contact with manifest human ambiguity. It narrows the range of encounters one is likely to have. For those functionaries who must deal directly with ambiguous men, task rationalization limits formal confrontations to restricted occasions. Generally, the functionary sees more ambiguous men, more superficially. A restricted occupational interest facilitates what Becker calls "fetishization," the narrowing of one's perspective to a manageable microcosm. The institutional interest in ambiguous men is fragmented into subinterests whose circumscriptions aid an evasion of the implications of ambiguous men. A limitation of formal duties promotes a diversionary emphasis on them, promotes what the sociologist Robert Merton terms a "displacement of goals."

Multitiered stratification enhances the illusions of those persons who work their institution's magic on ambiguous men. The men between the two extremes of such a hierarchy have both subordinates and superordinates and can use the former as auxiliaries to buttress an illusion and the latter as hierophants to confirm this illusion. The men at the top have the entire organization to foster their sense of power, and at the same time they are likely to have the least substantial contact with ambiguous men. The men at the bottom are likely to have the most substantial contact with ambiguous men, but they can look up to many tiers of superiors in the mysteries of "competence."

In that a "competence" institution becomes grand in terms of the scale and the complexity of its cant, settings, trappings and organization, that institution's ideology becomes substantial and the institution itself becomes rigid, less resilient perhaps—but more durable. That which is large and lasting impresses small and transient men. A grand institutionalization of a "competence" reduces the theatrics necessary to support it. With their institutions as proof of their efficacy, functionaries can perform their duties calmly without frantic attempts at self-persuasion, without torch light parades or bacchanalian hoopla.

However, whatever the state of the institution, some dramatization is necessary to a "competence" since power is manifest in doing and since neither professionals or their institutions can forestall mortality. Enacted, a "competence" is a drama with professional leads, laymen support and perhaps a chorus or organization men. In that there is deception, it tends to be mutual, since the drama is staged to persuade all involved, and all play their parts.

The public's trust in the professional is not blind. In broad terms, laymen can see the empirical efficacy of a "competence"

72 as well as the professionals. They also generally have some familiarity with the professional's ideology and with the purposes of his various techniques. Certainly, laymen play in the show roles that require a knowledge of the profesional's act.

The public wants to believe. It pays tribute to the professional with deference and money, helps supply him with trappings and settings, calls on him for explanations and remedies and hopes in his power. Laymen proffer these manifestations of trust, even though they doubt, and perhaps even though they know, the professional's real limitations. This apparent faith bolsters the confidence of the professional who must cope with his own inner misgivings.

The professional wants to be believed, in part, so that he can believe in himself. He labors to be a weighty personnage and to produce an impressive show, and in so doing he works to supply society with a soothing pretension. The professional's public front requires elaborate backstage preparation since it must impress and yet appear effortless.[11] For optimal impact, the professional must be conversant with the lines and the postures of his calling. His "competence" must be certified by his sect. He must have endured an onerous training and trial. He must act convincingly even though he is uncertain, even if, like some alchemists, he stages the proofs of his powers. The consummate professional fulfills these requisites not only to meet public expectations, but also to persuade himself of his efficacy.

The auxiliaries who deal most directly with ambiguous men are likely to be the most skeptical of "competence" dramas. These men set the stages, witness the failures at close hand and work without the mezmerizing aura of professional prestige. Yet, the auxiliaries, too, willingly engage in the dramatization of "competence." In part, they play their roles because such is their job—their livelihood. They also garner the reflected glory of the professionals or the institution. But, such cynical motives are not their only motives; the drama itself attracts them, however much they protest its deceitfulness. Auxiliaries, too, want to believe.

When done with style, a drama of "competence" enchants. Any man taken up in a chorus of hosannas resounding from the egresses of a cavernous cathedral believes on some level of his being, and for the moment believes poignantly. He and others are acting as if they believe. The world is arranged as if the

[11] Irving Goffman, *The Presentation of Self in Everyday Life*, Garden City, NY: Doubleday, 1959.

"competence" is true. On such occasions, a man is both inspired and calmed, and the glory is so redolent he can almost taste it. More modest productions are more modest affirmations of faith, but the magic allures in any quantity.

Generally, men are ambivalent toward their society's institutions of "competence" whether or not they are part of these institutions. Men both believe and disbelieve at the same time, or put differently, they both hope and doubt. Such "dual-think" leads to much apparent hypocrisy. With his death imminent a man who has deprecated religion may summon a priest. A man who has asserverated that all doctors are charlatans may rush a stricken son to a hospital. When the chips are down, men tend to "find religion," but it likely was with them all along. Practitioners and their assistants may appear far more cynical than they are. On the other hand, a man who appears certain is almost certainly not. The unflappable professional quakes in the quiet of his soul.

Men desire salvation, especially when mortality looms before them, and within a society this presence is always sufficient to promote a sustaining interest in credible affirmations of "competence." Constant demand and the imperatives of credibility foster efforts toward more sublime and weighty productions. Thus, "competence" becomes the province of professionals and institutions that delineate and substantiate their societies' most satisfying answers to the ultimate concerns, and which affirm these answers with high drama. "Competences" that are institutionalized throughout a society become components of culture in the sense that their doctrines, in general form, steel all normative citizens for living. In that reality presses them, all citizens doubt, but in that they yearn for resolution, they tend toward the ways of their people.

The Backstage of "Competence"

The rituals of a "competence" are frontstage affirmations of a faith. They are open statements that profess an idealized reality that reflects the wishes of men. Such rituals require backstage preparations: education, rehearsal, certifications, scenes and the general maintenance of an upholding institution. This groundwork is congruent with the spirit of the performance, and thus can be acknowledged, if not flaunted, yet "competences" under duress require backstage support of another sort—support that if freely acknowledged would spoil a show of "competence."

Without reinforcement, "competences," regardless of their staging, cannot withstand prolonged or numerous encounters with resistantly ambiguous men, since "competences" are substantially specious. Thus, in the face of such contact, men of "competence" fortify their confidence with methods alien and often antithetical to the professed spirit and conception of their callings. Practitioners brace themselves with combinations of prejudice, ritual separation, obscenity reaction, diversion, MASH or induration. To preserve their imagery and credibility, the "competent" mislabel such behavior or keep it from public view, suppressing its implications even for themselves.

In another example of dual-think, men can sustain a "competence" with methods that belie it. Rationalization palliates the inconsistency by dressing the alien methods as aspects of a "competence." Reasoning that his obsession is dedication to his calling, a doctor may not freely admit to himself that he takes obscene delight in the plights of his patients. In similar fashion, fastidiousness can mask ritual diversion, MASH can be taken as an innocent release of tensions and induration can be tagged perspective.

Such delusion is rarely if ever complete. Absolute beguilement would imply an escape from reality and uncertainty, an escape beyond human capacity. Also, the effort necessary for deception belies a true belief in it. Under probing or in unguarded moments, men of "competence" tend to betray their true awareness. Still, the level of perspicacity does not negate the possibility or the reality of delusion. When it suits a valued purpose, men are able to live with lies, to believe them even while they disbelieve them. Men will willingly live with inconsistency to preserve a sense of certainty, and they will resist all efforts to unmask the inconsistency unless they perceive alternate means to buttress their certainty, alternate means which must themselves be inconsistent with their "competences."

Through staging and rationalization, alien methods can be more and less accommodated to the frontstage rituals and postures of "competence." Some methods are so antithetical to the humanitarian bent of "competence" that they are generally kept backstage, hidden from laymen, and barely acknowledged by the practitioners themselves. Being a forthright means of separation, aversion tends to be surreptitious. MASH vitiates both affinity and pretension and is thus relegated to the backstage. Obscenity reaction can be camouflaged as dedication, but nuance will readily betray it if its presence is not muted.

Diversion is a versatile tool used in keeping to and from business. Its presence is so unobtrusive that to conceal it requires small effort. Intricate "competence" rituals enable frontstage diversion. Men can tend directly to their business with ambiguous men and in so doing can so immerse themselves in cant and technique that their perception of human ambiguity is dimmed. Extensive preparations, institutional politics and personal concerns enable backstage diversion. Anything that the institution seems to require has an air of legitimacy. Pensiveness and musing, whatever their content, are quiet activities that can be entertained readily when the situation does not demand strict formality.

Induration is prominently marked by calm, a symptom that is easily seen as signifying wisdom rather than insensitivity. Allegedly, "competences" entail mysterious understandings and powers. The poise of "competence" professionals testifies to the truth of this claim. Equanimity bespeaks profundity to laymen, neophytes and the professionals themselves. Initiates eventually ascertain that, regarding the ultimate concerns, esoteric mysteries are empty, but, by this time, they have acquired professional defenses and grown somewhat inured to human amguity. This insensitivity becomes a sign of strength. The veteran gloats over the uncertainty of the neophyte, and the neophyte is awed and comforted by the calm of the veteran. Thus, the "competent" generally flaunt their induration.

The use of ritual separation is a special case, for this method is akin to normalization and transcendence in that ritual separation, in its more developed forms, is based on ideology and is institutionalized. Also, men of "competence" tend also to be the men competent in ritual separation. Doctors pronounce the dead and priests preside over funerals. Such ritual separation is frontstage activity in its own right. However, the degree to which ritual separation is tauted by the "competent" depends on its implications for their "competences." Those men "competent" in spiritual transcendence employ ritual separation openly to distinguish corpses and the unclean for normative men. Such use entails no apparent inconsistency since spiritual transcendence operates on an ethereal plane. Indeed, freaks may be immolated to save their souls in a combination of removal and transcendence. Also, since access to heaven is generally thought to be restricted, priests can cast men from a congregation without confounding the salvation of the chosen. However, normalizing "competences" would cure ambiguous men, and thus rehabilitators and reformers must make a subdued use of ritual separation. For physicians, death is the very symbol of failure; consequently, physicians tend to pronounce the dead with a minimum of fanfare. In diagnosis, ritual separation is covert. Diagnosis is used ostensibly to delineate maladies—only furtively to distinguish ambiguous men from normative men.

Awareness plagues men; however well-disguised alien methods are, a latent awareness of them perennially threatens to deface "competences." Again, men rationalize to defend their faiths. Base methods are attributed to individual weakness and veniality, and to extenuating circumstances; idealized "competence" is thought possible in some other place or time when practiced by the truly "competent." In quiet moments, a professional may curse as personal failings, his insensitivity, his ritual diversion, his ill-temper, his intemperate humor, his arrogance and his furtive thrill at inflicting pain and presume that his "competence" can be free of all these. In similar manner, laymen and auxiliaries bemoan the "idiosyncratic" shortcomings of professionals and themselves and claim that purer "competence" is possible. Circumstances are blamed. Men reason that conditions beyond their control impose limitations upon them. Too few resources, too much work, or inverted institutional priorities are seen as precluding a more humane approach.

Yet, any belief in pure "competence" is Pollyannish. A "competence" that solely reflects its ideology is impossible in the chronic presence of ambiguous men. An operative "competence" requires induration and diversion. At least traces of other methods are also likely to be represented: prejudice, obscenity reaction, ritual separation, MASH. In addition to these standard methods of assuagement, the social pretension and structured interaction with ambiguous men afforded by "competence" institutions may also be requisite. Since ambiguous men both fascinate and repulse, obscenity reactions and prejudices in some form are virtually inevitable responses to them. Ritual separation is a lofty method that serves the same purpose as aversion. The comic release of MASH would seem to be irresistible for men suffering the duress that accompanies protracted contact with resistant and gross human ambiguity.

Even though men at various times may be drawn toward every means to support their "competences," the manner in which a "competence" is supported is not fixed since some methods may be stressed over others. The means that men entertain reflect on them and their societies. A saint may feel repulsion welling within him and yet repress this feeling and all but minimal expression of it. He may grasp the purposeful diversion of prayer and iron discipline. A medical worker may eschew prayer and discipline and depend on MASH and the diversion of sociability. A misanthrope may dwell on repulsion and sadistic attraction.

A person's adjustment to ambiguous men does not depend on whim; situation and socialization substantially influence adjustment. The extent and the type of contact hold considerable sway. Rational, ideological adjustments are more possible with distance and minor ambiguity. The more ambiguous the ambiguous men, and the more contact with them, the more MASH, aversion and obscenity reactions are likely to emerge. Pressure fosters more primordial and less rational reactions. Also, the more tenuous a man's grasp of a "competence" and its trappings, the less he is likely to depend on the rituals and the conceptions of that "competence." Thus, within a "competence" institution the competence of the hierophants may differ considerably from the competence of the auxiliaries. For example, the adjustment of mental hospital attendants to the insane may hardly reflect the "competence" of their psychiatric superiors. The attendants have extensive contact, minimal prestige and minimal psychiatric training, and thus their situation and socialization differ considerably from those of the psychiatrists. Prejudices, MASH and obscenity reactions are likely to be mainstays of institutional attendants, while the psychiatrists with their cant, power, prestige and restricted encounters with ambiguous men are afforded the luxury of a sublime approach.

A mien of "competence" is not easily maintained. Generally, a "competent" man must be buttressed with professionalization, institutionalization and dramatization. In addition, he must be sustained covertly by alien means that if freely acknowledged would confute the truth of his ideology and calling. A professional's exalted position within his institution protects him from an exposure to human ambiguity that would compel a gross exhibition of alien techniques. The institution structures the professional's duties such that his use of alien techniques is disguised and is thus amenable to rational denial.

In that auxiliaries share a professional mantle and an institution's protection against undue exposure, they will mime the professional adjustment. In that they are bereft of this mantle and protection, auxiliaries will be compelled toward more primordial and less sublime adjustments. Depending on their own professionalization and position, aids can be frontstage represen-

78 tatives of a "competence" institution— or something between these extremes.

Laymen will likely have some grasp of the ideologies of the "competences" that are widely institutionalized in their society, and laymen will likely endeavor to use these ideologies to interpret the mortal state. However, in that these laymen are without proficiency in the "competences" themselves, a pretense of knowing cannot be maintained without a dearth of challenging experiences. In that "competence" institutions limit or mitigate the public's exposure to ambiguous men, the public is permitted an elevated view of human ambiguity. This end is served by any sequestration or removal of freaks that spares the public. In preserving the illusions of their society, the jailers and the disposers of ambiguous men perform their dirty work through base adjustments.

Society and Adjustments to Ambiguous Men

Society plays a considerable role in determining individual adaptations to human ambiguity. Cultural conceptions of man constrain overt postures toward ambiguous men. The social structuring of relations with them influences covert as well as overt adaptations. In that there is a division of labor in coping with ambiguous men and a restriction of this coping to special groups, an individual's social position becomes salient to his adjustments to human ambiguity.

A society's handling of ambiguous men reflects its conceptions of man. Since ambiguous men illustrate both the uncertainty of human identity and the need for salvation, they provide both the impetus and the test for myths by which men in society explain their mortal state and point the way to salvation. These myths provide craved assurance, and therefore society choreographs and controls public reactions to ambiguous men to support society's mythical interpretations. Thus, if some ambiguous men are viewed as damned rather than human, and if the world is painted fraught with embodied devils, rationale will elevate aversion to ritual separation and ambiguous men, as witches, may be stoned or burned at the stake but not welcomed into the bosom of society. If spirits drive one mad, the spirits should be driven out. If the spirits are contagious, the infected should be shunned. If all men are created equal and redeemed through humaneness, they should not be spat upon in the streets.

Adjustments that confound the prevailing conceptions of man and salvation will exist. The graphic reality of ambiguous men elicits all methods of assuagement, and frontstage affectations generally require antithetical backstage supports. However, these alien adjustments are muted. They are kept covert or related to social deviants—doers of dirty work.

"Competences" form part of a society's arsenal against ambiguous men. All ambiguous men are not game for a society's "competences," but only those ambiguous men which society consigns to them. The dead are buried and their souls may be damned. Fools, freaks and the diseased are not necessarily given over to rehabilitators but may be set apart from humanity ritually, expressively or literally. Lepers have been traditionally cast out. The inmates of Bedlam were objects of public ridicule.

Mythical interpretations are brought to play against the dilemma of ambiguous men through a choreography of the ideological means of assuagement: ritual separation, humanitarianism, spiritual transcendence and normalization. Spiritual transcendence is confined to death and the prospects of death. The jurisdiction of the other ideological techniques over living ambiguous men is divided according to the dictates of culture and social power. Ritual separation on one hand and humanitarianism and normalization on the other represent opposite approaches, the former serving to exclude ambiguous men from and the latter to bind them to humanity. These two approaches can be used alternately for the same types of ambiguous men, or they can be used together as long as one approach is kept covert; yet within a society each approach is generally associated with certain types of ambiguous men. Which approach is the dominant posture against a given variety within a society depends on how that society labels it. In one society a lunatic may be stigmatized; in another he may be rehabilitated. In the former case humanitarianism will be covertly manifest if the lunatic is maintained, and in the latter case ritual separation will be covertly manifest if he is committed to an institution; yet in both cases the frontstage tone tends one way or the other and this tendency is set by society.

In that ritual separation prevails as a technique, base aversion and obscenity are unleashed, since all three of these are means by which ambiguous men are distinguished from men. In that ritual separation strips a man of his humanity, it condones less sublimated efforts in the same direction. If through due process a man is labeled, "fool," why should he not be abused or mocked? Only humanitarianism would bar such action, but humanitarianism is the antithesis of ritual separation.

The ethic of humanitarianism and normalization does condemn prejudices and obscenity reactions, but in doing so it complicates a society's adjustment to ambiguous men. Human- itarianism is perhaps the most comforting adjustment since it would banish fear and thrust open the doors of experience, but in practice it tends to be a parlor adjustment due to the difficulty of maintaining it in the presence of ambiguous men. Humani- tarians cannot vent their anxieties directly upon the heads of ambiguous men. In a society steeped in humanitarianism, am- biguous men should not be ridiculed, tormented, mocked, ostra- cized or stared at, and yet the compulsion to react in these ways becomes irresistible for persons without the panoply of "com- petence" who must endure the presence of acutely ambiguous men or the protracted presence of all but minimally ambiguous men. In that ambiguous men are thrust upon the public, the public must contend with tendencies that would-be humanitar- ians must loath. With the ethic of humanitarianism and nor- malization prevailing, the presence of ambiguous men becomes more difficult. Only their removal can mitigate this strain. Thus, in societies that maintain this ethic, ambiguous men are seques- tered to spare the general public. The institutions themselves become elaborate systems that elaborately conceal the requisite animosity, voyeurism and separation. Developed humanitarian- ism requires a division of labor vis-à-vis ambiguous men that overt ritual separation does not approximately require.

To reconcile the humanitarian ethic with the removal of ambiguous men, society must execute this removal such that a humane interpretation of it is plausible. An ostensibly beneficent exile is required. Thus, ambiguous men should not merely be cast out, but housed together apart from society for their own good. Hostels for the afflicted should not be prisons but institu- tions that benefit their charges.

A humanitarian asylum would highlight the humanity of ambiguous men by according them the dignity of acceptance as men. However, the difficulty of maintaining a humanitarian ethic in a convocation of ambiguous men is insurmountable without aid of either a powerful spiritual or medical "compe- tence," since an acceptance of ambiguous men cannot be toler- ated by men unless they have reason to hope that man possesses an essence beyond the body or that the body can be cured. A possible exception to this rule exists in homes that are substan- tially maintained by the afflicted themselves, in homes where men of sound mind and passable dexterity work to persuade each other that their affliction is compatible with manhood; yet in for normative men or to appear and behave more normally, they exemplify the rule. Generally, without a foundation of "competence," would-be asylums degenerate into pounds, as have many mental institutions and nursing homes of recent history.

Perhaps a semblance of humanitarianism can be achieved only if hospices become hospitals—if normalization aids humanitarianism. The desire for a real and positive mitigation of human ambiguity is so great that active humanitarianism might not exist without some trace of it. Even inspired religious orders care for the sick by normalizing their appearance: by cleaning them, clothing them and nursing them toward health in that such seems possible. Normalization is chiefly the province of medical "competence" professionals and institutions, and thus hospitals become their bases in that they can upgrade their act sufficiently to supplant the priests and their institutions.

Hospitals and asylums cannot be entirely what they are supposed to be in humanitarian terms due to necessary but antithetical backstage adjustments. Yet, these establishments can be more and less humanitarian. Internally, they can be overtly separatist, and as long as their facades bespeak humanity, public pieties may remain unruffled since what is walled from the public is covert in terms of society. However, facades will not be enough if a society's humanitarianism turns ardent.

Strong faith in a strong spiritual or medical "competence" is a necessary (though not sufficient) prerequisite for an ardent humanitarianism. Societies with either faith might take their humanitarianism earnestly. If they do, they will foster muckrakers, and then the inner workings of hospitals will be pressured toward an overt humaneness. Thereupon, these institutions will require the elaborate rituals and ideologies of their powerful "competences" to conceal the animosity and separation which are necessary to close any prolonged contact with manifest human ambiguity.

The Gregor Effect

In the accounts at the beginning of this book, Gregor and grandfather become acutely and resistantly ambiguous men, and in so doing incur renunciation by their fellowmen and by their blood relatives. This rejection seems both cruel and wrong. Gregor and grandfather have committed no crime; their state is beyond their control. Yet, they are rejected, necessarily. The

82 normative characters do not behave wantonly, but are constrained by circumstances. Human identity is frail. Men are insecure and weak. They are dominated by a drive for self-orientation. They must defend themselves against the implications of human ambiguity. They will defend themselves with certain means of assuagement, according to the ways of their society, and individually, according to the means at their disposal.

The more abnormal a man appears, the greater is the tendency of normative men who perceive him to reject his manhood. A man who grows increasingly abnormal will eventually cease to be ambiguous, and will then be rejected unequivocally. Yet, ambivalence dies hard; the declining trajectory of manifest human ambiguity is long. Bodies and even bones are not readily let go; but bodies must eventually come to ashes or dust and these will be let go. Gregor and grandfather suffer rejection, although not total rejection while their presence is felt. Their plight is an inevitable consequence of their advanced incapacity to appear or behave as normative social actors.

In a sense, the treatment of Gregor and grandfather is quite humane. For such sad representations of man, they receive considerable care. The Samsas domicile a cockroach within their home, feeding it every day. Grandfather is maintained at considerable public expense and visited—however reluctantly. While they live, neither Gregor nor grandfather is cast out of society entirely. Gregor and grandfather are undeniably ambiguous as well as abnormal, and being undeniably ambiguous they inspire ambivalence in the form of efforts to reject and to accept their humanity.

The ambiguous man is not quite a congener to any man. The stylized ministrations of "competence" professionals denote no love, neither does the lewd curiosity of the less-sophisticated. The ambiguous man is too abnormal to be accepted as a man, yet too human to be rejected as a man. Thus, though he cannot be welcomed in, he cannot be kept out as long as he is present. Any hand stretched out to him is clammy and unsure. Any rebuff is to a relative. There can be no definitive reaction to ambiguous man.

The more ambiguous a man appears, the more intense the ambivalence he inspires. An acutely and resistantly ambiguous man bears a poignant paradox. Composure in his presence is difficult in that his presence is not evaded. Any individual who confronts him openly will be fearful and fascinated. Alternately or perhaps concomitantly, this individual will deny the ambiguity before him by trying to perceive a man and by trying to perceive an alien. His actions will be confounded, both humane and inhumane.

Such inconsistency is confusing, and thus straining. A man's orientation requires an accommodation, and in that none is forthcoming, fatigue results with more desperate measures: aversion or obscenity reaction which may undermine the self-image of the man, causing him further duress. The families of Gregor and grandfather suffer their dilemma greatly. Ultimately, they grow irritable and angry.

The dilemma of ambiguous men is a challenge as well as a threat. In that men accommodate their own ambivalent reactions to poignant human ambiguity, they become heroes garnering a sense of power and some handle on their fate. Men can become competent in assuaging manifest human ambiguity through mastery of certain subterfuges. Apparent success can generate some exhilaration. Yet, the dilemma and the ambivalence remain, however palliated and covert, and awareness of these continues to haunt the most intrepid heroes.

I use the term *Gregor Effect* to mean this basic reaction of men to manifest human ambiguity. The physical presence of ambiguous men confronts men with a poignant dilemma since it challenges their image of man and thus their self-orientations. Men are fearful of the confusion but fascinated by the mystery of ambiguous men. Men will work to resolve the ambiguity, but in that it cannot be manifestly relieved, they will treat the source and the ambiguous men themselves, ambivalently, as the former endeavor to see men, to see aliens or to avoid the question. This ambivalence will entail some rejection, however humanitarian the perspective of the men. Men will seek accommodation to the presence of ambiguous men via certain means of assuagement that would deny the ambiguity by excluding ambiguous men from or including them in humanity, or by disdaining or avoiding their significance. Accommodations against acutely and resistantly ambiguous men will entail inconsistent means; those that conflict with an assumed posture will be kept covert in that this is possible. Such accommodations depend on delusion. In that men cannot hide their ambivalence from themselves, they will be strained. Men will feel powerful in that they can hide their ambivalence, tolerate manifest human ambiguity, and more powerful, if they can seem to lessen it. Thus, men are drawn to the challenge of ambiguous men, drawn to use them as props in heroic plays of ascendency over the mortality of men.

84   The families of Gregor and grandfather, with perhaps the exception of grandfather's sister, are overwhelmed by the Gregor Effect. They find no suitable accommodation to the ambiguity before them and are reduced to base adjustments. The Samsas are hardly to be decried considering the uniqueness of their situation. Grandfather's family had the medical establishment, a "competence" institution that should have comforted the family and pointed its way toward adjustment. Yet, either the family failed to follow or it was never led. The latter alternative is more likely for reasons that will be disclosed. Ideally, societies render the Gregor Effect more palatable.

To rise above the gut confusion that the Gregor Effect can elicit, men in social concert develop interpretive ideologies and support them with elaborate rituals. This social sublimation of the Gregor Effect exemplifies the heroic transcendence of which Becker writes. Since reality does not verify a positive resolution to the dilemma of human ambiguity, men turn to theatre. Consensual and contextual verification serve for a missing empirical confirmation. The priests, the shamans and the doctors are the heroes who, together with their retainers and with pomp and circumstance, draw men into or cast them from humanity, according to the dictates of faith. Countervailing tendencies are rationalized or hidden. Heroes and their public collaborate in a play of certainty.

A CONSIDERATION
OF NURSES' ADJUSTMENTS
TO HUMAN AMBIGUITY
WITHIN A HOSPITAL CONTEXT

Nursing Routine
and Philosophy

Introduction

The purpose of this empirical section is not to prove that the Gregor Effect exists or that it operates as I have described. Such proofs would be very difficult if not impossible; certainly, they are beyond the scope of my study which was exploratory rather than experimental. My research was undertaken to answer a question that had haunted me for several years. The Gregor Effect is the answer that my experiences suggested to me. Here I shall proffer the arguments and describe the situations that led me to the hypothesis that I outlined in the first section.

During my college years, I worked for five summers as an attendant in a general hospital (hereafter "General Hospital") of about 300 beds. As an aspiring sociologist, I was immediately impressed with the intensity and the richness of the society that abounded about me. I was intrigued by the variety of personnel and the complexity of the organization that provided the elaborate health care of today's hospital. The scene was such a whirl, so may persons scurrying about, so many things to be done, so many persons with whom to contend. Coordination of effort was a consuming and endless

6

process. Rather rigid status hierarchies and rather confounded lines of authority led to an array of rubs and dramas. Politics and public relations seemed ubiquitous concerns among administrators, physicians, nurses, auxiliaries, technicians, patients, visitors, housekeepers, maintenance men et al. There were alliances, feuds, fiefs, prima donas, rules and regulations, sex role differentiation, sex roie contention, much evidence of class distinctions, some evidence of ethnic discrimination, power struggles, language barriers and gossip galore—much fodder for sociological rumination.

Almost as eye-catching as the social frenzy was the technological elaboration of the hospital. A civilian could not help but be impressed with the argot, the apparatus, the techniques and the mystery of modern medicine. The panoply was so apparent, so real, manifest in the design of the buildings, in the interior decoration, hanging from the ceilings, lining the halls, suffusing the air.

I developed an amateur's interest in medicine, and a more intent interest in hospital society, especially the nursing service of which I was nominally a part. This group offered much opportunity for application of sociological lore, as nurses and their minions are so beleagured by multifarious pressures from all sectors of the hospital scene and from a crush of variegated responsibilities.

Yet, as I followed my sociological interest, I was bothered by an observation. This hospital was fraught with horrible events, and yet hospital personnel behaved as if they were oblivious to them or only minimally affected. These horrors were the depredations of mortality and calamity that afflicted many patients. Most patients seemed hardly indisposed; certainly, they were not grossly deformed or debilitated; yet within the hospital could be found numerous examples of human tragedy and portraits of men that have not been matched for horror even by the vaunted excesses of modern cinematography. In my first trip to the morgue, I discovered the naked remnants of an elderly lady lying on a bare metal table, her back arched unnaturally, her head thrust back glaring at me with large clouded, blue eyes, her mouth agape with viscid mucus, her visage tallowy, her hair a thatch of straw, her body completely gutted and flapped open. To her right on a counter was stationed a delicatessen meat slicer, to her left lung a grocers' scale. The air was clammy and pungent with the stench of gangrene from the assorted arms and legs shelved in the morgue refrigerator room. On the floor the

vignettes of horror were less reminiscent of Poe, but as patent in
their own fashion. Stashed in rooms and cubicles were men
suffering all manners of deformity and debility.

That this horror played so small a role in the lives of the
hospital workers seemed neither a sign of depravity or institutional inadequacy; indeed, it seemed almost fitting and proper.
In large measure the hospital was what it "should be." No
vermin crawled along the baseboards. The premises were clean
and orderly, well heated and ventilated. The plant contained the
equipment necessary to its function. The personnel all seemed
trained to their tasks in line with the latest fashion in medicine,
nursing, social work, scientific management or hospital administration. The staff seemed dedicated for the most part; that the
staff was officious and even convivial rather than morose was in
keeping with the hope and the determination which the staff
was supposed to foster in patients. Patients seemed to suffer no
gross neglect. They were cleaned, groomed and tended.

I myself was quickly taken up in the ambience of hospital
work. I fraternized with patients, fumed at unreasonable demands from my numerous superiors, expounded on the petty
politics of my position, shared gossip and good cheer and grew
increasingly impervious to the plagues before me. No definite
feeling replaced the butterflies and the horror. The social requisites of my position seemed almost to crush out an interest in
"bigger" questions. Regarding ambiguous men, I suffered almost
a loss of feeling. At first I wanted to see them, but in time I saw
them without affect. There were men whom I wheeled up to my
floor, provided with patient care for weeks, and in the end I
wheeled them to the morgue without more than fleeting sentiment. Verily, a rotten remark from some nurse would generate
more intense and lasting emotion.

My own nonchalance and that of my co-workers puzzled me,
especially in light of my growing perception of the limitations of
medicine. As a boy, I had thought of disease primarily as acute
and infectious, and remediable via the chemical wizardry of
modern medicine. Once in the hospital, I saw mostly chronic
and functional disorders, many of which hardly responded to
medical means. A host of patients were not to be spared even by
new "still experimental" break-throughs or timely surgical in-
terventions. I watched men worsen; I watched them die; I
watched them persist as grotesques and caricatures of humanity.
Thought of these people raised a sigh within me, and mention of
them raised a sigh from my fellows, but this hardly seemed a

suitable response. Certainly, people from outside the hospital did not react as offhandedly to such graphic stimuli.

The thought grew within me that this apparent equanimity was aided by a number of conditions endemic to that hospital work which deals directly with patients. Perhaps, calm before severe afflictions is a function that hospitals as institutions are designed to provide. I mulled over this idea during my later summers at the hospital and arrived at a number of hypotheses. Eventually, I decided to return to the hospital for a more thorough investigation.

My empirical study centers on the adaptations of nursing service personnel within a general hospital to their patients in that these patients do not appear or behave as normal men. Convenience was a factor in my choosing my former co-workers as subjects; yet there is a more pertinent reason for my settling on this group. Within a hospital setting the nursing staff has the most extensive and the most prolonged contact with patients. It is most incumbent upon nursing personnel to accommodate patients to hospital living and to provide them with humane acceptance. Originally, I planned only to have registered nurses as my subjects, but as my field research progressed I realized that licensed practical nurses and nurses' aides were so similar to RNs in their adjustments to human ambiguity that I could consider staff nursing personnel as a whole.

In the fall of 1975 I returned as a participant observer to the hospital wherein I had worked for five summers. For the next year I sojourned as a volunteer attendant on five nursing units: the six-bed coronary care unit, the nine-bed intensive care unit, the emergency department, a 44-bed surgical unit and a 44-bed medical unit. Five 40-hour weeks marked my shortest time on a unit. I kept to the 7–3 shift throughout.

In the following discussions I will draw on my previous summers of experience as well. During this time, I worked on every nursing unit in the hospital with the exception of maternity, and spent considerable time on all three shifts.

My participant observation was supplemented with several interviews and an open-ended questionnaire of which I distributed about 250 copies and received 114 completed returns. The questionnaires were handed out to all nurses and auxiliaries on all three shifts in 13 nursing units or all units in the hospital with the exception of pediatrics, out-patient, the recovery room and the operating room. Eighty-six respondents were registered nurses; 15 were licensed practical nurses; 13 were aides and attendants. This breakdown, as lopsided as it is toward registered nurses, represents generally the proportions in the nursing staff at that time.

The questionnaire was designed to elicit personalized responses. My desire was to learn my subjects' thinking as opposed to their choices from set alternatives. Many of my questions required small essays to be answered fully. Consequently, my questionnaire was lengthy and arduous, a fact that was frequently brought to my attention by my subjects. The success of the questionnaire was mixed. I did not receive as many returns as I might have, certainly too few for any statistical virtuosity. Many answers were skimpier than I would have liked. Yet, I also received an array of views on some very interesting issues. The results of the questionnaire corresponded to my observations.

The participant observation was no easy search. After a short time, hospital work tends to mesmerize and dull. The fatiguing regimen of constant motion, constant tension and constant social demand renders one numb. Cursorily, the reality of the hospital world seems plain, yet the deeper nature of this reality remains frustratingly beyond the reach of a mind clouded and preoccupied by the surface currents of the hospital experience. Many evenings I found myself virtually unable to comment on the events of the day. That my subjects seemed to share this predicament gave me some hope that this muteness was a clue of sorts; yet the muddle could not be but frustrating.

I suspected that the true significance of manifest human abnormality is repressed for nursing personnel and latent in the hospital scene. But assaying this "true significance" proved difficult so overlayed is it with structural-functional encrustations. The multiple functions of nursing procedures, stances and milieu confounded the uncovering that I sought. There were so many alternate explanations for everything. For example, the nursing staff seemed to suffer a malaise that was at various times more and less pronounced. Morale would ebb; job satisfaction would dip. Staffers would grow irritable or melancholy. Alternately, they would stay suspended within themselves, or cling to each other's company for bouts of common complaining. Perhaps, this state results from a periodic weakening in a daily contention with sickness and death, from the impact of manifest mortality breaking through, but plausible explanation is also supplied by Stanley Udy's 31st principle of organization. This statement actually refers to assembly-line work, yet frequently the description is also apt for nursing in hospitals:

Short, truncated work cycles, fractionated work, little control over job content by the worker, combined with disciplined time pressure, produce low job satisfaction and low morale. Such a condition is likely to be reacted to through defensive informal organization, if ecological conditions are propitious to group interaction, and reactive individualism and withdrawal where they are not.[12]

Even admissions cannot be taken at face value. A number of persons whom I pressed, "admitted" that despite appearances they were bothered by the conditions of many patients. These nurses and aides reasoned that they would be overwhelmed if they dwelled on horrors they have so little power to alleviate. Mundane affairs and petty complaints provide an outlet and a manageable experience, but they do not hold as much attention as they seem. Such admissions would seem to be just the evidence I seek, yet can I trust this evidence? Perhaps, my subjects were rationalizing their apparent lack of concern and, under pressure from me, were professing something that does not actually exist. A nurse who is thinking about the tasks she must perform and stewing on an altercation she just had is concerned with those things. Who is to say that she is concerned with that to which she is giving no thought and about which she is feeling no emotion? Even intermittent, fleeting awareness of mortal horrors does not necessarily mark a more profound subterranean concern. What is more, the conscious preoccupying concerns of the nursing staff, the problems of routine, of working relations, of coping with the public, of confronting multifarious pressures, of performing a vital and technical task are hardly different from the concerns of persons in other service or technical industries. Other people gossip, daydream, feud, congregate and get on with their work—other people who are not confronted with the afflicted.

Still, I concluded that the Gregor Effect exists and that it operates within hospitals, though I could not base this view on evidence of direct cause and effect relationships. Those structures, concepts and behaviors that serve the Gregor Effect are not caused by it, at least not directly and explicitly, since they issue from many forces and serve multiple functions. Actions that allow one to avoid manifest human ambiguity may also play to organizational requisites, needs for self-actualization and qual-

[12]Stanley H. Udy, Comparative Analysis of Organizations, *Handbook of Organizations*, edited by James G. March, Chicago: Rand McNally & Co., 1965.

ity control. The nurse who becomes more involved in management rather than the direct provision of patient care is moving herself up the social ladder as she removes herself from ambiguous men.

The Gregor Effect is by nature not apparent. Its presence can only be inferred. For my nurses and hospital, circumstances are suggestive. If a number of mysterious, seemingly disjointed pieces together actually form a house, one can presume that a house is being built and that there is a reason for the clandestine construction. The house exists. I have surmised and discussed the reason for the stealth; now I must unveil this house, indicating the pieces as best I can.

Mundane World of Nursing

No cothurnus marks the routine of work of nursing personnel. The ambience of nursing units is not tragic, but mundane and businesslike. The work of nurses and aides is largely repetitive and is carried on largely in a habitual manner. Nurses' concerns in their work are comparable to the concerns of workers in other fields. Nursing staffers dwell on relations with co-workers and on the execution of tasks. As with other persons involved in serving the public, nursing personnel are much concerned with proper etiquette and the problems of public relations. Common diversion characterizes their coffee and lunch breaks in which talk revolves around dieting, eating out, sales, interior decoration, upcoming weddings, general gossip and the like. Nurses are often fatigued, but this fact is not surprising considering the number of hours they spend on their feet, the number of interruptions with which they must contend and the extent and difficulty of their tasks.

For the most part, nursing personnel seem to be hardly perturbed at the graphic conditions of their patients. On general medical and surgical units, there are always patients who are straining through their last days, who are in pain, who are deformed or who are unable to behave as people should. On special intensive care units, this situation is more extreme. Persons in the most severe conditions come through the doors of the emergency department. Such concentration of suffering and debility would seem to be poignant, yet nursing staffers hardly seem to notice. When they enter the presence of a sorely afflicted patient, their countenances are not likely to betray more than a flicker of emotion. When they leave his presence, they are not likely to give him more than a fleeting thought. Their thoughts, if they waver at all, will quickly return to mundane considerations.

Such banality in the face of human mortality is what I have seen. The results of my questionnaire tend to corroborate my observations. I asked: "What do you consider to be the most unpleasant aspect of your job?" Not one person answered forthrightly that illness or suffering disturbs most. Only 12 percent of the respondents (14) mentioned situations that arise directly from the sickness of patients. The answers I received were of the following variety:

> The lack of understanding the Hospital Administration seems to have of the nursing profession as it is today.

> As an LPN, patients usually consider me as a student nurse. This is an insult to me. I realize this is because they haven't been informed as to the difference but I get tired of hearing "Oh, you're not a nurse" or "You're not a real nurse."

> When I am considered fair game for verbal and physical and emotional abuse by doctors, administration, patients and families.

> Not unpleasant—just aggravating is trying to get MDs to write clear and complete orders and communicate with staff (at times) about patient's progress.

> Dealing with families of patients for whom there is no hope—especially victims of trauma—it is difficult to see them day after day and not be able to offer them some report of progress.

> Having to care for people who abuse the emergency room for non-emergencies; usually people who milk the welfare system dry running to MDs with minor complaints. Part of the reasoning for this, I feel, is the visit to the ED is the social highlight of the week or month of these people.

> Having to deal with families and their questions when it should be the doctor doing the answering but more than half of the time they can't be bothered. Also, covering up for a doctor.

> The rotation of shifts as often as we do. I know I'm not myself on the 11–7 shift and I know I have a tendency not to put forth my best effort at times—due to fatigue and not wanting to be there at that time.

> Receiving criticisms from superiors who are no more capable of handling a situation than you are.

> Unrespectful treatment from patients and relatives when you

yourself have done all and above that to care for them physically and emotionally.

Watching elderly patients as they watch patiently for the visiting family who never come.

Physicians' inability to relate to nursing personnel, and *patients* themselves, also patient's families.

Cleaning feces. Having contact with doctors.

Dealing with visitors. We are really understaffed and cannot give as much care as we should. Visitors do not understand this. They also see nurses as handmaidens of the doctors, not as professionals and cannot see that we have many other duties besides making tea for their mother, etc. Most visitors seem to feel the nurses aren't busy and don't work. It is extremely unpleasant to deal with people who don't feel I'm doing the best I can (which I try to do about 95% of the time!) Also, taking all the garbage from nursing supervisors, administration, doctors, visitors, patients and anybody else who's bitching out.

Inability to give good patient care, lack of time and help and trying to fulfill a need that the medical profession shirks!

Concealing or dodging the truth when the patient or family wants to talk because the doctor hasn't or wouldn't confront the patient.

Being too busy—understaffed to care adequately for patients. Going home at night thinking of all the things that might have been done with an extra pair of hands, and being so tired—not being able to sleep until wee hours of the morning.

I asked: "Are there patients with whom you have found it difficult to work? If so, what sorts of patients are these?" Only one person claimed never to have found patients difficult, but only six percent (7) attributed trouble to medical problems. Eighty-nine percent (101) admitted that they have difficulty working with some patients due to the social behavior of those patients. One person claimed to have difficulty with patients who have certain medical problems and certain personalities. Here are some examples of the answers to this question:

People who abuse the emergency department on a regular basis— these people are people on welfare who come in for every runny nose.

Patients who seem to revel in their illness and "enjoy" poor health arouse negative feelings in me, which I'm sometimes able to set aside. The most difficult type of patient for me is the (usually male) person who, although accepting a lot of caring, teaching energy, indicates he has no intention of acting on what's being taught him.

Patients who refuse to do for themselves and treat nurses as paid maids. Some patients do not recognize nurses as educated professionals but feel that the nursing staff is obligated to wait on them even if it is not necessary.

Yes, the patient who is demanding, arrogant and who thinks the nurse owes him constant, subservient attention.

Patients who are very picky and call after you as though you are their personal maid or waitress.

Of course, there is always someone that is difficult to deal with. I have found for the most part that these people are angry, hostile, and or frightened. Not necessarily due to my own actions but at the system. With much patience and time, however, they can be reached.

The above two questions were designed to ascertain whether the graphic horrors of illness jump to mind for nursing personnel when they think of the most difficult aspects of their work and relations with patients. Obviously, these horrors did not jump to mind for my respondents. These nurses and aides seemed to feel themselves most disquieted by time-task pressures, by social difficulties similar to that which waitresses encounter or by aggravations with superiors or the system. They complained of such things even though they were informed that I was studying adaptations to manifest illness.

As my questions progressed, they became more pointed, but my subjects did not become more inclined to admit a problem with manifest human abnormality. I asked: "Have the deformities of patients ever bothered you? If so, will you give me examples?" Seventy-three percent (83) claimed that they had *never* been bothered by deformities. Twenty-five percent of the respondents (29) claimed that they had been bothered at times, but they tended to refer to specific instances rather than categorical conditions:

A few, for example—a grossly distended abdomen (down to patient's knees) that was draining foul smelling fecal material. The smell was the worse thing.

Not usually, although I once was surprised to find that I was giving "locale care" to a hermaphrodite (in a state hospital infirmary).

Only once when we had a man who had cancer of the mouth and half his face was gone. He had maggots and we had to irrigate his wound twice daily. We irrigated it through an opening in his eye and it came out his mouth.

Yes—a 15 year old girl, we had, had a large open wound of her right femur—gross injuries are about the only thing that bothers me.

When I first began nursing many deformities bothered me but as with anything else you tend to get used to them. I worked in a rehab unit and amputations were common but even to this day if a patient is in bed and I take off the sheets I still get a shock to see only one leg.

The initial "shock" of a deformity bothers me but after that, I can become accustomed to it. The deformity that bothered me most was an elderly lady who had skin cancer on her anterior and posterior left chest and left arm. The ribs were visible and the stench of the wound was really bad. Changing her dressing took a good 30 minutes and it was a very painful experience for her. Often it left me sick to my stomach if I dwelled on it.

Only gross traumatic deformities affect me. A young boy with a large laceration of his forehead, exposing bone. A man who fell off a ladder and landed on his face totally deforming it. A young girl with a severely injured leg that turned necrotic. Man in an airplane accident who badly ripped his facial skin. In addition to foul smell from certain injuries, the impact alone of deformity shocks me. It's hard to conceive the injuries a once healthy, intact, well being when I see the body so disfigured.

I asked: "Are you ever bothered by patient's motor deficiencies? If so, will you give me examples?" Eighty-four percent of the respondents (96) wrote that they had *never* been bothered by patients' motor deficiencies. Thirteen percent (15) wrote that they have been bothered, but a majority of these claimed to be frustrated only by the slowness of such patients and the concomitant difficulty in physically caring for them.

I asked: "Are you ever bothered by personality disorders? Examples?" Thirty-six percent of the respondents (41) denied ever being bothered by personality disorders. Thirty-two percent (37) claimed to be bothered by alcoholics. Only twenty-eight percent (32) answered that they are *sometimes* bothered by personality disorders not related to alcoholism.

On the other hand, a question concerning social behavior drew a much different response. "Does the rude or disorderly behavior of patients ever both you? Examples?" Seventy-eight percent of the respondents (90) answered this question affirmatively. Eighteen percent (20) answered it negatively. The affirmative answers rarely referred to just specific instances, but referred to common complaints:

> Yes, loud drunks; loud, screaming, crying, hysterical Puerto Ricans.

> Yes—often quads will go through a period of depression where they become rude and take out their frustrations on the staff. I try to be reasonable and help them deal with their feelings but I don't take disrespect.

> Yes. Patients admitted to hospital to satisfy drug habit or for shelter from the elements until they can afford more alcohol.

> Yes, certain alcoholics who are regulars in ED are abusive. One woman pinned me against the wall and I might have been hurt except for a doctor who pulled the patient away from me. Also, they threaten to report you and cause a scene in the lobby.

> Dealing with physically violent behavior, as well as extreme verbal abuse is sometimes difficult to tolerate. Continuous use of some of the heavier curses among individuals makes me wish they could change their vocabulary.

> Yes, definitely, I once had a woman patient who thought I was a waitress to serve tea to visitors. The fact that I was charge nurse, it was supper time so half the staff was gone, and I was giving out medication made no difference. If a patient is confused, I can laugh it off, but otherwise I feel there is a point when the line must be drawn.

> There is no excuse for some of the rude patients in ED especially those who are irritated by waiting and the ED is very busy. Everyone wants to be seen first and immediately.

> No, there are reasons for them; it's up to the professionals to try to find the reasons.

> Of course, especially when I am treated as a slave or servant by the "I pay your salary" type.

> Yes. Nursing has lost respect; patients and visitors are flip to you and what can you do about it? *ZERO.*

The number of licensed practical nurses and aides in my sample was too small for any significant cross tabulation. However, tables of the results of the above questions seem to show no evident relationship between answers and the nursing education of the respondents; in other words, that a respondent was a registered nurse with a university degree, a registered nurse without a degree, a licensed practical nurse or an auxiliary did not seem to significantly influence answers to the foregoing questions. Also, the religion, the age and the family status seemed to have no bearing. Nurses from the intensive care unit seemed perhaps a bit more moved by deformity and debility. In the coronary care unit, the intensve care unit, the emergency department, and the large medical and surgical units, the breakdown of answers was about the same.

The consensus is likely even greater than it appears. I pressed some persons who claimed never to be bothered by deformities, and they admitted that there were some cases in which startling deformities had distressed them. Other persons who claimed to be discomforted by deformities admitted that their discomfort was not great or lasting.

I could append here many accounts of nursing personnel at work, accounts which would illustrate how they react strongly to peccadilloes, aspersions and disruptions of the mood or pace of their routines, and how they fail to react, at least apparently, to most manifestations of illness. Here are three examples from my observations.

1. An emergency department nurse, who fumes over the misdeeds of welfare patients and fulminates over the arrogance of certain doctors, stands impassively as ambulance attendants wheel in a bloodied and battered man. The tautness of her expression betrays a certain tension, but from what does this tension arise? The patient is aware, and as the nurse cleans the wounds on his face, she talks to him quietly, soothingly. Her touch is gentle. She seems the angel in white. But her eyes are steady and do not betray what is within. Perhaps, nothing is in a suspension of feeling and thought. Perhaps, there is something of which she is unaware—of which she would not be aware. An assistant comments and the nurse smiles freely. When the event ends, the needles broken, her room tidied and restocked, the event seems never to have occurred except that the nurse is tired, but a procession of screaming kids with cut fingers would have made her just as tired.

   I have asked nurses on occasions, such as this one, what they have felt and thought. Not one found the words to answer me. I myself have had similar experiences with patients, and have barely found the words to answer myself.

2. An enormously obese woman of 59 years is admitted to a medical-surgical unit of 22 semi-private rooms. She is to undergo exploratory surgery and is frantically apprehensive about the prospects of cancer. She smiles nervously and trembles most of the day, but manages to convey to us, the staff, that she is a lovely person—loving and generous to her family.

After her operation, she seems anxious to know the outcome. On five consecutive days, she queries her doctor but he evades her. After the fifth day she asks no more. She has five weeks to live in her semi-private room. Her lower legs and feet are black; from the beginning it has been arduous for her to hoist herself out of bed. Soon after her operation she becomes barely able to move herself at all. The staff, in twos and threes, must move her. We move her in her bed, several times a shift, and as often as every half hour. Nonetheless, she develops cavernous bed sores that compound an agony already great from the depredations of cancer. Certainly, she receives medication, but relief seems to last only a few minutes.

Our huge lady moans and cries incessantly, sometimes softly, sometimes stridently. Her visage is always twisted. She puts on her light every few minutes.

Initially, there is some display of compassion for this wretched woman, but her disruptive presence withers whatever real compassion there might have been. She beckons frequently and thus disrupts the routines of the nurses. As the weeks pass, the nursing staff grows subtly hostile. The mention of her name draws hard, knowing looks. The sound of her voice screeching through the corridors elicits expressions of exasperation. Being assigned to her becomes something of a sentence. Ultimately, one dour 3–11 I am sitting in the nurses' lounge with two nurses, both of whom are sitting on the edges of their chairs and drawing slowly, silently on cigarettes. The call light blinks on, and then comes that familiar and dreaded cry for help. One of the nurses grimaces and says, "I wish I could throw her out the window." Shortly, thereafter, while I am not on duty, the tormented lady dies and is transported with some difficulty, I am sure, to the morgue for dissection. I remained stationed on this same unit for another month, and never in that time did I hear mention of this woman's plight or name.

The hostility was not so hard as it might appear to a

casual observer. Behind it churned frustration, weariness,
impotence and indecision. The nurses did not criticize this
patient as they do most complainers. Her behavior was not
seen as improper. She was difficult socially. She disrupted the
nurses' work and could not be pleased. Also, she presented a
problem with which the nurses would not or could not cope.
This patient created a turbulence on the unit. She disrupted
an ambience in which the horror of disease is a diminished
factor. The nurses were indeed moved to react to her disease,
but only indirectly. She called attention to her plight and that
is what called attention to her. She presented nurses with a
social, navigational problem. She asked for help; the nurses
had neither the time nor the inclination to answer her constant pleas and did not know how to help her in any case.

3. Carrying a large dressing tray, a nurse strolls solemnly toward
a patient's room. At the door she breaks into a broad grin and
struts in. "How are you today?" The patient smiles wanly,
sits up on the edge of his bed and pulls up his nightgown to
reveal a large wet dressing on his upper left side. As she
makes preparations, the nurse continues to talk in an exaggerated yet jocular manner about the weather and the patient's
flowers and cards. Gingerly, with gloved fingers she pulls
loose the old dressing, exposing a gaping purulent wound. The
patient squints down at it as if it were not part of his own
body. "Much better!" exclaims the nurse as she sops up the
ooze with sterile sponges. "Yes, it does look better, doesn't
it?" admits the patient hesitantly. Deftly, the nurse proceeds
with her work, the irrigation, the new dressing. "There you
are! Now, you let me know if it sops through again." She is
already cleaning up and ordering her tray.

Soon she is out the door, and into the next room where
a girl of 14 sits propped up in her bed, a queen amidst a
retinue of stuffed animals, a cascade of cards, and a disarray
of cigarette butts, movie magazines, pop bottles and the like.
The nurse stands sternly at the foot of the teenager's bed. "I
put on the light because I was wondering where my gingerale
was," perks the patient. "Gingerale!" bellows the nurse with
feigned exasperation. "I told you I'd bring it when it comes
up. Now, what's with this water here?" Cool, clean wash
water sets before the patient. The nurse parks her tray on a
chair, grasps up the wash basin and heads for the bathroom.
In a minute she returns. "Come on now, let's get this show
on the road. WASH!" She plunks down the basin and gently

lifts the girl's covers, peers at the dressing on the stump of her leg. "I'm told you may be up in a wheel chair in a day or two." The patient smiles, indeed she has been smiling gleefully throughout. The nurse briskly tugs the curtains around her and is out of the room.

I am with the nurse. I have been with her all along. I ask whether the wound or the stump bother her. She answers that the wound does not but that the stump does somewhat. She proceeds to tell me that the girl's leg had been crushed in an auto accident. Her doctors wanted very much to save this leg and it was actually rotting before they were persuaded to amputate. They amputated the leg just above the knee, but the girl has no feeling or motion in the stump which has refused to heal. The stump is hideous.

The next stop for the nurse is the lounge for a cigarette break. There, she talks about problems with neighbors' children. In a few minutes, she is off to the nurses' station to check the lunch assignment to make sure that she is not scheduled with another nurse of whom she is not particularly fond.

I was not left with a definite impression that the nurse was perturbed by the stump or not perturbed by the wound. In the daily world of nursing, the significance of manifest disease is not obvious. Navigational task and social concerns are so much on the minds of nursing personnel that disease seems almost tangential to them. The scene is perplexing, almost disjointed. Nursing seems in many ways to be a job only, a job in which many requirements are met with many faces. Even tender loving care seems to be turned on and off as the occasion warrants. One wonders what works within these harried nurses.

Most nurses of my acquaintance would consider unfair the picture of nursing that I have drawn thus far. They would claim, rightly, that they work strenuously for patients and give them much kind consideration. In my questionnaire, I asked: "What do you consider to be the most rewarding aspect of your job?" Seventy percent of the respondents volunteered that making patients comfortable or seeing them recover is the most rewarding aspect of nursing. As a whole, nurses view themselves as compassionate. I asked a number of nurses if they care that patients are sick. The answer was generally a resounding and sometimes indignant "yes." When I affronted nurses with some

of my evidence, they tended to counter: "How could we dwell 103
on such things; we would go mad or be dreary all the time."

If one followed a dedicated and competent nurse through the course of a busy shift, one would likely be impressed by how she meets the multiple demands of her work. The leg work alone seems ample inducement for varicose veins. Among the treatments, the charts, the basic physical patient care, the strains of staff relations, this nurse manages a kind word and an attentative ear for her patients, and a bit of jauntiness to cheer them up. On some days, that she manages this at all seems miraculous. If one gets a feeling for her work, one is not likely to question the focus of her effort. Ready explanation jumps to mind for any action that seems less than humanitarian. She seems so hemmed in by imperatives. She is hardly to be blamed that she often does not hear what patients tell her or that she does not ponder their fates.

However, if one remains dispassionate and watches the nurse without attempting to rationalize her acts, one sees a somewhat different picture. The nurse seems engaged in an elaborate act, the production of which consumes much of her attention. Her behavior denotes more a concern for her duties than for her patients. She seems to care for them, and yet also finds them tiring and aggravating. She keeps her distance.

This unofficial focus of nursing is noted at times. Patients and visitors often criticize nursing personnel who become incensed at such a lack of understanding and appreciation. Nurses and nursing educators also notice this focus and complain of staff shortages or hospital priorities, or endeavor to create programs that will make nurses more patient-oriented, more perceptive of the patients' needs.

The Gregor Effect and the Frontstage
of Nursing "Competence"

Manifest human ambiguity is not a preeminent conscious concern of nursing personnel because the institution of which they are a part disdains or avoids its significance through an elaborate choreography of means. In an ultimate sense, hospitals as institutions exist to diminish the poignancy of ambiguous men. Hospitals are heroic systems of denial, specializing in equanimity before manifest mortality. Individual nurses deny human ambiguity through thought and actions that are supported and to some extent compelled by conditions inherent in their nurses' milieu. The ambivalences of the Gregor Effect, the attraction and the repulsion and the equivocal efforts at amelioration that irrefragable human ambiguity inspires are institutionalized so that they are not apparent.

Nurses work against disease and its dehumanizing effects. Mortality is their enemy, and yet it is also their cause. Nurses place themselves in the path of mortality because the challenge of it charges their work with significance. Nurses seek and battle their adversary as an affirmation of life and as an acclamation of self. As sickness is endemic to their situation, nurses' desire for it is not obvious. One generally hears references to the other inclination. Nurses bemoan the work debilitated patients make for them, and note their regrets that certain patients are failing. Nurses do not like to see their patients worsen; yet I have heard nurses complain that their patients were so "up and about" that working with them was not "true" nursing. Indeed, one cannot *nurse* patients who seem well. In relation to such patients, nursing tasks become purely service tasks, and nurses tend to feel degraded to maids. Nineteen percent of my questionnaire respondents (22) admit to feeling some special pleasure or satisfaction when a medical emergency occurs. An additional 17 percent (19) feel some satisfaction when the emergency ends well for the patient.

Befitting the enigma of resistant manifest human ambiguity, nurses' denial of it is confounded, a fact that is masked by the nursing profession, as a philosophy and as a corresponding performance. In fact, nurses do display a full range of reactions to manifest human ambiguity. Nurses' actions humanize and dehumanize ambiguous men, and suggest and disdain the significance of their plight. The frontstage postures themselves serve multiple and antithetical ends, the latter of which are also served by backstage postures. Frontstage nursing does set the dominant tone for nurses' reactions to ambiguous men, but not the only tone, nor could it possibly set the only tone unless medicine could cure all patients.

The ideology upon which hospitals are founded entails two conceptions of man—one more closely associated with medicine and the other more closely associated with nursing, but both integral to the perspectives of nursing personnel. These conceptions serve to rationalize human abnormality so that it is less horrific and to define "man" so that living ambiguous men can be accepted as people conceptually.

In the medical view, the human body is an organism whose qualities and actions are determined by physical–chemical events in accordance with laws governing a material world. Deviations from health, variances from the ideal type of man are conceived as resulting from material circumstances as opposed to malevolent will. This "demystification" of disease serves to quell inordinate fears of the threat ambiguous men pose for men. Ambiguous men are not fiends or magicians but physical beings.

The reifying lenses of the medical perspective further diffuse the impact of ambiguous men by dissolving the gestalt of man into its component parts. Perception if focused upon heart, skin, arm, thigh or psychosis, but not on the totality of an ambiguous man. Of course, perception of a man is not readily thwarted and is perhaps never completely dispelled as long as signs of man are apparent. However, the medical perspective can divert attention from the person. This diversion is more or less easily sustained depending on how compelling a patient presents courage and character within a given situation. In psychiatry the medical perspective may be relatively less effective than in urology. The medical perspective may be most successful in surgery with anesthesia and in post-mortem dissection since in these the patient does not draw attention to character through behavior.

The reification of the individual is one of two aspects of the medical perspective. The second aspect aids in the acceptance of the ambiguous man as a man. One cannot feasibly confront a disease without confronting a patient who, if cogent, will expect the social consideration due a man. The practitioner may be reluctant to surrender his view of patients as things, but in that he is compelled or desires to do so, his ideology provides another protective perspective. When the medical man stands back and sees an ambiguous man, he endeavors to think of him as a man-with-a-malady. The ambiguous man's incongruous elements, his stigmas, are conceived of as being separate from him. Ambiguous men become men without fingers, men with tumors and men with neuroses. Maladies that are hidden within the body are no perceptual threat, but their symptoms can be. These symptoms are also segregated. A jaundiced man is not a yellow man, but a man with jaundice.

Since another man is manifest only in his physical presence, the more stigmatized an ambiguous man is, the less effective the medical perspective is in making a man of him. It is difficult to see a man unequivocally in a being who has no face or personality. When reality refutes the credibility of an ambiguous man as a man-with-a-malady, there is a strong tendency for medical men to indurate to evidence that should signal "man" and to reify the ambiguous man as a thing comprised of things.

Optimally, the reifying and the man-preserving aspects of the medical perspective work in tandem. The malady is conceptually separated from the man, and then this malady is focused on as a thing derived of things. In this way, a positivist perspective is restrained from dehumanizing patients. Induration in conjunction with this approach is topically applied to anesthestize the malady without compromising the perception of a man. Unfortunately, this ideal combination is rarely maintained in confrontation with acute and resistant human ambiguity.

In recent years, social scientists and "radical" physicians have endeavored to impress upon the medical profession that its hard line positivist presumptions are in error, that personality, attitudes and social adjustments may be responsible for physical and behavioral stigmas. Ultimately, these social components can be assumed into a positivist world view; yet, in an immediate sense, they imply treatment of people rather than maladies, and thus they imply a general breakdown of the neat division of man from his body and from his disease. Thus, a social-psychological perspective threatens the entire medical perspective as conceptual armor. For this reason (among others) the medical profession has resisted and will continue to resist the social-psychological perspective. Generally, patients whose ailments are undeniably psychosomatic or social in derivation kindle impatience, frustration or even disgust in their physicians. In that nursing personnel hold to the medical perspective, they also shun nonmedical rationales, but nursing entails more in its view of man than the medical perspective. This added breadth has made nursing educators more attentive than medical men to social rationales.

Nursing combines a medical conception of man with a humanitarian conception that is more totally its own. In that nurses are medical auxiliaries, nursing is a stepchild of medicine; yet in that nurses serve patients with tender loving care, nursing is a humanitarian institution.

Professional nursing was initiated in this country with the opening of the Bellevue Hospital training school in 1873. This program and many that quickly followed were designed to train nurses to bring managerial efficiency to hospital wards, to provide trained assistance to physicians, and to provide patients with humane and nutritive care. From its inception until the decline of the hospital schools, which began in the 1950s, professional nursing was seen as a quasireligious calling, and nurses were construed as paragons of virtue, servers of humanity and angels in white. Nursing education stressed good character, service and a humanitarian view of living ambiguous men as men in need. The medical and the managerial tasks of nursing have increased over the years, especially for the more educated nurses, but not so much as to preclude a pronounced humanitarian perspective in nursing as a whole.

Medicine itself is not devoid of humanitarian outlook. Once this outlook figured as prominently as the medical perspective, but an overwhelming reliance on the medical perspective has been fostered by medicine's growing preoccupation with medical technology and the abrogation by physicians of direct responsibility for nutritive and maintenance care.

Nursing personnel must deal more substantially than physicians with patients as personalities, and therefore the humanitarian perspective has remained an important aspect of nursing. Also, nursing personnel possess a smaller repertoire of medical techniques and rationales and practice medicine much less exclusively and with far less fanfare than physicians.

Conceptions of man cannot resolve the dilemma of ambiguous men due to men's narrow perception of "man," but these conceptions can aid an adjustment to manifest human ambiguity if they are fortified with affirmative rationales and actions. Within a modern hospital, both the medical and the humanitarian perspectives are corroborated by ideologies and related ritual systems. In that medical technology explains medically the more minute aspects of man's physical being, it lends credence to a view of man as a physical being. More substantial support for the medical perspective comes through the prospect of physical rehabilitation. This prospect provides hope that ambiguous men can be cured. This prospect persuades, and rehabilitation itself confirms that men are subject to physical events and that ambiguous men are indeed merely men-with-maladies, maladies that can be excoriated. The purported purpose of medicine is normalization. To this end, men of medical competence learn and practice a host of treatments most of which are conceptually validated through intricate rationales.

Hospital humanitarianism is Christian in origin, but largely secular today. Philosophical rationales and principles have replaced theological as supports of this view. Not being tied to spiritual transcendence, these latter day ethics of compassion and the community of man are vague—bereft of compelling argument. A godless humanitarianism is no match for medical rehabilitation as the dominating purpose of the hospital as an institution; yet, humanitarianism has its place in the mundane living together of patients and nursing personnel within nursing units.

Humanitarianism is affirmed rather than confirmed by its rituals. Tender loving care is a humane gesture from one person to another. Even common courtesy exhibits faith in the humanity of the recipient. Obliquely, nurses' nonchalance about disease and their air of mundane industry are humanitarian. Nurses exhort patients to "get on with living," and help them to do so through the business of nurse-patient encounters.

For reasons explained in Section I, humanitarianism is a satisfying but a weak means of assuagement. Traditionally, it has been alloyed with spiritual transcendence. Acts of charity were also acts that aided the salvation of the actor and perhaps the salvation of the recipient. Rehabilitation almost always played a role, too, in that nutritive care was used to cure, and potions were administered. In close contact with ambiguous men, humanitarianism must be associated with at least one or the other of spiritual transcendence and rehabilitation (normalization). Within the modern hospital where medicine reigns, humanitarian acts are generally seen as salubrious. Tender, loving care is not only charity, it is also therapy. Nursing personnel build patients' morale and offer them social acceptance so that they might recover.

In return, medical technology and techniques buttress humanitarianism in that they enable a perception of ambiguous men as men-with-maladies. This perspective on manifest human abnormality is not truly the same as the humanitarian that locates the essence of man in the intangible; yet for all intents and purposes, man-with-a-malady is a serviceable conception of ambiguous man for a humanitarian bent as long as this person is not so extensively and resistantly stigmatized that this conception becomes incredible. In that medical techniques heal and relieve, they promote the dignity of man and show that ambiguous men were men all along. In this sense, medicine serves humanitarian ends.

The medical perspective and medical rehabilitation are not entirely congruent with the conception or the ethos of humanitarianism. There are occasions when this disparity becomes apparent to nurses who share both views. The medical reification of man is in a sense the antithesis of the humanitarian perspective. Interest in concrete conditions and diseases can lead to callous disregard for the human sensibilities of patients. For the limited prospect of a limited prolongation of life, medical techniques may be used that result in the humiliation or the degradation of patients.

Nursing personnel are sometimes caught between medical and humanitarian perspectives. In terms of what they do, medicine almost always prevails since physicians reign. Yet, nurses feel the strain of the inconsistency especially when medicine fails to deliver in the sense of providing either the hope or the reality of rehabilitation. As will be shown, when medicine fails, there is a tendency for nurses to yearn for a more humanitarian approach.

To a limited extent, nurses have sought to avoid the coldness of the medical approach by turning to psychology and sociology. As these "sciences" relate to ambiguous men, both serve to explain, and to a far lesser degree to suggest, methods of rehabilitation. In this sense, they resemble medicine and serve medical ends; yet psychology and sociology are far more akin to humanitarianism. For psychologists, sociologists and humanitarians, the presence of man emanates from his physical being, but is not one with it. Humanitarians search ambiguous men for their intangible personalities. Human behavior is perhaps the most persuasive evidence of the human soul, and thus it is what humanitarians seek most. Psychology and sociology interpret abnormal behavior so that it can be conceived as a variation of a human theme. Psychology and sociology can sanction humanitarian rituals, and in turn, their rituals can be imbued with humanitarian intent. However, except in limiting the patients' use of analgesics and tranquilizers and their desires for "unnecessary" medical procedures, human science is not used to stem the use of medicine or medical hegemony within the hospital. Values sway the use of medical technology, and desires for rehabilitation and survival are the dominant values.

Nursing personnel conceive of the afflicted in terms of a medical and a humanitarian perspective both of which would attenuate the ambiguity of these afflicted. In the medical view, the issue of human ambiguity is avoided with a concept of ambiguous men as men-with-maladies. In the humanitarian view, living ambiguous men are men in need. In support of these two perspectives, nursing is both rehabilitative and charitable. It is rehabilitative in that it uses nutritive and medical means to cure or to forestall disease. It is charitable in that it serves patients and affirms their human dignity with tender loving care.

Medical and humanitarian perspectives, ideologies and rituals are considered here strictly as means for assuaging the impact of ambiguous men. To this end, nurses *use* medicine and humanitarianism. That physicians rely less on humanitarianism does not mean that they are not compassionate. It does mean that they are less inclined to *use* compassion to mitigate manifest human ambiguity. Nurses use compassion and they sometimes feel it, but the one is not the other. Ritual compassion is not the same as true compassion, although one may evoke the other.

Nursing's conceptions of man and its rationales for disease are abstractions that endure before the presence of ambiguous men through the aid of a number of strategems and conditions which will be discussed at the appropriate time. Ritual doing has already been considered since it is a creature of ideology. Affective neutrality, professional distance or, in common parlance, "not being too involved" will be mentioned here also because it is a principle in itself and a part of nursing (and medical) professionalism.

Traditionally, doctors should not treat members of their own families, and in General Hospital there is a standing rule that a patient must not be admitted to a unit in which a relative works. Especially in years gone by, nurses have "specialed" (served as private duty nurses) relatives; yet in so doing, these nurses have foregone or attenuated their professional distance and perhaps much of their professional "competence." In the course of their work, health professionals should not become "emotionally involved" with patients since such involvement allegedly impedes professional judgment and functioning. Caring for relatives is discouraged since one is already involved with them.

Whatever assistance professional distance provides professional performance, this distance provides definite support for the professional perspective. In effect, professional reserve is a restriction of behavior and bearing on the part of the professional to the roles which comprise his calling. Nursing's medical-humanitarian views of man and illness are enhanced in that nurses interact with patients via medical and humanitarian rituals. Nursing roles affirm *Nursing perspectives*. In that a nurse plays other roles for an ambiguous man, and he thus becomes more than a fleshed version of "patient" and "man," this nurse's professional conceptions are likely to be undermined. To look too closely is to see too much.

In passing conversations, a number of nurses and aides have told me that they have not been able to maintain a purposeful calm when dealing with seriously ill or dying friends and relatives, a calm that these nurses and aides ordinarily manage in the hospital. One nurse informed me that when she was a recent graduate, she was especially proud of her cool dexterity in the operating room, so much so that she decided to assist in her mother's gall bladder operation. This nurse set up the operation in a matter-of-fact way and remained cooly professional until the scalpel cut into her mother, whereupon this nurse fainted.

Medical and humanitarian definitions, rationales, rituals and professional reserve comprise nursing with a capital "N," the Nursing that pertains to confrontations with ambiguous men. The elements of this Nursing in some ratio comprise the frontstage adaptations of all normative nursing personnel—comprise their conscious denials of manifest human ambiguity. In that they exist, postures that are incongruent or antithetical to the conceptions of the spirit of Nursing tend to be kept covert. Within the hospital, nurses and aides should not overtly resort to hate, mockery, violence, voyeurism or evasion.

Perceptions and Conceptions in Nursing

Nurses and aides use a lexicon of rationales and labels to explain and to identify types of patients. Such conceptualizations and designations set the choreography of active relations between the staff and individual patients. The medical and humanitarian views of man are the broadest conceptions used to define patients and are automatically applied to all patients. These conceptions set the official tone of Nursing. Many more specific conceptions and labels are used to define and to identify individual patients and to guide staff relations with them. These labels are appended to patients by nursing personnel according to what they know about patients via records and reports, and according to what they perceive about patients directly. Recorded and reported medical diagnoses are given to most patients. A diagnosis "explains" a patient's condition, suggests his prognosis, and indicates the course of his treatment. Nurses learn a number of attributes regarding patients from both reports and perceptions. Such attributes as age, sex, ethnicity and social class are learned indirectly and directly, and have considerable bearing on treatment. Finally, nursing personnel stereotype and categorize patients. Patients are seen as senile patients, cranks, alcoholics, responsible adults and so forth.

Regarding the perception of manifest human ambiguity, rationalizations hold some sway, but for the most part, this perception depends on the human ideal type of the beholder and the appearance of the beheld. Appearances are more poignant than labels. Human ambiguity is a creature of perception. The perception of ambiguity determines the effort made to deny it or to disdain its significance.

Conceptions structure relations with patients, but perceptions influence how this structure is used and how it is supported. Indeed, perceptions of human ambiguity are the ultimate impetus for the construction of conceptual solutions. Beyond the bare bones of formal Nursing, the informal typifications arising from nurses' perceptions of patients determine how Nursing and its backstage supports are used in dealing with individual patients. Can the patient walk? Does he have a face? Can he talk? Is he cogent? Perceptual answers to these questions are more relevant to the social treatment of a patient than is his diagnosis. The perception of human ambiguity triggers means of assuagement that are not built into the Nursing task and strengthens reliance on those means that are.

I have heard and read much about nurses' reactions to dying patients. Generally, some "view" of death is probed. A statement or implication is made that patients are regarded and treated differently because they are dying. From what I have seen, such an approach is misdirected. The knowledge that a patient is dying does not so much influence the postures of nursing personnel toward this patient as does this patient's presentation of himself. Dying patients who seem normative and who draw no attention to their plight are treated, for the most part, like patients who do not share so dire a prognosis. Patients who seem merely senile are treated much the same whether or not they are dying. Cogent patients who openly discuss their demise are handled differently than mute patients whose appearance bespeaks their end. Unless something of a personal relationship has developed between staff and patient, the prospect of death seems to influence nursing only when the patient broaches the subject or appears undeniably moribund.

Whatever their diagnoses, patients through their physical presentations of self either undermine or augment Nursing as an adjustment to them. Humanitarianism is easier before patients who seem more normative, and if patients' gratitude acknowledges Nursing beneficence, so much the better. Faith is rehabilitative power is easier with convalescent patients. The more dramatic the recovery, the more dramatic the demonstration of such power. Nursing is more difficult and less adequate with 113 patients who seem more abnormal and whose manifest humanity is deteriorating.

Frontstage Supports for Nursing "Competence"

If a rehabilitative-humanitarian perspective is to be credible in the absence of am immortalizing medical efficacy, and in the presence of resistantly ambiguous men, two interrelated conditions must obtain: (1) Context and drama must foster an illusion of potent medical efficacy, and an ethos of humanitarianism. (2) The manifest human ambiguity must not be so prevalently poignant that this illusion and this ethos cannot be maintained. In General Hospital both these conditions prevail sufficiently for some faith to be placed in the Nursing perspective. Nursing roles form a part in the requisite drama. The roles of physicians, technicians and patients themselves complete the play. Nursing units and medical specialty departments provide contexts fraught with the appropriate symbolisms. Generally, the patients are not so ambiguous as to threaten seriously the Nursing perspective, due to context, roles, affluence, analgesics, medical cosmetic effects and rehabilitation.

General Hospital provides nursing personnel with a context that aids and compels their practice of Nursing. The design and the decor of their milieu, their number and organization, the delineation of their tasks enmesh nurses and aides in a reality in which Nursing seems both their duty and a plausible foil to human ambiguity.

General Hospital is many things. It is almost as much an office building as it is a medical-nursing facility. However, staff nurses and aides work with patients with circumscribed areas comprised of medical specialty departments and nursing units. X-ray, the operating room, cystoscopy, sigmoidoscopy, the laboratory, isotope and the like are medical workshops festooned with the apparatus of that trade. In a sense, these primary scenes for medical performance are chapels for the affirmation of the medical perspective. Nursing units also bespeak medical utility, but their symbolisms are somewhat confounded as they reflect the dual perspective of Nursing.

Nursing units' functional layouts and almost austere decors proclaim a lean medical determinism, but they also suggest a monastic simplicity. Many of the features that tell the cold material reality of science and technology also echo the humility and other-worldliness of the spiritual ascetic. In the larger nursing units, patients' rooms are similar cells, similarly appointed and furnished, linearly arranged. These rooms are just big enough for necessary movement. If chairs are pushed to one side, the beds can be shifted and carriers, wheel chairs and most portable gear can be brought in and out. The decor is institutional. Curtains are of durable synthetics and walls are painted in unmemorable tones. Behind and above the beds branch examination lights on extension arms and wait outlets for oxygen and suction machines. The impersonal, patent sameness and the simplistic functionality of the rooms denote medical purpose, but they also denote the stark egalitarianism of an abstract humanitarian conception. A description of the coronary care unit illustrates this point further.

The coronary care unit is small but commodious, spartan but adequate. There are six rooms for six patients. Five of these rooms are arranged in a line across from the nurses' station. The sixth room is on the far side of the utility room on the nurses' station side. A short hall divides the five rooms from the sixth room, utility room, nurses' station, bathroom and nurses' lounge. As is standard in General Hospital, the nurses' lounge is so cramped that two persons cannot stand side-by-side across its width. Throughout the unit, the flooring is asphalt tiles. The walls are muted green and beige. The five patients' rooms across from the nurses' station have green draped glass doors and partially glass walls. Each patient's room contains a bed, a bedside table, and over-the-bed stand, a vinyl easy chair, a sink and a mirror. The entire unit is scrubbed aseptic. There is no clutter; everything is kept in its place. Plate glass windows emit ample light. A painting reproduction graces a wall of each patient's room, but such divertissement hardly impedes the banausic ambience of the rooms or the unit.

The trappings of medical technology are evident but not intrusive. Except for an occasional buzzer and the gasp of itinerate Bird respirators, there is no regular mechanical noise. A monitor juts from a wall of each patient's room as a metronome whose silent blips punctuate the gravity of the unit's task. The crisis paraphernalia of cardiac care sits in and on two carts in the hall.

The layouts and the accoutrements of other nursing units vary from CCUs, but the ambiences in these units are substantially the same. The presence of medical technology is more poignant in the intensive care unit. The large medical and surgical units

contain semiprivate rooms, and they are noisier and less orderly
than CCU, but only so much as to make them several degrees
less somber.

The context within which nurses' work fosters medical pragmatism and abstracts individuals, ambiguous and not, into patients and thus into humanity. A nursing unit is a world of
interchangeable parts that are not individually but only categor-
ically significant. Each motorized, adjustable, railed, wheeled,
steel bed with its plastic coated slab of a mattress has accommodated hundreds of patients. No one can say which patients
have been served by which beds, or how many persons have died
on a given bed. Each bed is true to its type. Beds are wheeled
from room to room, and thus even context cannot individualize
them. As it is with beds, so it is with all else which the
institution consigns to the service of patients. If patients' rooms
were shuffled, putting them back in their original order would
be difficult if not impossible.

Patients barely impede the standardization of their surround-
ings. Flowers are propped on window sills and cards are taped to
closets, but such embellishments are extrinsic and are removed
ultimately along with their owners. When a patient leaves either
for home or for the morgue, no reminders remain behind—no
clues to his fate. His place is quickly assumed by another patient.

Set in a patient's cell, garbed in a patient's clothes, framed by
disposable cups, basins and water pitchers, a patient is as solely
a patient as context can make him. Socially, he is as one-
dimensional as he can be made. Since he is one of many men
who have been, are and will be patients in his place by virtue of
this place, he is an object by which mankind is served. Nursing
units serve humanity; they serve individuals incidently.

Nurses and aides are themselves interchangeable functionaries.
Organizationally and contextually their direct relations with
patients are restricted to prescribed Nursing rituals of medical
and humanitarian significance. A formal nursing hierarchy and
an informal nursing society enforce this stance through the
threat of dismissal or disapproval.

Nurses and aides work under conditions consciously designed
to make Nursing their currency with man-made patients. A
nurse, identified as a nurse, dressed as a nurse, encounters
situations in which the implements for Nursing are at hand, the
scene for Nursing is set, Nursing is exemplified by other nurses,
and Nursing is expected of her by all socially normative
witnesses.

Patients can disrupt this structured order, but at General Hospital, more often than not, they do not. Nursing personnel must perform and credit rehabilitative-humanitarian roles if these roles are to assuage the manifest ambiguity of patients. Since these roles are played vis-à-vis patients, performance and credibility depend substantially on the appearances and the behavior of patients. Typically, patients must not act so as to preclude Nursing's rehabilitative-humanitarian mien. They must not appear so resistantly grotesque that nurses and aides cannot support a hope for their patients' recovery or a belief in their humanity. In General Hospital these conditions were generally met.

If nurses are to execute Nursing roles, patients as a group must enact complementary roles, or at the very least must offer no insurmountable impedance. In fact, General Hospital's patients frequently play complementary roles and generally accept the suppositions of Nursing. As a whole, patients do accept nursing personnel as rehabilitators and humanitarians, and respect their professional distance. Patients think of their diseases as things, and view themselves as men-with-maladies and as individuals.

Nursing personnel expect patients to behave in an "appropriate" manner. This manner is not set, but it is circumscribed. Nurses and aides assess the physical and the mental competence of patients. In that patients are deemed able, they are expected to respect staffers as knowledgeable rehabilitators and to follow their directions pliantly. Furthermore, able patients are to be duly grateful for services rendered, and are thus to acknowledge the humanitarianism of the staff.

Patients are not to draw "unwarranted" attention to their afflictions. Staffers assess the severity of their patients' conditions and estimate the pain, if any, these patients are suffering. In light of these assessments and estimations, nurses determine the lamentation that is acceptable from each of their patients. Generally, little plaint is condoned. Patients whose maladies are deemed especially severe are allowed "bad days"; yet prolonged bewailing or snivelling is condemned for all patients. The most stricken patients are expected to exert tremendous effort to keep their suffering to themselves.

Nursing personnel reveal these expectations in their criticisms of patients. Nurses seem to be forever grumbling about whiners, recalcitrants and ingrates. Such patients are belabored at the nurses' station, in the lounge and at lunch. Occasionally, on hearing such a complaint, a staffer may demur, but she does so by suggesting that the given's patient's circumstances are more extenuating than presumed or by citing occasions when the patient has behaved properly. Generally, consensus is readily formed regarding the improprieties of patients. Patients need do very little to be censured in the nurses' lounge. One moan, one refusal, or one gripe is frequently sufficient.

In large measures in General Hospital, patients do fulfill staff expectations. I was continuously amazed, considering the social diversity of the patients, that they as a group were so quiet, so compliant and so grateful. Many patients of my acquaintance hardly referred to their sickness, and many of these patients were dying. Any 19-year-old nurse's aide could generally anticipate prompt obedience from any cogent patient. Although patients were not typically effusive in their thanksgiving, in gesture and in tone they often did acknowledge nursing beneficence. I was much impressed at how accommodating most patients were. Even patients who seemed that they might be obstreperous as "civilians" were fairly complaint as patients. In a unit of 46 patients, nurses and aides would rarely complain about the behavior of more than several patients. This same high ratio held in all the nursing units I studied, including the emergency department.

To some extent patients are cowed, being indisposed strangers in an overpowering milieu, but they also play their roles in their own interest. Patients have a stake in Nursing "competence" in that they want to recover, in that they want to be treated well, and in that they want to share Nursing's denial of their ambiguity. For those patients who are up to the performance, relations between patients and staff follow definite norms. Nurse–patient "interaction rituals" characterize encounters between staff and patients. The play is known to staff and patients alike. Able patients match nurses' expectations by expecting nurses to be dedicated and competent rehabilitators and servants of humanity. When nurses fall short of patients' expectations in this regard, able patients, in their turn, complain as stridently as nurses.

Able patients desire nurses and aides to be sociable and seemingly concerned, but I have never met a patient who openly wished to be adopted by the nursing staff or by individual nurses. Patients usually support nurses in their ken for professional distance. In large measure, familiarity between patients and staff is a fantasy knowingly entertained by both parties much as is the cordial informality between public relations man and their clients—and waitresses and their patrons.

Those patients who are unable to partake of nurse–patient rituals fall into two categories: those patients who do and those patients who do not disrupt Nursing rituals. Most unable patients at General Hospital do not impede the nurses' act. Such patients are comatose, very weak or benignly demented. In that they respond, they do not respond appropriately, but their impropriety is discounted by nurses. These patients become, in a sense, manikins toward whom nursing personnel can practice Nursing. This arrangement is not as satisfactory for frontstage Nursing as is ritual interaction with able patients; yet manikins prohibit neither rehabilitative or humanitarian rituals.

Disruptively unable patients pose a far greater problem for Nursing. These patients uninhibitedly flout order within nursing units by wailing, general and stout resistance, or violent outbursts. A rehabilitative-humanitarian mien becomes difficult in the presence of a shrieking patient, or when a patient spits the food one is feeding him into one's face, or when one must forcibly stop a patient from walking out the door. Permissible means for controlling such a patient are limited. A patient may be sedated or tied down with specially designed restraints but, sedation is a questionable method and restraints are only marginally acceptable. Many nurses use restraints reluctantly.

However, in General Hospital the contrariety of patients rarely precludes Nursing. More often than not, patients actively assist nursing personnel in their roles, and thus assist their assuagement of manifest human ambiguity. The only quality a patient needs to play his role is a coherent, discernable personality; most patients have this quality.

General Hospital serves many ambiguous men, some acutely so, but most patients are not poignantly manifestly ambiguous. The modicum of manifest human ambiguity arises for a number of reasons. The hospital, being a community hospital, refers many elderly patients to nursing homes, many critically sick patients to medical centers, and many debilitated patients to rehabilitation centers. The patients' status reduces the visibility of afflictions. Affluence and medicine tend to normalize the appearance of patients.

The behavior expected of people as hospital patients is far less demanding than that which is expected of them generally, and thus people as hospital patients have less occasion to exhibit debilities. In this regard, being a "hospital patient" is a distinct advantage over being merely "sick." At home, individuals can be

deemed "sick" and be thus accorded certain allowances, but
their status at home is always tempered by longstanding if muted
expectations of another sort. Within a hospital, patients are more
totally patients. With impunity, they can loll in bed where any
weakness or incoordination is minimally apparent. They need
not think much for themselves or manage lengthy discourses.
The compliance and the appreciation associated with the patients' role can be managed as limp surrender and a faint smile.
Hospitals are instituted to care for patients and thus long-term
patients do not receive the resentment they would if there were
imposing upon their families or the general public.

Deformities are masked. A sheet tucked under a patient's chin
covers much. Casts, bandages and dressings clothe.

In large measure, American affluence averts the evils of mal-
nutrition and allows the use of medical technology. General
Hospital's patients rarely suffer from dietary deficiencies. They
are almost never so racked from hunger that their bones protrude,
or their bellies swell. Being well-nourished, the patients are
generally well-formed. National affluence enabled these patients
throughout their lives to benefit from the cosmetic marvels of
modern medicine, not the least of which is dentistry.

The success of medicine against infection and of surgery
against gross deformity has resulted in patients' being less palp-
ably abnormal. A medieval saint drank pus that she not find
repulsive the afflictions of the needy. Modern medical humanitarians confront a most aseptic challenge. The stench of purulent
wounds does not permeate wards and corridors. Writhing plague
victims do not press one upon the other. Even torrid fevers are
less frequent. Antibiotics have virtually begotten a generation of
patients with chronic, degenerative diseases which in all but
their last stages are far less visible than acute infections. Surgery
saves limbs and their functions. It removes growths and recon-
structs features. A sutured wound is ever so much less garish
than an open wound. In short, one does not frequently encounter
in General Hospital scenes reminiscent of those in newsreels
from the Hospital Ship Hope.

General Hospital is no overt facsimile of hell. Suffering is met
with analgesics and anguish with sedatives. One sees gnashing
of teeth, but not much, relative to the number of patients one
encounters as a member of the nursing staff. Display is socially
discouraged but the success of this stricture would be much less
without both the real and the placebo effects of drugs. Nurses'

faith in drugs is so great that they become almost aggravated when patients complain of sustained pain. In such instances, nurses tend to reason that the patients are faking or that their medications are not strong enough.

Recoveries and fresh faces sustain a faith in the rehabilitative powers of medicine and tender loving care. Many patients do recover or improve. However, whether they do or do not recover, patients do not remain indefinitely at General Hospital, and the turnover fosters an impression of rehabilitation. Six months is an unusually long stay at this hospital. Patients do return, but often they are admitted to different units, and even when they are readmitted regularly to the same unit, many short stays do not render the same impression as one seemingly interminable stay. Patients who die are quickly removed in carriers which conceal even the shapes of their bodies. Their places are quickly filled with living faces.

Thus, as a group, patients are not so restive that Nursing cannot be done and so resistantly monstrous that Nursing cannot be believed. Nursing does structure the relations between nursing personnel and patients. Nursing is the staff's conscious, front-stage adaptation to manifest human ambiguity. The rehabilitative humanitarian ethos of Nursing reigns. Whatever nurses and aides do to patients is either clothed in this ethos or done thoughtlessly or covertly.

The above discussion may have rendered the impression that there are no or few ambiguous men at General Hospital. There are enough of them so that in every unit, except the emergency department, manifest human ambiguity is always a presence. The ambiguous men are inobtrusive enough to permit Nursing to be almost always the dominant posture of nursing personnel vis-à-vis patients, but they are generally obtrusive enough to require more than Nursing. Some patients are exceedingly ambiguous. Many others are moderately so, emitting telltale signs of mortality. Patients deteriorate as well as recuperate. Many linger for months with no prospect for active lives. Nurses do not have hope for all patients.

A series of covert backstage methods eases the impact of those patients whose conditions graphically undermine the rehabilitative-humanitarian ideology of Nursing. Some of these methods are covered by Nursing's official regimen. Others are not covered. All of them enable Nursing by assuaging ambiguity, but would overwhelm Nursing if they became too prominent. Such is more likely to be the case as the ambiguity of patients becomes more pervasive, more poignant and more resistant. In my experience in General Hospital, these conditions were approached at times in the intensive care unit and generally in the presence of the senile elderly. In both cases, the frontstage supports of Nursing were unable to subdue the ambiguity of certain patients sufficiently to allow "proper" Nursing performance.

The hospital's most startlingly debilitated patients are concentrated in the intensive care unit. A number of nurses that had by far the greatest propensity for irreverent humor (MASH) I saw anywhere in the hospital. During my stay on ICU, patients were occasionally treated in a manner bespeaking neither medical professionalism or nursing humanitarianism. Antics were enacted before the patients as if they were nonpersons or not present, or patients were jostled about and addressed as if they were life-size puppets in a Punch-and-Judy show. Such occasions were but short interludes in a more standard nursing regimen, but they definitely broke the Nursing ambience. One nurse who was at the center of many MASH events reasoned that such raucous activities and almost rough treatment are good for patients in that they startle patients into an awareness of ongoing life which is important to their survival. Thus, MASH is given a Nursing rationale; however, to watch this MASH dispassionately is to doubt that Nursing is its impetus or its effect.

Senile patients sometimes resist the ministrations of Nursing. They refuse medications. They refuse food. They do not turn when the nurse says, "Turn," or stay when the nurse says, "Stay." If nursing personnel are to do their duty by such patients, coercion is necessary. Yet, whatever its ultimate rationale, such force is not evidently rehabilitative or humanitarian. The strong arm can hardly be seen as a medical technique. Nursing personnel would not force a patient deemed to be mentally competent, and thus coercion would seem to belie humanitarianism. Senile patients are tied down; they are dragged on walks; spoons are shoved down their mouths. Many nurses seem to find these activities disquieting; at least they seem somewhat hesitant or reluctant. Most nursing personnel ultimately cover their actions with a feigned humor, as if the coercion is not to be taken seriously. Grins meant to be indulgent and knowing are stretched across their faces. Feeding is done to the tune of "feed the baby." Two husky nurses waltz a patient propped between them, a tiny patient whose feet barely touch the floor—waltz her out to "see" the nurses at the nurses' station. "Look who we have here! Isn't she cute!" A hardness edges this fun and games, a hardness not in keeping with Nursing, at times threatening its preeminence.

At General Hospital the manifest ambiguity of patients does not generally push nurses to such extremity, though nurses do commonly use non-Nursing methods. These covert means of which the above are obtrusive expressions will be discussed at length.

Limits
to Idealism

Humanitarianism and
the Limits of Medical Heroism

Nursing personnel do witness horrors against
which they employ a number of hedges. Among
these hedges are a certain reserve concerning
medical heroics and a concomitant sense that
certain troubling circumstances should be different, that a humanitarian concern for the comfort
and the dignity of patients should at times super-
vene where the tests and the treatments of rehabilitative medicine are scourging unsalvageable
patients or maintaining their tortured existences
and presences. Nurses and aides are not entirely
taken up in the medical dramas that play about
them despite the elaborate staging and the coop-
eration of most patients. As medical auxiliaries
and nursing professionals, nurses are plied with
too much exposure to inept medical performance
and the failings of medical "competence" to be
overawed. Also, they do indeed confront circumstances in which medical performance is not in
keeping with their humanitarian ethos.

Nurses are equivocal concerning medicine.
Generally, they accord persons of medical "competence" the highest prestige. Historically, nurses
have become increasingly involved with medical

practice, such that they now exhort themselves to make nursing diagnoses, to initiate medical action and to challenge physicians on judgement and procedures. Such shoulder rubbing with the priests of medicine tends to be limited to the more educated and experienced registered nurses; yet all nursing personnel are proud of their participation in the medical task, however peripheral that participation might be. All nursing personnel are privileged spectators, a status that links them with medical heroism, but also impresses upon them the limitations of this heroism.

The medical illusion is limited for nurses by two factors: (1) Nurses are not priests of medicine, and therefore do not fully share the physician's aura of power. Nurses are seconds and stage hands who set up and mop up. Their duties are more service than medically oriented, and thus nursing experiences are not so conducive to medical pretensions. (2) Nurses have closer and more prolonged contact with individual patients within the hospital than do physicians, and therefore nurses are likely to be more impressed with patients' personalities and the deficiencies of these personalities. Nurses are also more likely to be impressed with the failures of medical ritual. Physicians "hit and run"; nurses must live with the results.

Nurses' feelings about doctors are confounded. To reside on a nursing unit is to be impressed with the disrespect nurses feel for doctors who are mercilessly berated for being either over- or underzealous in their use of medical techniques. Nurses chafe incessantly at the pomposity of certain physicians. Some of this plaint is undoubtedly the sour grapes self-assertion that subordinates commonly vent against superordinates, but for the most part nurses' complaints are specific. On the other hand, doctors are treated as superior beings whose criticism and praise are taken much to heart despite disclaimers. Nurses are true believers in medical utility, although not in all circumstances. Generally, they are as appalled as physicians if a patient's condition has become "needlessly" critical because of the patient's failure to seek medical care. With the exception I shall discuss presently, nurses' grievances with doctors are not so much directed against the medical profession as against individual physicians who are not cordial or do not practice medicine as competently as nurses think they should. Despite the grumbling, the nurses I asked were generally satisfied with the medical competence of the physicians with whom they worked. Although the bouquets are not so rousing as the blasts, nurses think highly of certain

doctors who approximate the nurses' ideals concerning medical
practice.

As physicians are superiors, nurses accord them greater latitude in manners, but in general nurses apply their own professional standards to physicians. Nurses want to see medicine practiced with dedication and competence and become incensed when physicians are remiss in these areas, but this reaction is similar to that which remiss nurses incur and is thus not a source of the special reservations nurses hold toward physicians and the medical profesion. Similarly, physicians are sometimes deemed to be insufferably arrogant, but this ad hominem concern is not the major bone of contention. Humanitarianism is the issue. Nurses would have physicians support a Nursing ethos and thus frequently believe physicians are insufficiently concerned with the dignity and the comfort of their patients—that physicians often do not think of their patients as human beings.

I asked: "Do you think that relative to doctors, nurses generally care more, less or about the same about individual patients?" Seventy-one percent of the respondents (82) think that nurses care more than doctors. Seven percent (7) think that nurses and doctors care about the same. Ten percent (11) answered that caring depends on the individual doctors and nurses. Nine percent (10) did not answer this question. Only four percent (4) think that doctors care more than nurses about individual patients. Many respondents mentioned nurses' greater contact with patients:

In most cases more because we spend longer time spans with the patient—we know them better—are able to develop more significant relationships. I suspect that with some people the intimacy of shared activities such as bathing, toileting, back rubs etc. provides an atmosphere for deeper sharing.

More. We have the most contact, see the most suffering, supply the most comfort and general care.

Since nurses spend more time with the patients I think we care more about the individual patients. There is a pattern I've noticed. When a patient is admitted in critical condition, the doctors do take a great interest in their charge and are very concerned about their progress. Unfortunately, due to the great number of patients/ MD, specialization reigns and the patient becomes not an individual but an inanimate object that should respond in such a way to a particular treatment. Once the crisis has passed, doctors irregu-

126   larly see their patients and then only briefly. It is my opinion that nurses tend to worry more than the doctors. Many times a sudden change occurs and you get all hyped up and call only to be asked, "What did you bother me with that for?"

—ICU Nurse

Nurses care more as they are with them for 8 hr/day as opposed to less than 8 min/day.

A number of respondents cited venal motives as limiting physicians' interests in patients:

I think nurses care more than the majority of doctors. Doctors seem to think of time and money and tend to cut the patient short.

More. I think to doctors they are a way to make money. Half the doctors don't even know their patients' names.

Unfortunately, I do feel that the nursing staff cares more about the patients than do most doctors. Not all, but many doctors do not like to be called on 11–7 even if there is a valid reason. It is not uncommon to have many of them hang up on a nurse, that is to say, if they call back at all. My most recent experience was when a patient shot a blood clot to the groin. "We'll take care of it in the morning!" and hung up.

Some respondents see nurses as advocates for patients:

More about the patients! Even though we sometimes get grief from the doctors, I think nurses are willing to take the grief from the MDs in order to help patients.

Nurses care more about patients than doctors and often serve as their advocate.

These answers exemplify the more equivocal responses:

It depends on a lot of factors. Both doctors and nurses care more for the people they've gotten to know than for people they don't know, and when a patient is unassigned to a doctor, the chances are that, through their greater exposure to the patient, the nurses will care more about him than the doctor. Some sensitive and kind doctors seem to care more about their patients even ones they've only just met, than rushed and task-driven nursing staff.

I think patient–nurse relationships have a lot to do with the
degree of caring. I think on a small floor where the nurses have
more time to spend with patients, the degree goes up. On larger
floors, doctors care more; that depends on who the doctor is too.
Some care a lot; some not at all.

—CCU Nurse

Only one respondent chose to explain why she thinks physicians
are more caring. "Doctors care more because they know the
patient and have closer contact with him." This respondent
happens to be an emergency department nurse whose contact
with individual patients is momentary. However, while I was at
General Hospital, I heard this particular answer a number of
times from physicians. These physicians were all private physicians, and their claim thus has a ring of truth; yet more often
than not, I would side with the nurses. The country doctor is
gone, at least in the vicinity of General Hospital. Physicians here
typically have hundreds of patients and offices that have become
clinics with complements of medical aides. Certainly, while they
are in the hospital, patients usually do not see much of their
doctors. The harried physician bearing great responsibility and
dividing too many hours among too many patients remains
almost necessarily a remote figure to most of his patients. That
he practices medicine tends to become an overweening reality
for the physician. Other factors are involved. His lofty status in
itself distances him from many patients. Certainly, most physicians seem more comfortable with and considerate of persons
who share their elevated status. At General Hospital, there are
physicians who transcend all obstacles and manage to be especially sensitive to the concerns of both patients and nurses. On
the whole, however, I believe that General Hospital's nurses are
more moved by the dictates of humanitarianism than are its
physicians, and I believe that this nursing bent results from and
is used to structure nurses' more intimate service relationship
with patients.

Nurses use a humanitarian prospect to compensate for gaps
they perceive in medicine's illusion of power. As medical auxiliaries, nurses spare physicians the full realization of their limitations by protecting physicians from protracted and unceremonious contact with patients. Physicians command, perform and
depart, leaving patients to nursing care. As with all auxiliaries in

such a position, nurses cannot easily evade reality's challenge to an illusion of potent efficacy. Most functionaries in this position would be compelled toward reliance on the base, nonideological means of assuagement. Nurses do use the nonideological techniques, but they also turn to their humanitarian perspective that does not require rehabilitative effort and which in its broadest sense, colors death in quiet tones as long as death comes with "dignity."

Physicians seem more intent with denying death and using "heroic" medical techniques than nurses. When at General Hospital, I never heard a doctor tell a patient of impending death. The patients who knew seemed to have realized their plight without official assistance. Nurses frequently complain that physicians give patients and sometimes their families unrealistically optimistic reports. Physicians often order or perform tests and procedures that hurt or mutilate with the slim possibility that these efforts will extend life that can never again be approximately normal.

Nurses seem more willing to accept the prospect of death and would more frequently inform patients of their dire conditions. Nurses would also limit medical hegemony, by withdrawing all but palliative treatment and medications from the patients nurses deem to be medically unsalvageable. In place of medicine nurses would employ their own tender loving care and perhaps the tender loving care of the patients' families. This point of view is exemplified by the following comment from an intensive care nurse:

> I could list a few unpleasant aspects, but the one most prominent is facing death with patients and families. I wish I could have a course instructing us how to handle these situations. I am a very emotional person, but usually contain myself well when facing these people. Having worked as long as I have on ICU I try to extend myself more in these circumstances and allow the families unlimited visiting hours as death approaches the family member. I, myself, try to keep the patient well-medicated and free from pain—I've found it helps the family to see the patient comfortable and quiet. It is most upsetting and frustrating to see someone die in great misery and discomfort. Many times the situation we nurses face is denial by the doctors that their patient is going to die. Inevitably (and I have seen it happen), they tell the family the patient is doing fine. If we disagree with the doctors and ask them to face reality, they get really upset (since it is a defeat for them)

and nothing is accomplished. Allowing the family members to become involved in the patient's care (i.e., backrubs, positioning in bed) helps all around, especially for the patient as he does not feel alone. However, with unresponsive patients families are sometimes more upset, particularly if the victim is ill as result of a sudden accident— guilt feelings and feelings of "how can he do this to me" come out. Sometimes I find myself avoiding these people and trying to occupy myself with some unrelated task just so I won't have to talk with them. I feel I don't know how to cope with their problem and walking away is the easy way out. *Never* have I seen a patient be told he is going to die, thus denying him the truth he is entitled to help prepare him for it.

Almost all of my questionnaire respondents would limit the use of "heroic" medical methods. In answer to my question: "What do you think of "heroic" medical or surgical efforts to prolong life? When do you think they are warranted? When do you think they are not?"—only three percent, three persons, claimed that "heroic" medical or surgical efforts should *always* be used when there is a chance of prolonging life. Four percent (5) did not answer this question. The remaining 93 percent (106) would limit "heroic" means employed to save terminal patients or elderly patients who have no prospects but pain and debility:

> I cannot see it for the very elderly who have been sick for a long time (CHF, heart disease, severe infection, etc.). Nor for the terminal cancer patient who has suffered enough—he does not need us to prolong his suffering or his family's anguish. The problem often is with the doctors who do not honestly communicate with patients and their families about conditions of their patients. Yes, save the life, if there is hope that he will live productively—not as a vegetable.

> "Heroic" is something I have to feel. On an elderly, terminal patient—no— they should have the privilege of death in dignity and understanding. Although, I guess that goes for all terminal patients. No sense in prolonging the inevitable, after all avenues of treatment for care have been judged, assessed and justified.

Some respondents suggested that some assessment of the quality of life should be used as a criterion for initiating heroic measures:

> Consider them unwarranted in most instances. *Possibly* used for young. Most of the time these attempts are unsuccessful; if life is maintained, a questionable way of life for patient and family.

For the most part asinine. I feel that they are warranted when the person has a chance for regaining a fairly "normal" lifestyle for a pretty decent length of time. When "heroics" create needless suffering, in some cases, death is better than life.

They are warranted if the person desires it or if the prognosis is favorable. It sickens me when a doctor seemingly practices on someone (usually an elderly person) to prolong their life and suffering. I wonder if heroics are so much to restore or prolong life as they serve for the MD to avoid death/failure. With medicine life seems to be the only alternative, doctors don't seem to realize that death "with dignity" is sometimes a better alternative.

In the same vein as this last response, one respondent said:

"heroic efforts"—frequently abused mostly when MD is unwilling to give up or needs practice and will therefore resuscitate any-one.

Finally, a number of respondents believe that patients or patients' families should have the final say in whether "heroics" are initiated:

I feel any patient admitted to emergency should be given every benefit and all medical skill possible. Age makes little difference here since one would know little about the patient's history. Next, I think the decision (without guilt) should be left first to the patient, then second to the family, unless again it is an emergency situation; then if the patient's prognosis is good, everything should be done; if the prognosis is poor, the patient should be able to leave life with dignity, without pain and with peace of mind.

I think that the first thing to consider is how the patient feels. If he wants to live longer at any price, then we as professionals should go the route and provide the best service we can. If the patient is aware of the hopelessness of his condition and wants to refuse the care that we can offer then this should be his right. If there is hope, then this too should be made clear to the patient, who should have the final say. Too often patients are not dealt with properly and remain ignorant of what hope there is, what the risks are, what the quality of life is that we have to offer, what the complications are, etc. People should be given a choice and that choice should be respected!! Most physicians shy away from an honest relationship with a patient. This is very wrong! People are not stupid. We are dealing with an educated public, this is not the dark ages. If the patient cannot make this choice by reason, then a responsible member of the family should be allowed to make it for him without being made to feel guilty. Almost everyone has expressed strong feelings about such matters at some time in their life and usually to a family member.

As further evidence of nurses' willingness to accept death in principle, a majority of my respondents profess to believe that at least passive euthanasia should be practiced. I asked: "Do you believe in euthanasia—passive or active?" Seventy-three percent (83) of my respondents claim to believe in passive euthanasia. Thirteen percent (15) believe in active as well as passive euthanasia. Nineteen percent (22) are against all forms of euthanasia, and eight percent (8) had no opinion.

There is considerable sentiment among my nursing respondents that patients do not die with dignity at General Hospital. I asked: "Do you think that the patients who die in this hospital generally die with dignity? If not, please explain." Thirty-three percent (38) claim that patients who die, die with dignity. Forty-eight percent (55) claim that patients generally do not die with dignity. Sixteen percent (18) maintain that some patients do and some patients do not die with dignity. Three percent (3) had no opinion. Many nurses and aides once again mentioned an over-zealous use of medical procedures as a reason for undignified death. Signaled out for mention were "codes" that are emergency cardio-pulmonary resuscitative efforts:

Usually not on CCU—too much broohaha with codes, when it usually has become apparent that it's no go.

No—many are not even told of their problem and many patients' lives, especially those with terminal disease, are prolonged to a ridiculous extent.

No! They are kept alive for legal purposes only, not for comfort measures. Let's say they are tortured.

No. They should just be left alone to die in peace.

No—doctors don't let patients die with dignity but prolong the suffering with tests and procedures that demean the patient. Doctors are also afraid of med.s and frequently restrict med.s to patients who are terminal and suffering intense pain.

Some do, some don't. Some are kept going on a code so long it's really disgusting, especially when everyone knows the patient is dead.

No—patients never have anything to do with their own deaths. They are just done to.

No. Some of them do not die with dignity—especially those who are 90–98 years old. They are to be kept alive until they reach 100.

Rarely, there is no dignity in a Code and far too many are called.

No. You need a "doctor's" order to die at the time your physical being "decides" to.

Medicine is not always seen as the culprit. Nurses and aides sometimes cite failure of humanitarian concern among themselves or institutional indifference as causes for the undignified deaths of patients.

No. Either they are brutally battered about during a code (and I realize this is necessary) or they die due to problems of old age in which case their last days consist of being tied to a chair, etc. The biggest thing that bothers me is people talking to elderly patients like they are children or treating them like children. When I'm 80 years old I don't want a 20-year-old putting pink bows in my hair and calling me cute!

No, how can a person die with dignity with strangers coming in and out 24 hours a day. The only way a person dies with dignity is at home with those he loves. I might add that a patient does not die with dignity in a private room on L3 as seems to be a general consensus here.

The process of dying as I've observed it here is really not dealt with. Patients die but how they feel about it and what they and their family want done is not discussed.

Not always—victims of gross disfiguring trauma sometimes regarded as horror show, not as people.

No, they usually die alone and are found in their bed or have been coded for an hour with no result.

No! Particularly in the emergency department where your acquaintance with the patient is short. You don't know him or his family usually. The patient becomes "that body," "that DOA," or "it." I've always found this attitude difficult to contend with.

No. First of all, we strip them of their clothing and dress them in hospital jonnies. Secondly, most of them are referred to as a room number and bed number. We have taken them out of their home and brought them here to die. Many would prefer to die at home in their own clothes and in their bed. They are with strangers who neither know or love them. Often times, they are overmedicated or tied down. Dignity? No way. Where is the family unit? The family becomes visitors! How many patients are fortunate enough to have a doctor that will go along with their wishes? How many times do we put two dying patients in together? Great company! How often can they hear their grandchildren or hold them? How many die alone and are found?

Codes are frantic but organized efforts by nurses, doctors, and technicians to revive patients whose hearts have stopped or are threatening to stop. Codes are grossly violent. Time is of essence, and a powerful sense of urgency prevails. To set the patient's heart beating regularly, his chest is slammed with a closed fist, and then repeatedly jerked-compressed with such force that ribs are sometimes broken. In the meantime, the patient's clothes are pulled, ripped and sometimes cut from him. The patient's head is thrust back and a rubber tube is shoved down his gullet. In preparation for this, vomit may have to be fingered from his mouth. He often wretches as the tube is thrust down. An ambu bag is attached to the free end of the tube and a technician or nurse repeatedly compresses it to inflate the patient's lungs. By this time, nurses, technicians, aides and doctors—some working, others merely watching—are massed around the prone patient. Electrodes are strapped above his wrists and ankles, and wired to an electrocardiograph machine. An intravenous line is started. If the patient's veins are not amenable, he may be stuck a number of times, and eventually a cutdown may be done. Numerous medications are drawn up and injected. More likely than not, the chest thrusting will give way to defibrillation; two electrode paddles are pressed against the patient's naked chest, and electricity convulses his body, hopefully, to jolt his heart into regular activity. The patient is frantically beaten, stripped, cut, punctured and shocked before the eyes of five to fifteen dispassionate strangers. The sight can be utterly hideous. The patient may be purple, convulsing and vomiting, his hair matted, his body greased with clammy sweat, his eyes rolled back in his head.

Such a scene can hardly be perceived as dignified, and to die under such conditions can hardly be seen as a dignified death; yet when codes are successful in saving a viable life, they are the very essence of medical heroics. Swift critical intervention has cheated fate. Participants in such a drama are rightly proud. However, when codes are unleashed on the boney, sagging, tallowed bodies of ancients, the glory seems less tangible to nurses. When a patient has been coded numerous times, when his only prospect is a sputtering life, when the code itself seems a futile gesture upon a moribund body, the code itself becomes a stark demonstration of medical failure. The protective illusion is smashed, and the broken and battered presence of the coded patient presses defenses of nurses.

Codes are not the only efforts that strain the medical credibility. Any grossly paining or mutilating act of unmaskable futility will tend to inspire humanitarian reservations. Nurses on a large surgical unit were disgruntled over a craniotomy performed on a senile 83-year-old man. The man returned to the unit as senile as before.

On the intensive care unit, the phenomenon of the ventilator (respirator) to sustain life troubled some nurses. One man in his late 60s was dying on the unit. His doctors admitted to the nurses that he was dying and yet would not withdraw his life support medications and apparatus. The man had suffered numerous operations and months of agony and severe debility. Ultimately, he was laid out in the intensive care unit, tracheotomized, attached to a respirator and fed intravenously. His lungs would fill with fluids and a blackish slime would collect around and in his tracheotomy. Periodically, a nurse would have to suction out his lungs and tracheotomy. As the long thin red catheter was slipped down through the trach, there would be a loud sucking noise; the man would wretch and scowl fiercely, and copious amounts of viscid mucus would be drawn up into the suction bottle. This man was so weak that he could barely move. When he was moved by nurses, he scowled and stiffened. His arms were tied down because periodically he would summon enough strength to pick at the tubes which sustained him. In that anyone could tell, he seemed to be aware of his condition, and did not act out of confusion. This patient was present in this condition on the fourth week of my stay there. When talking about him among themselves, the nurses would preface his name with "Poor"; he was always "Poor . . . ."

Nurses will willingly participate in medical drama and procedures as long as these maintain some semblance of rehabilitative utility even if the techniques and the tests are painful or mutilating. Many medical procedures do compromise human dignity. When patients are reluctant or recalcitrant, nurses often advocate, if only mildly, the prescribed course. The operation will be a likely benefit. The amputation is necessary. The doctor needs to know and, therefore, the patient should submit to a torture chamber array of tests in which blood samples are repeatedly drawn, strong purgatives are taken, a thick metal tube is stuck

up the rectum, and a number of contorted postures on a chilled
steel X-ray table are required. If half a patient's face must be
scraped away to save him, this must be done. Only when an
appearance of rehabilitative efficacy cannot be maintained for
nurses, and the techniques graphically reveal the frailty or the
mortality of men, only then would nurses generally call a halt to
the use of such techniques. Only when such extreme methods
seem highly questionable in terms of rehabilitation would some
nurses leave the choice to use them strictly with patients and
families.

Where medicine rules incredibly and actually highlights the
ambiguity of man, humanitarianism serves nurses as an amelio-
rative rationale and prospect. The humanitarian rationale allows
nurses to think that medicine is the cause of the horror they
witness. The humanitarian prospect enables nurses to hope and
perhaps to believe that what seems so horrible can be corrected
or at least made comfortably tolerable.

Since "excessive" use of medical means does enhance the
graphic ambiguity of patients, a prohibition of this use would
ease the experience of nurses; yet it is questionable that the
savings would be commensurate with the expectations fostered
by the humanitarian prospect. If actualized, the dream would
likely be deflated by reality. "Death with dignity" and humanitarian care in general are not to be had merely through changes
in medical practice.

Perhaps, nurses inwardly realize the value of the prospect and
the limits of the reality since their humanitarian conviction is
not so ardent that they act effectively on their disaffection with
medicine. Nurses do sometimes petition physicians for restraint,
but I have seen meager results. Medical orders are followed and
medical drama unfolds at the direction of physicians.

In actual fact, many and perhaps most unviable patients are
not subjected to "excessive" medical means, but are given over
substantially by their physicians to the humanitarianism of
nurses. Indeed, nurses, at times, complain among themselves of
abandonment, citing physicians' failures to provide proper palliative care in the form of bedside manner and pain medications.
However, whether or not physicians assist in humanitarian care,
and some do, this real medical reserve tosses the proverbial ball
clearly into the nurses' court. Many patients live out their last
days in General Hospital with unobtrusive medical interference,
such as medicines and regimens to increase or to decrease their
body fluids, to nourish them, to prevent blood clots, to regulate

their heart rates or rhythms, to regulate their blood pressures or to help them breathe. Such therapies hardly impede bedside nursing; the skin care, hygiene, feeding, and soothing, caring, humane presence that mark the humanitarianism of Nursing.

When nurses are given the field, their bedside manner does not eliminate the indignity and the horror of death or of many nonlethal afflictions. A number of my questionnaire respondents noted that nursing does not meet this challenge. No nurses or aides openly fault the humanitarian ideal. They fault the failure to achieve it. They dream of a purer "competence" which would mitigate the poignant ambivalence and the uncertainty inspired by ambiguous men.

The Prospect of a "Purer" Humanitarian "Competence"

In that nurses perceive their own care to be inadequate to provide patients dignity, nurses tend to suppose that a dignifying humanitarian care would be possible if certain reforms were instituted. In other words, they dream of a "purer" humanitarian "competence" as a way of keeping faith with the humanitarian ideal in light of shortfalls in actual performance. Medical reform has already been considered. The other reforms that I have heard proposed by General Hospital's nurses fall into one of three categories: (1) instituting a socio-psychological orientation, (2) easing time-task pressures and (3) ameliorating the institutional nature of hospital care through family participation. I argue that all three of these proposals would not ease nurses' adjustment to human ambiguity and that they would hinder present adjustments. I also argue that these reforms would likely cause considerable dissatisfaction—less so for the second reform. Family and visitor participation I shall consider at length since the problems associated with it arise from the nature of nurses' status, role and competence.

Instituting a Socio-psychological Orientation

Some nurses claim that nurses need more socio-psychological training to understand better and to fulfill the needs of dying and sorely afflicted patients. These nurses would make a science out of humanitarianism. They would have consciousness-raising conferences in which problems would be brought up and perhaps solved via a case study method in which each troubling patient's situation would be a special case. The assumption or hope inherent in this approach is that socio-psychological understanding will lead to a truly humanitarian nursing that would far better solve the plights of patients.

In fact, many nurses of my acquaintance are impatient with conferences and consciousness-raising sessions; they argue that these sessions are not "realistic," and that they take time from patient care. Time-task pressure is seen as precluding a developed socio-psychological approach, but other reasons are indicated by these nurses' delight in being too busy to attend or to convene these sessions. I get the impression that many nurses consider them specious. Certainly, psychological care is of limited use for patients who are incoherent or comatose. For patients who are aware, the establishment of a profound interaction is tricky and difficult. The understanding that applied social science provides for nurses is likely to be only marginally useful to them in assuaging human ambiguity.

Even the nurses who claim the greatest faith in psychological care are diffident in using it. These nurses seem to concentrate their efforts on selected patients. Meaningful conversations seem to be had with only those patients who are most willing and most able. Even then, the nurses' efforts are tame. Philosophical issues are hardly broached. In rarely more than a scant few minutes, the nurses commiserate and serve platitudes about "being strong" or "this too shall pass away." Tender loving care becomes merely more conscious.

In that socio-psychological sessions and cant exhort nurses to humane sensitivity, providing them with things to do for patients and glib explanations, socio-psychology does nurture humanitarian perspective and activity; but this nurturance is limited. Socio-psychology can provide no answers to the ultimate concerns and it cannot broaden the human ideal type or accommodate ambiguous men to it convincingly. Indeed, a "scientific" probing of reality and of reasons for prejudices and fears may be unsettling for patients and nurses in the actual presence of manifest human ambiguity.

When cant becomes overblown, it may achieve less than humanitarian consequences. The nurse who spews topical dogma may defeat her alleged purpose. While I was on the coronary care unit, a dying patient, a veteran of many hospitalizations, was visited by a nurse he had met in another unit. This patient was both brave and sociable and had become friendly with many nurses throughout the hospital during his many stays. The nurse who now visited him began a discussion about death and dying, citing ideas and findings from recent literature on that subject. Her venture was unusual in my experience for I never before had heard so weighty a discussion between a nurse and a patient. Unfortunately, this nurse's efforts were indelicate. As she was leaving, she made an interesting admission that she now felt "much better." However, the patient had grown visibly distressed. Two nurses on the unit noticed what had happened and became upset.

Most nurses will avoid the discursive thicket and concentrate on the gentle touch and soothing tone of standard tender loving care. Except for pleasantries and encouragement, of what use are words when there are no explanations? Most nurses seem to sense this reality; those nurses who do not are deluding themselves somewhat. Social understanding serves to diminish social prejudices or at least to make nurses more aware of them; yet regarding ambiguous men, socio-psychological nursing is not much different from traditional, angel-in-white nursing. Both schools stress "understanding" and humanitarian concern. Despite the claims of some young nurses, regarding ambiguous men, I have seen no tangible difference in the humanitarianism of the older nurses from hospital programs and the younger nurses from college programs. Tender loving care, in practice, is precisely the same for both groups. Individual differences reflect the maturity and the sensitivity of individuals.

Easing Time-Task Pressures

Many nurses cite "extenuating circumstances" for a dearth of proper tender loving care. These circumstances are task-time pressures due to understaffing and institutional priorities. I asked: "Do you think the nurses tend to think more about the task, technical and paper work aspects of their work than they think about the individual needs of patients?" Thirty-nine percent (45) of my respondents reported that nurses tend to think more about the task aspects of their work. Another 23 percent (26) reported that nurses exhibit this tendency some of the time or that some nurses do. Some nurses mentioned insufficient staffing.

> Depends on the situation and the nurse. For a nurse to have a heavy patient assignment along with being TL (team leader) and having one team member it's hard to meet individual needs.

> Unfortunately, I have to say yes more than no. The biggest reason why is lack of staffing (i.e., secretary, aides). Also, when it is very

busy and there is a lack of nurses, the priorities lie in a very task
oriented way: *only* do meds, treatments and, above all, your charts!
During these times, the needs of the individual patients always
seem to come secondary. It is difficult to prevent this sometimes
when you have 3–4 ICU patients with about 5–6 necessary things
to do every 1–2 hours.

Other nurses stressed task pressures and official priorities:

No, but sometimes it's very difficult to think of the individual
patients because of paper work etc. Ironic, isn't it!

Yes—very often—sometimes it seems nurses are termed "good"
depending on how quickly they perform their "tasks" and get
them well done.

I feel for the most part the nurses remain aware of the needs of
their patients but whether they have the "time" to attend to these
needs is another question. That is why we so often look so
involved in the task oriented role—there are days when you have
all you can do to get through the technical orders involving a
certain patient.

Unfortunately, yes—because it is the overall attitude and the
feeling is a "good" nurse gets her work done. This is most evident
among supervisors, head nurses and older nurses. The newer
school teaches nurses to be more psychologically oriented and
more aware of the individual needs. Hopefully, we will soon see
the trend changing.

Not one of my respondents ventured that sensitive concern for
individual needs is nonessential. Not one suggested that such
care is impossible for certain patients. Respondents either maintained that nurses tend to think more about the individual needs
of patients or implied that nurses would care substantially more
about these needs if time-task pressures were not so great.

Time-task pressure can be a real impediment to the practice of
tender loving care; when this is the case, a relief of this pressure
would likely improve such nursing. However, sufficient staffing
for intensive patient-oriented nursing would not likely result in
such for most patients. Generally, nurses do not use their free
time to intensify their contacts with the more ambiguous
patients.

On medical and surgical floors there are "slow" days occasionally when the staff finishes early the prescribed regimen of
morning care. What do the staffers do then? Generally, after they
have fidgeted about looking to help co-workers, they congregate

in twos and threes, sometimes at the nurses' station or lounge, but such daliance draws wrath from supervisors and busywork from head nurses. More popular are the rooms of favored patients, where the staff feel welcome with enjoyable company. These patients are never sullen and rarely are they stricken with anxiety. The patients chat with their nurse visitors or watch television with them.

Ironically, the rooms of patients on the other end of the sociability scale are also favorite asylums. Incoherent elderly patients require "total" care that translates into a complete bed bath. These patients are often the last patients to be "done," and as they do require considerable work, their nurses are often still working on them when other staffers have finished their patient assignments. Since finished staffers generally look to help others who are not finished, the rooms of confused elderly patients become natural rendezvous. The staffers dawdle here because such patients can be treated as nonpersons. The nurses can relax, be themselves and enjoy their own company.

Hectic days are not coveted but neither are slow days. Nurses do not want to rush their work, but contact with patients is comfortable only if they are especially sociable or if the contact is couched in immediate purpose—nursing tasks. Many nurses voice their dislike of "slow" days, because they "drag." These nurses prefer comfortably busy days—days when there is always something to do, but there is never a rush and "everything gets done." Nurses feel unsatisfied with abbreviated or hasty patient care, with "a lick and a promise" as some call it. Yet, slow days are uncomfortable since nurses are expected always to be "professionally" occupied, especially on the day shift, and most nurses do not take "professionally occupied" to mean special humane or socio-psychological consideration of patients who are not good company.

Time-task pressure is itself a diversionary means of assuagement and a provider of such means. Thus, to reduce it so that diversion becomes difficult is to weaken the competence of nurses.

Ameliorating the Institutional Nature of Hospital Care Through Family Participation

Some nurses believe that humanitarian care within the hospital would greatly benefit from the help of family and friends. Some nurses lament the functional, impersonal ambience of the

hospital and suggest that only family and friends can provide
optimal warmth and sympathy. A few nurses maintain that many
of the dying elderly should be at home with their families and
not in the hospital at all—that such an alien place with its
dispassionate functionaries cannot provide the care for death
with dignity.

The use of family and friends would not in itself improve the
humanitarianism of nurses; indeed, such use would entail a
transfer of humanitarian responsibility. Keeping dying patients at
home or transferring them there would certainly be a way of
avoiding the problem of death with dignity in the hospital. In
that visitors' efforts could be incorporated successfully into
patient care, they would also spare nurses responsibility for
difficult patients.

In fact, many nurses would not welcome the help of visitors,
while with some reservation, some nurses would welcome help.
I asked: "Do you have any ideas on the place and role of visitors
within the hospital?" Thirty-four percent of my respondents had
totally negative views on visitors. A considerable number of the
rest had doubts. Using examples, I start with two that represent
the positive view of visitors as potential providers of patient
care:

> For the most part, I think they are necessary and valuable to the
> patient and to themselves. The need to talk to someone is great
> for everyone and more so for a hospitalized person. Time just drags
> in the hospital, hence, encouraging time for self-pity. Doctors
> rarely talk at length with their patients; nurses are often occupied
> with numerous duties and can't many times spend more time
> than their treatments call for, leaving visitors as the last resort.
> Patients look forward to a visit from family or friends. There
> should be rules to abide by (length of stay, amount per patient,
> etc.) Sometimes they can convince elderly people to eat if nurses
> are unsuccessful and I also feel if family members wish to involve
> themselves with the patient's care, they should be allowed to do
> so.

> Families should be incorporated into the recovery of the patient.
> This is not always possible but should be worked out as much as
> possible. The family usually represents home and recovery. They
> are very important. . . .Good visitors can help speed recovery and
> should be part of the team if at all possible. An added source of
> communication and tool.

The negative responses are terser.

None—no visitors at all.

Visiting much too long—visitors much too many.

In most cases visitors are a drain on the patient's strength.

I have no idea what the usefulness is of most visitors.

Yes—they should all stay home!

The place of most visitors should be at home and *when* allowed to visit be it only half an hour maximum. Visitors for the most part tend to be more of a nuisance for the patient.

In my experience as a patient, I've found visitors good only in small doses. Visitors often become sort of an "uh, ah" squad and only serve to upset the patient by talking about "Uncle Harry dying of the same thing," etc.

Most visitors should be banned. There are very few visitors that cheer up the patients—most grump about their own problems and don't listen to what the patient is saying. On the other hand, visitors are necessary so as not to totally isolate the patient. I wish they could be a little more understanding.

Yes, I feel most of the time that they serve *no* useful purpose except to make *themselves* feel better.

A number of respondents implied that visitors are nuisances for nurses.

I think that visitors should act as visitors and leave the care of patients to the nursing staff completely.

No visitors, which, of course, is not right but I do like the hours they are not in the hospital.

They should be cooperative, polite and not make unreasonable demands on the staff.

Immediate family should be kept informed of patient's welfare and in certain cases take part in patient's care and recovery. But when asked in some cases to leave room should leave.

Only as diversion for patients; otherwise they are more of a hindrance.

They should not be allowed to constantly badger nurses about patients' conditions. If doctors related to families more, this would be eliminated.

They should visit quietly, allow patients to rest, not badger them or nurses.

I think visitors are very important but I don't think they should interfere with nursing care or make unreasonable demands on staff.

I find visitors a necessary evil.

There are several reasons for nurses' disaffection with visitors; all of these reasons entail what nurses see as disruptive intrusion on their work and terrain. This disruption affects the flow of nurses' work, their self-images and the very ambience of nursing units. Members of any occupation would chafe at such infringement; yet nurses have a special reason to be supersensitive since the infringement strains their "competence" before human ambiguity.

This burden is not likely to be lightened much through an enlightened handling and use of visitors, as visitors remain institutional outsiders with primary relations with patients, and nurses remain institutional insiders with secondary relations with patients. Some visitors aid more than they burden nurses, but these visitors are either demure or special. Even if visitors could be used to provide heightened social support for patients and if visitors aided the nurses' humanitarian orientation, visitors would still burden nurses in the course of their work, and more significantly, visitors would still strain nursing "competence."

In select and controlled "doses," visitors add a human touch to nursing units. Nurses are moved by the joys and sorrows that seem to bloom in the closeness of familial encounters. Touching interludes warm the nursing scene and nourish nurses' faith in their humanitarian calling. Visitors who are sweet, considerate, earnest and perhaps humorous are appreciated. Visitors who grieve proclaim the value of life and are respected as long as they sorrow reservedly. The limits of welcomed visitor presence are narrow.

During my time in the intensive care unit, I noted that visiting families were treated and regarded disparately. I asked several nurses about their reactions to families and these nurses corroborated my observation.

A number of special conditions pertain to ICU. The ICU is an open ward and thus interactions between nurses and families are easily observed. ICU's visiting regulations are especially strict, only two 20-minute periods per day, and visitors are limited to immediate family. ICU patients are all critically ill, and their families have cause for concern.

144   Some families are given special consideration by the staff. Nurses purposefully spend time with them, stretch rules to answer their questions and commiserate with them. In addition, members of these families are sometimes admitted to the unit at proscribed times. I have known nurses to call families daily to report on their relatives' conditions. The nurses I questioned on this favoritism suggested that they just "take to" some families more than others.

From what I have seen of them, favored families are nice middle-class people who seem very much concerned about their loved ones and who are grateful, uncomplaining, deferential and friendly toward the nurses. They manifest another quality that is not so tangible, a cleanness, a sweetness that moves nurses and seems to suggest in itself human dignity. Families do not acquire a favored status instantly. A rapport must be developed, a rapport requiring the patient stay on the unit for at least a number of days, preferably many days; yet by no means are all or most long-term visitors accorded favored status.

Average families are treated with due but no special consideration. They do not complain stridently; indeed, they are generally silent or discreet. They come and they go. Ethnicity or class may bar further rapport with nurses, but personality is a factor too.

Unfavored families are wailers or people who criticize nurses in anything but the most diplomatic tones, or people who seem irrational to nurses, or insufficiently concerned about the patient. Nurses pointedly avoid such people. When such visitors enter the unit, nurses frequently murmur their displeasure and their intention to avoid contact.

Families are generally assessed as a unit. Sometimes only part of a family will be given unfavorable status; yet almost always favorable status is bestowed only upon families in which the frequent visitors meet the nurses' standards.

The unfavored families I saw hardly seemed formidable. They were apprehensive and suspicious for the most part, and some were histrionic in their grief; yet they did not scream at the nurses or pull out the patients' tubes or make a debilitating disturbance (apparently) of any kind. Their sin seemed to be that they discredited humanitarian and professional pretenses by undignified display—by not caring, by a meanness of spirit or by questioning the judgement and the motives of nurses.

Favored families often introduce a note of tragedy to the unit. A number of ICU nurses told me that they sometimes do not realize the horror of patients' conditions until they see it mirrored

in the faces of relatives. These same nurses admitted that dealing
with the grief of relatives is especially difficult for the nurses,
more so for relatives they have grown to know and like. Why
then are nurses drawn to commiserate with favored families?

Nurses do not evade the tragedy associated with favored
families because the nurses' experience of it is controlled, and
because this limited experience has a certain humanizing and
cathartic effect for nurses whose work days are so clinical and so
irreverent. Due to limited visiting time, the cost for the release
is rarely more than 15 minutes a day, often less, and certainly
not every day. The favored families are especially dignified and
possessed of a radiant warmth; they do not have the chill of
existential fear—the dread of the abyss about them. Thus, the
limited burden of favored families is bittersweet and is
welcomed.

ICU nurses have relatively limited contact with visitors, and
that contact is tamed by the unit's intimidating aura of critical
purpose. Nurses who work the 3–11 shift in the general units
and all shifts in the emergency department have less restricted
contact and for this reason face additional problems with visitors.

Visitors distract and obstruct. During visiting hours, charge
nurses, laboring through stacks of charts, are repeatedly diverted
by apprehensive, inquisitive or demanding visitors. During visiting hours, nurses must frequently wade through visitors to
work with patients. The visitors are physically obstructive; they
beleaguer the nurse with questions, statements and requests;
they scrutinize her every move.

Visitors often annoy nurses. Unlike patients, visitors are not
dependent. They frequently consider it their duty to safeguard
the patients' interests. The nurses generally do not recognize the
visitors' authority and consider their interference to be meddle-
some, unless it is deferential—petitioning instead of telling.
Visitors intermittently fail to recognize the professional status
of nurses. Many visitors do consider nurses to be "the handmaidens" of physicians. This attitude grates on nurses. All nursing
personnel loath being treated as servants.

Beyond supportive companionship and baby sitting, there is
little visitors can add directly to patient care. Care is provided by
the hospital establishment. Within a modern hospital, the ways
and means of this provision are not apparent, and visitors are
rarely versed in health care organization and technology. Thus,
visitors' efforts to direct patient care in the more substantive
areas of medical nursing are frequently misdirected; often they

exhibit minimal understanding of actual nursing responsibilities and competence. On their part, nurses do not have the time or patience to instruct an army of visitors—many either stupid or antagonistic—in the mores of nursing units.

Visitors seem to find the hectic and preoccupied nature of hospital nursing most incomprehensible and aggravating. Overwhelmed by modern medicine, most visitors resort to active concern for what seems to them to be the most patent of patients' requirements such as desires for a new pillow, water, a bedpan, pain medication or a bed change. Nurses are, however, frequently too busy to attend immediately to these noncritical needs. Stewing in the semiprivate rooms or standing at the nurses' station, the visitors do not see how busy the nurses are, or the visitors do not understand the significance of the nurses' current activities, or the visitors are made oblivious to the evidence with concern for the patient, with thoughts about the responsibilities of hospitals or with thoughts about the cost of hospitalization. At times, however, visitors have apparent cause for complaints.

Even when they are doing nothing urgent, nurses sometimes fail to jump at request because they are weary of or resent hustling at the beck and call of visitors for what to the nurses are banal services, however essential these may be to the immediate comfort of patients. Thus, a conversation may be completed or a nurse may dawdle before delivering a bedpan or water. This hauteur infuriates visitors, while their resentment infuriates nurses.

For the most part, nurses and aides regard proper visitors as spectators, and it is difficult for visitors to presume too much of an active role in patient care without breaking hospital regulations, subverting doctors' orders or offending nurses and aides. The hospital bears the official responsibility, and visitors are generally ill-informed outsiders. Yet, even knowledgeable outsiders must step lightly—a fact to which I can attest from personal experience.

During my time at General Hospital, my grandfather was dying at another community hospital similar to General Hospital. After my day of participant observation, I would visit him. He was more and less confused, and one day I found him covered with diarrhea in his bed. This was the 3–11 shift and I had noted on entering that the unit's staff seemed small and very busy. On another afternoon such as this, my grandfather, my mother and I had waited 20 minutes for help with another "accident." I resolved to clean my grandfather myself; after all, I did this sort of work all day for other people. Yet, I was torn; I wanted to care for my grandfather, but I knew how presumptuous I was being in terms of the operating ethos of nursing units. In the few moments it took me to locate a nurse, I wondered how my proposal would be taken. I realized that I would have to be especially diplomatic lest I impugn the dedication of the staff. Thus, my case spewed forth in a tumble of qualifications: "I do this all the time. . . .I can see you're very busy. . . .I would really like to. . . ." The nurse seemed startled, then uncertain. She admitted that the staff was very busy, and at length she hesitantly guided me to the linen, all the time asking me if I was sure and reassuring me that they (the staff) were willing.

On two other occasions, I found my grandfather in similar straits, and I did my duty clandestinely. On the second occasion, the staff must have discovered the situation before I arrived since after I had finished, two aides trooped in with towels and sheets. They were nonplussed to find the job done and even more nonplussed to find that I had done it. Clearly, I had offended them, and I quickly proferred my explanation, which mollified them but left them seemingly uncertain as they left the room.

My mother, who is a nurse, also came to serve my grandfather in this and other little ways. The last occasion where she found him in a mess was during the day shift, and she thought that she had better inform the head nurse of her intentions. The head nurse's response was an officious and somewhat gracious, "I wouldn't think of it." With a few gestures and words she dispatched a nurse and an aide. My mother waited at the end of the hall.

As patients' official guardians, nurses must contend with some visitors. No special relative is charged with protecting the patient from the detrimental effects of too many visitors, too long visits or the wrong visitors. This responsibility is an onerous one for nurses. Viewing the nurses as strangers, relatives may not recognize the nurses' role of guardian. Also, due to guilt, frustration or grief, families frequently suffer from bad feeling when a member is ill. Nurses are periodically subject to this familial hostility because they do bear responsibility and because they are there.

Visitors' desires for information frequently place nurses in difficult positions. Visitors ask nurses about patients' conditions, prognoses and care. Nurses confront such questions because physicians are generally difficult to reach and/or are uncommunicative when reached and because nurses are a captive audience; they are there. Nurses are caught between the visitors' compelling desire to know and a circumspection that the preeminence of physicians necessitates. Nurses generally do not know what the physician has told the relatives of a given patient. At times, physicians lie to or mislead relatives; at other times, relatives misinterpret physicians' statements. This misinformation places nurses in a bind when visitors seek assurances. Thus, nurses commonly do not know how to answer serious questions proffered by visitors. This indecisiveness makes unpleasant encounters with probing visitors. On the other hand, the fact that nurses can circumvent difficult questions spares them. From listening to their complaints, I suspect that most nurses would rather that the physicians fulfill their responsibility to inform patients than that this responsibility be shifted to the nurses.

By their very presence, the unhappy visitors of sorely afflicted patients dampen the denial that seems the ethos of modern hospitals. As I have already suggested, task-driven nurses often are not fully conscious of the presence of tragedy until visitors graphically reflect it. The moving presence of grief and dread may not gall nurses and it may add a human touch to their work, yet it must make their work more onerous in that it impedes psychic escape from the weight of human mortality and in that it requires nurses to face difficult interactions with the visitors themselves. Not being the patients' intimates, usually not feeling as the visitors do, the nurses do not easily rise to the somber requirements of the occasion.

Some of the foregoing difficulties might be diminished by reforms directed at familiarizing the public with hospitals and health care, and insinuating families into the care of patients. However, the logistics of institutionalizing *substantial* roles for relatives would be torturous. The quality control of medical and nutritive care alone would be agonizing with hundreds of heterogeneous free agents roaming the hospital, all with an inalienable blood right to independent action. Dismissing or disciplining a mother would not be as easy as firing or disciplining a nurse.

At present, relatives serve only at the pleasure of nurses or doctors, and there are numerous instances when this seems a wise policy. I cite one example. In the emergency department when mothers bring in small children who have lacerations, the mother is sometimes allowed to stay with her child and is sometimes told to "wait outside" while her child is sutured. Sometimes this decision reflects the whimsical policy of the attending physician, but more often than not the mother stays or leaves depending on how the nurse or the doctor assesses her influence on the child. Experience teaches emergency department personnel that the attitudes of parents sway the child, especially when the parents are fearful. Thus, if the mother seems a calming influence, she stays. If she seems a nervous wreck, she must depart.

Floor duty nurses generally welcome the occasional visitor who unobtrusively comes to feed, to calm or to cheer a patient, and some nurses would like to see more (not much more) of this kind of contribution, but the prospect of more substantial involvement is not welcomed by nurses. The human relations and task coordination demands of nursing are great enough as they are. Maintaining smooth relations with hospital working visitors, coordinating nursing with their presence and policing their uneven efforts would be perhaps an impossible task. Also, such an incursion would undermine nursing "competence," the adjustment of nurses to the human ambiguity of their patients, by deflating nursing heroism and vitiating the staging of humanitarianism.

Just as despite nurses' complaints, most patients are "good" patients, despite nurses' complaints, most visitors are "good" visitors. They are a proper public, properly awed by Nursing as a humanitarian calling and as a medical profession. Glory always seems more tangible when it has an audience, and capacity seems more credible when it is respected. Formal relations between visitors and nurses enhance nurses' faith in Nursing and their sense of self-importance.

If an awareness of medicine as it is actually practiced were thrust upon the general public, medicine's illusion of power could not be so grand. The limitations of medical efficacy and the limitations of particular practitioners would cloud the public's trust in practitioners, and this doubt would undermine the practitioner's faith in himself. If the public saw no specialness and mystery in the mundane techniques of medicine, the aura of medicine would fade. The distance between public and practitioner would close. The prestige of the practitioner would dip. Familiarity breeds restraint if not contempt. Medical heroism would be a less sturdy shield for all those who now benefit from it, which includes nurses and the public itself.

Nursing units are the nurses' shops. Here they practice their trade. Nurses are aware that their practice is less than ideal; but as with people from all occupations that entail high moral and procedural standards, nurses want to maintain an image that approximates the ideal. As an example of dual-think, nurses believe in their "competence" even though they are cognizant of conditions that prohibit a truly "competent" performance. Thus, nurses do not want visitors so mindful of the realities in given nursing units that norn-affirming formal interaction becomes impossible, and pretense is vitiated.

In this regard, patients do not present nearly as much of a problem as visitors might. Patients are labeled "sick" and, for the most part, accept their nonchallenging dependent role. The patients toward whom actual nursing practice is likely to seem least ideal are generally the most ambiguous or afflicted patients, and these patients are likely to be too unaware, too confused, too pained, too self-occupied or too immobile to note nurses' adjustments to them or to impress nurses with their adjustments. Some patients become so familiar with nursing units that they act as, and are virtually accepted as, insiders. Generally, these patients are not themselves apparently much debilitated, and they tend to share the nurses' operational perspectives. Long-term visitors can themselves approach this status, but only if their patient relatives are convalescent. The intimates of the most ambiguous men must possess perspectives that contrast with the nurses' perspectives.

An everpresence of visitors would impress nurses with their true feelings toward patients and would impede their actual adjustments toward patients. Family and friends have primary relationships with patients, whereas nurses have secondary, service relationships with them. The constant presence of "primary" concerns on the nursing units would greatly alter their ambience. Powerful emotions would cloud the workaday world of nurses. A spectrum of turbulent feelings: anguish, resentment, anxiety, frustration, love, hate and fear would impede any tranquility to which nurses might aspire and would certainly sap the diversionary potential of routine nursing. From what I have seen, I suspect that nurses and relatives know that nurses as strangers cannot care as relatives do, but since most patient care is provided when visitors are barred, this reality does not weigh upon visitors or nurses as it might. The profounder identification of visitors would impress nurses with the relative superficiality of nurses' concern on one level, and on a deeper level it would impress nurses with their evasion of the significance of human ambiguity.

Harder to use would be the backstage methods by which

nurses presently compensate for the shortfalls of medical and humanitarian heroics. In the eyes of the dearly beloved or sorely afflicted patients, induration would seem cold insensitivity; social diversion with co-workers, a lack of dedication; MASH, an outrageous irreverence, and a desire for the action of codes or other medical emergencies, a ghoulish perversion. Certainly, in the days of nursing in private homes, nurses compensated for the presence of families and they would likely compensate for the extensive presence of families in hospitals if facilities were provided for families so that nurses, families, auxiliaries and patients were not constricted in hallways and patients' rooms. Yet what the everpresence of visitors would mean is a substantial change in current nursing competence. As hospitals are now, nurses have much to hide.

Several nurses in the intensive care unit were so accustomed to using MASH that they seemed barely able to constrain themselves during the 20 minutes when visitors were in the unit. Yet, discretion is requisite. How could parents of a boy with a crushed brain positively react to nurses who squirt each other with water filled syringes, or put ice down the back of an anesthesiologist or yell at an elderly patient, "Quit it," spanking his hand when he tries to pull out his intravenous line? So, the nurses withhold the urge for expression as best they can during visiting minutes and rarely allow more than a knowing smirk or an aside.

In general, when visitors protest a lack of Nursing propriety, nurses have ready, plausible retorts. "If I did not laugh, I would have to cry." "We are busy and much pressured and cannot always provide what visitors or patients want when they want it. Everyone must wait his turn." "Certainly, some of us care more for one another's company than for the patients' company, but we know one another so much better." "We are bothered by patients' conditions far more than it seems, but we just can't let it get to us, and so we think about other things." "Visitors just don't see or care to see how much we do. We are not servants and do not have the time to be servants." "The doctors write the orders; we just follow them." We have to feed these old patients, to walk them, keep them in bed, and they don't sometimes want to do any of this. So we kid them along and give them a tug. What else can we do?" "That family is a pain in the neck. You have to push through them to get anything done. They won't move." "Yes, we'd like to think more of patients, but we have all this paperwork, and the supervisors and all the ridiculous rules in this hospital." I have heard or overheard each of these statements and many others like them. If other nurses were present, there were generally nods of approval.

However, despite the rationales, the accusing eyes and words of visitors unsettle nursing personnel, since in that the above rationales are weak, they fail to soothe, and in that they are true, they highlight a reality of which nursing personnel are aware but of which they do not wish to be made too aware since such mindfulness must undermine the medical and humanitarian scaffolding upon which Nursing "competence" is built. Nurses do not want to acknowledge the full extent of their uncertainty. They do not want to experience (consciously) the full scope of the Gregor Effect: the attraction and the repulsion, the acceptance and the rejection, the fascination and the terror, which ambiguous men elicit from men. Nurses do not want to acknowledge the self-aggrandizement that their profession entails. They do not want to accept the selfish side.

Nursing—its rehabilitative medicine and its nutritive humanitarianism—is the frontstage, temporal wisdom by which nurses would define their certainty. Nursing's backstage underpinnings and counterpoints exist as embarassments or as naughty spice; yet they exist necessarily in their present form due to present conditions, but necessarily in some form in any case. They represent the other side, the counterparts of faith and compassion—counterparts that must be considered implicitly or explicitly by any would-be reformer who would be even marginally effective. I shall outline Nursing's backstage presently.

Nursing and the Limits of Human Dignity

"The dignity of man" is a humanitarian concept that refers to coherent and positive human identity. Disease is the ultimate nemesis of this "dignity." "Death with dignity" entails an inherent contradiction. "Debility with dignity" is a difficult proposition—more difficult as the debility is greater.

Yet, "dignity" is a term that is much associated with hospitals and Nursing since they are associated with humanitarian ideals. Since these ideals are secular, they charge nurses with a duty to work for the restoration or the preservation of dignity that is corporeal and social. Guided by the medical perspective, nurses endeavor to heal the diseased part and to emphasize the human part of the patient. In that an unwhole man is not restored, nurses goad him with tender loving care so that the man will

shine through his mottled being. Tender loving care poses the
greatest test of humanitarian faith since it requires some level of
social contact and commiseration. Nurses seem to see their
greatest responsibility to the "dignity" of patients as the provi-
sions of social contextual supports for positive human identity.

Nursing's methods for augmenting human dignity are most
effective for those patients who can be integrated into a social
system in which patient and nurses play their respective roles as
a normative daily routine spiced with everyday humor and
pleasantries. The frenetic activity in nursing units spells purposeful living. Patients are prodded into getting on with the
business of living, and this determination fosters an uplifting
temporal hope. The business between nurses and patients, as
reflected in banter, negotiation and mutual effort, is man-to-
man, here and now. There is nothing particularly transcendental,
otherworldly or Shakespearean in Nursing's maintenance of
human dignity.

Unfortunately, many patients, especially dying patients are not
apt to be dignified into positive manhood by tender loving care
or anything else which nurses might do. In many cases, many of
Nursing's humanitarian techniques seem as futile as medical
codes for unviable patients. Patients who cannot present a coherent personality are especially troublesome. For secular nurses,
the personality is the seat of the soul. They can largely manage
to regard patients as people-with-maladies until the personality
is abnormal or imperceptible. Social interaction with patients so
afflicted either becomes limited or it becomes a blatant demonstration of the patients' inadequacies.

In practice, humanitarianism is a feeble means of assuagement;
therefore, humanitarian effort is more alloyed toward more
ambiguous men, or it becomes a tortuous exercise. Since sociability is largely impossible with patients whose personalities are
greatly defective, the humanitarian effort is generally slackened
for these patients. Nurses may feel the greatest humanitarian
strain with patients whose extreme debilities are bodily since
the intact personalities of such patients elicit humanitarian
regard.

The sustainment of human dignity is not merely an altruistic
exercise. The motivation for humanitarian deeds is partly selfish.
Nurses' humanitarian "competence" benefits from the dignifying
of patients; nurses are humanitarians in that it is feasible.

This feasibility is limited and so therefore is the humanitarianism of nurses. Acute manifest human ambiguity would mock

nurses' efforts to render its victims plausible social actors who move, act, talk and think as men should. Thus, the efforts are hedged. The most ambiguous men are the most irremediably undignified. Within General Hospital gross deformity is limited, but chronic diseases and the depredations of aging bereave multitudes of their human dignity almost silently.

At the age of 20, I came to General Hospital, believing that wisdom came with age. I expected to hear stirring soliloquies from older patients facing their deaths and the hardships of disease. I believed in the transcendent power of the human spirit. I still do believe in this power, but I was certainly disappointed in what I saw. Many patients seemed totally unable to contemplate an ethereal approach to dignity, or indeed any approach at all.

For most patients, death does not come in short order upon a healthy man, as in the movies, but is presaged by deterioration and humiliation. One's mental and physical vitality ebbs, one's body bloats, rumples or withers, and thus the elemental foundations of social honor are worn away. Although this situation affects men at any age, it is most often the plight of the hospitalized elderly. An ailing elderly person grieves for his entire generation and likely sees scant temporal prospects for himself. He cannot do anything as he once did. He is dependent with minimal opportunity to serve. Life sputters and horizons narrow to immediate comforts and discomforts. "Is the food too hot or too cold?" "Must I stay up in the chair?" "Please don't be so rough." "Did you clean my razor?" For many of the ancient, no intelligible words come at all. Far from seeming wise, many ancients seem to be morons whose petering deaths are inglorious.

Whether or not he is further tormented with a code, the person who gasps out life with congestive heart failure or emphysema is undignified except under extraordinary circumstances. Many die as this man—cancer-rotted: He was reputed to be a lovely family man. I met this grandfather when his disease was already progressed. By then he was a subdued, skeletal man whose morning care was entrusted to me, the attendant. He was to be washed and gotten up in a chair each day. For the most part, he lay impassively in his bed, but the prospect of being moved upset him greatly. He would stiffen and shrink at the thought. Thus, I had to be most gentle, and I talked with him though he was loath to answer. "How many grandchildren do you have?" "Are you retired?" His answers were distracted and short. He had bed sores which I periodically asked a nurse to dress. He left the

hospital for a while, and when he returned to my unit, he was 155
near death. His medication was so strong it befuddled his brain,
and he would murmur incoherently as if plagued by nightmares.
The pain seemed to eat through his stupor. I do not know what
had been done to this man, but as he had a number of dressings
and drainage tubes, he had probably suffered some surgery.
Nurses cared for him now, but at times I helped for he frequently
fouled himself with liquid feces. To spare a more aware patient,
a senile old man was moved in as his roommate. The ordeal
lasted for two weeks; a nurse entered his room and found him
dead. When I came to help wrap him up, his tubes and dressings
had already been removed. What I saw was a decrepit Christ
from whose slit wounds oozed a black purulence and whose body
lapped a pool of stool. This man's ordeal was mute as far as the
nursing personnel experienced it. He did not make pronounce-
ments on the way to his cross or as he hung from it. When he
died, the nurses were likely writing charts or casting lots in the
nurses' lounge.

Patients suffering pain are also not discursive or amenable to
the cheer of daily living. Richard Sergeant writes that the immediate reaction to severe pain is astonishment.[13] Pain can be so
bad that it is impossible to imagine beforehand and difficult to
remember afterward. Pain clamors for attention, and enormous
effort is required to divert attention from it.

Patients who cannot or will not cooperate in the care and the
sociability by which nurses would dignify them are patients
toward whom humanitarian Nursing is largely (though not entirely) inadequate as a "resolution" of human ambiguity. This
inadequacy does not preclude nurses' thinking of undignified
patients as "men"; however, the more ambiguous men are, the
more a humanitarian view of them must be sustained by backstage nonhumanitarian means, and thus the more actions belie
philosophy. At least for some nurses some of the time Nursing
cannot define their frame of mind.

I asked: "Have patients ever been so deformed or incapacitated
that you could not or found it difficult to think of them as
people?" Only 18 percent (21) of the respondents answered this
question affirmatively. However, the one negative answer that
expanded on "No" displayed an unconscious irony: "No—NEV-
ER! I think no matter what condition you must remember there
is/was a person there, and they should be treated as such."

[13] Richard Sergeant, *The Spectrum of Pain*, Rupert-Davis, 1969.

Although in the minority, the respondents who answered affirmatively were much more likely to explain, and their explanations
are revealing. Almost all of them stressed a dearth of personality
as the great dehumanizer:

> Comatose, paralyzed patients whom you have never seen awake
> and alert and never talked to, somehow seem unreal. You have no
> concept of what this person was like and it makes it so difficult
> to explain but there is absolutely no feedback—no interaction
> with these patients and I feel this does make a difference.

> Deformities, as I have had occasion to deal with, don't seem to
> have that effect on me. An elderly, senile and physically incapa-
> citated person, one that does not in any way respond as a person,
> one that at no time in my experience responded to me as a person,
> yes.

> Some long-term stroke patients who could do no more than
> grimace and moan in no apparent response to anything, I found
> hard to see as people. Patients to whom a lot must be *done,* that
> is, suctioning, venipuncture, measurements of all kinds—pro-
> longed very intensive care—tend to get lost in the shuffle as
> people.

> Patients who have been in a coma for a period seem like a dead
> body without a mind—lifeless piece of flesh. I find myself bathing
> and caring for them quickly so as not to think too much of what
> I'm doing.

> Yes. A 90-year-old lady with a stroke (one of several) unable to
> move at all or talk. She barely responds to her environment, yet
> eats like an automaton. I attempt to remember she was an active
> human, but she is so vegetative—"unhuman" now, it's hard to
> treat her like a person.

> No—not if they're awake. Patients who are comatose, nonrespon-
> sive and probably nonviable become rapidly unimportant to me as
> people.

> Yes, we have had a couple of patients injured in auto accidents
> that had severe brain damage and were being maintained solely by
> drugs and respirator. Caring for an individual with complete
> absence of responses is merely task-oriented and morbid as it
> sounds; it's like caring for a corpse. Also, with quadraplegic
> patients, I sometimes view them as a "head" since that is basically
> all that is functionally remaining.

One respondent described the variable focus of the medical
perspective:

While changing very messy dressings, for example of decubiti, I have to think only of what I am doing, that this a dirty wound that must be irrigated and debrided in order to heal; after doing the dressing, I can think about the patient.

That nurses generally see themselves as humanitarians is to be expected since humanitarianism is part of their frontstage stance; in their actions nurses exhibit less than total humanitarian acceptance of ambiguous men, especially those men with feeble, distorted or imperceptible personalities. However, there are two humanitarian ways to which nurses shore up their sense of humanitarianism toward sorely ambiguous men. One method, touch, can be almost universally employed. The other, a celebration of patient heroism, must be used most selectively.

The sense of touch is not usually used to discern the presence of other men; yet it is an important means for supporting a humanitarian perspective in the presence of ambiguous men, because almost all living men feel like men. In appearance and behavior a patient may be grotesque or a "vegetable" but to the fingers he is a living man; to rub his back or to bathe him is to be reassured of his humanity. A corpse feels altogether different. Long after all regard for social sensibilities is abandoned regarding a patient, he still likely receives the tender loving care of the touch.

I suspect that when nurses claim to provide humanitarian care to the most afflicted, they are thinking in terms of this tactile care, the bathing, the clean, smooth sheets, the fluffed up pillow. The bedside care of severely debilitated patients is a lengthy task; and yet one which is generally not done begrudgingly. There is a magic to this touching: an affirmation of a man and a sense of ordering and cleansing. As with all methods, tactile care is more effective toward patients who radiate some personality. In General Hospital heroism is most often and openly associated with medicine; yet there are nurses who find their heroism in the tactility of bedside Nursing.

Sickness tends to make its victims self-absorbed, more so as it is greater; yet now and again, a patient weighed down with intermittent agony, great debility and the pall of death will radiate his humanity in such a way that nurses are captivated and respond with the heightened sympathy of ideal humanitarianism. Such is the patient hero, the complement of the Nursing hero. The patient hero is the exception among the sorely afflicted which affirms the humanitarian creed of nurses. His personality seems to transcend his body, thus fulfilling the promise of secular humanitarianism. When there is a chance, he fights, and when there is not, in a realm where death and failure are rarely broached, he acknowledges his fate unflinchingly. He quietly, soulfully says: "I am going to die" or "I know I am permanently paralyzed," and the nurses retort, "Oh, no you're not" or "Don't think that way" or "What makes you think that?" but they are inwardly impressed. This man disarms mortality. He will live with dignity or die with dignity. Any despair is hidden, or shows but momentarily. Above all he is strong. He toughs his way from day to day, enduring pain with barely a complaint, struggling to do for himself. He punches through the formality of the nurse–patient relationship by appreciating the nurses, learning their names, taking an active interest in them. Thus, his becomes a bigger presence than other patients'. In their spare moments, nurses visit him, crowd around him, while other stricken patients—the frightened and the withdrawn— cower alone in their rooms. The nurses dwell on the hero, bear the thought of him, cry for him. The nurses and the hero together dramatize humanitarian Nursing and epitomize its pathos and power.

Thus, human dignity cannot be bestowed upon all patients. Nurses are less inclined to try for nonheroic patients for whom the prospects of dignity are limited or for patients who do not cooperate with the routine and sociability by which nurses would firm patients' identities. In that active humanitarianism is lacking, other means of assuagement assume the slack. Several of these means are byproducts of Nursing as it is practiced in General Hospital and elsewhere, and are therefore masked by Nursing. All of these other means arise from the countervalent tendencies of the Gregor Effect.

Accommodation
of Nursing Practice

The Institutionalization
of Distance and Diversion

Occasions for diversionary focus are incorporated
into the nurses' situation to such an extent and
in such a way that some distraction becomes
virtually inevitable, and yet "natural" and unob-
structive. The medical perspective itself is a diversionary focus. When a nurse dwells on her
technique and the wound, she is diverting her
attention from manifest human ambiguity.

Tasks and task pressures are another source of
diversion. Nursing tasks are varied, and Nursing
responsibilities are considerable. Most of the
time, time-task pressure is substantial for most
nurses. Responsibility for medical procedures and
the general medical welfare of patients is considerable. Thus, nurses must be somewhat task-
oriented as opposed to patient-oriented. In their
care of patients, nursing personnel are often essentially "ritualistic" in the standard sociological
sense of the word.

Hospital society provides the greatest occasion
for diversion. A hospital is so intensively and
complexly social that living is drawn outward
into active interactions. Nurses are given little
opportunity to ruminate on the presence of hu-

8

160 man ambiguity. Their situation requires the expiation of "doing." Even without patients, nurses would be constantly pressed for social performance by their co-workers. As was demonstrated in Chapter 6, nurses and aides seem preoccupied with mundane navigational concerns, in other words, social concerns in the common sense. Considering the navigational requisites of their work, nurses would be concerned with etiquette, gossip and the like even if all their patients seemed normative men; that they are not all seemingly normative provides these "social" concerns with a special function of diversion.

"Social" concerns are versatile diversions. Not only are they preoccupying, they are also excellent cover for expressions of the frustrations and the fatigue that must accompany close association with ambiguous men. Nurses often lament social pressures and difficult social relations (and task-pressures) as sources for *nurses' malaise* (which I shall discuss)—the fatigue and the ineffable dispirit that intermittently plague nurses. Certainly, these factors do contribute to nurses' malaise, but the Gregor Effect contributes as well.

Social diversion for nurses depends upon the quality as well as the intensity of their social situation. If an intense social posture were focused directly upon a particular ambiguous man, its potential for diversion would likely be minimal. As they are, nurses' relations with co-workers and with patients are structured and defined such that diversion is facilitated.

General Hospital is part of a large volume, service industry, and as such it is akin to the likes of United Airlines, McDonald's and Ramada Inns. All of these would compensate for a dearth of familiarity in a highly rationalized, mobile society by staging specious intimacy in secondary relationships between their functionaries and numerous, transient clients. Nurses should apply their smiles and sociability indiscriminately to any patient. Nurse–patient rituals provide a point of human contact. Since the nurse enters the patient's private space, and since their formal interaction is conducted via conventions of tempered informality, the point of contact seems often more substantial than it is. The relative stability and solidarity of the nursing staff and the number and the rapid turnover of patients work to impede a transcendence of the secondary relationship between nurses and patients. As agents of the hospital, nurses are close to their patients, but not too close. Thus, ambivalence is structurally accommodated. Unobtrusively, nurses are like spectators who stand by but are not too close to carnage from a traffic accident. The distance between nurses and patients is figurative, but real. As nurses' association with patients is limited, so nurses' identification with patients can be limited without an apparent rejection on the part of nurses. Focus can therefore more readily be shifted from ambiguous men toward a society of nursing personnel and toward the tasks of Nursing.

I asked: "Do you think that the nursing staff takes more pleasure in its own company or in its contacts with patients?" Forty-two percent of my respondents (48) indicated that the nursing staff prefers its own company over contacts with patients. Seventeen percent (20) protested that preference depends upon the staff and the patients involved. Twenty-one percent (24) claimed that the nursing staff enjoys both types of company equally. Eleven percent (12) had no opinion. Only nine percent (10) insisted that the staff prefers the patients' company over its own. Not one of the respondents who preferred the patients explained her position; "patients" and "with patients" were typical answers. Perhaps, these nurses and aides felt that no explanation was necessary because patient-orientation is a maxim of Nursing as a calling. Whatever the reason, nurses who prefer their own company often elaborated in line with this representative sample:

> More in its own company—unless there's an especially appealing patient or unless there are tensions among the staff on a particular day.

> Yes, to the first part—I'm a nurse because of patients but they're not my friends and I really don't know them very well.

> Usually, in its own company. Our patients are usually over 65 and partially senile; it is very difficult to take pleasure in a conversation where the patient thinks you're a thief.

> With their own company because they all feel the same job frustrations, and patients are part of that frustration.

> It is safer, less painful to hold back and stay with your healthy co-workers.

And all the equivocal responses were of this ilk:

> Depending on the type of patient you are dealing with day-in-day-out. If all patients are elderly and confused, yes, naturally you prefer pleasure with your interactions with the staff.

Though my respondents stressed, on other questions, "social" problems with patients (e.g., bad manners) and down-played problems arising from the debilities of patients, many nurses and aides in answering the above question suggested that an inability of patients to socialize leads nurses to prefer their own company. This irony implies that the availability of nursing camaraderie keeps the unsociability of certain patients from being prominently problematic. From what I have seen, nurses tend to keep more to themselves when their patients are confused, unaware or feeble, in that nurses do not linger with such patients more than bare nursing tasks require. It would seem that this shift toward their own company is entirely natural in the eyes of nurses; yet be this as it may, this shift evidences a difficulty in nursing confused, unaware or feeble patients and provides a means by which manifest human ambiguity is avoided.

In general, regardless of the patients' conditions, nurses are more socially involved with one another than with patients. Since nurses share mutual status and roles, the basis for mutual identification is greater. In that nurses work together over longer periods, the opportunity is greater for amity and enmity.

Nurses do not have to like one another to be preoccupied with one another. Feuds, altercations and competition among nurses also direct attention from patients. I do not suggest that nurses and aides feud, argue or compete any more than members of any other occupation, but nurses likely do as much. Grounds for dispute are plentiful: personality clashes, competition for positions or social honor, problems with the distribution of work and disagreements on the ways and means and standards of nursing. I never worked in a nursing unit in which there was not some long-standing enmity, however superficial, between some of the nurses; very often there were opposing cliques. I was told by certain parties on the intensive care unit that disaffection among the staff tends to grow when the patients on the unit are especially critically sick. This increase is likely an immediate response to the tensions that especially critically ill patients foster for a number or reasons—task pressure being one of them; yet whatever the impetus, this disaffection directs attention from the patients and thus diminishes the poignancy of their ambiguity.

Sociability and the problems of sociability with more normative patients are also distracting. Patients who are merely amusing or interesting may captivate nurses even more readily (if more superficially) than heroic patients. Patients who are demanding, rude or obstinate often get and keep nurses agitated.

Nurses are subject to multifarious pressures which dilute the impact of manifest human ambiguity by drawing the attention of nurses in many directions. Staff nurses must cope with the rest of the hospital establishment: doctors, supervisors, administrators, a plethora of technicians and maintenance personnel. Nurses are at the center of the "health team" in the sense that little is done to patients in which nurses have no part since nurses are most directly responsible for seeing that doctors' orders are carried out. All the above personnel initiate activity for nurses, frequently interrupting the flow of their work. All of the above sometimes hinder nurses' efforts by not performing their duties promptly or well. Hospital politics are consuming.

Weighed down with the multifarious pressures of the health care establishment and with the responsibilities and time pressures of their tasks, nurses can ill afford to sustain the burden that a full receptivity to sick persons would entail. In that nurses do not utterly exhaust themselves, they stylize their nursing to control their relationships with patients so that they do not initiate too much for the nurses. I use two stereotypes to illustrate my point; most nurses tend to fall somewhere between these types.

The happiest of staff nurses or aides seem to be those who generate "a head of steam," bursting in upon their patients with exuberant determination. Such a nurse speaks firmly to her patients in somewhat louder than conversational tones. She commands; even her questions are commands, but the commands are meant to seem good-natured. She laughs and spouts joyous persiflage. Her movements are brisk. An air of efficient industry emanates from her that cheers many patients and intimidates most of the rest.

Another class of nurses is comprised of "long sufferers" who bear an air of solemn duty. Such a nurse is slower, but paced. She is ostentatiously tolerant such that patients easily know when they are taxing her. Patients can readily see from her bearing that she has much to do and carries heavy responsibilities. Duty dictates.

Individual nurses develop an act vis-à-vis patients. Despite some appearances, the relationship between nurses and patients is formal. Nurses regularly meet and serve new patients. Thus, it is only natural that actual nursing becomes stylized. As a whole, nursing duties are set. Individual patients are treated differently in accordance with a number of factors; yet a style pervades, and individual nurses do act more uniformly than would be the case if they developed primary, informal relations with patients. The front that nurses present to patients is enough of a thing unto itself that nurses can dwell on it rather than the patients or use it by rote as a shield to protect diversionary private thoughts.

Nurses' comrades and enemies are found among fellow hospital workers; patients are customers whose names and faces are generally taped on short term memory. For nursing personnel the most real persons are usually co-workers. I doubt that nurses on large units are really all that much aware that their units contain 50 or so individuals.

For nurses who deal with at least several patients a shift, a dearth of true familiarity with patients fosters a *composite Nursing experience* that conceals from nurses gaps in their Nursing experience regarding individual patients, and therefore facilitates nurses' avoidance of certain patients and their implications. If some patients die, many live and recover. If some cannot be consoled, others can. If some are not grateful, others are. Nurses selectively play out their roles with the patients who are most conducive to given approaches and, without fully realizing it, avoid troublesome patients. Since nurses are usually kept hopping, they rarely have time for "full" Nursing with all their patients, and for this reason, nurses are not pressed with the disparities in their nursing. In a sense, nurses acknowledge the "composite experience" and its importance when they complain that all or most of their patients are "out of it," and thus imply that a more normative mix would be more palatable.

At the end of her day, this nurse looks back on a day of nursing that likely seems full to her. She provided two patients with complete bed baths from which she experienced tactile tender loving care. She had a humorous exchange with another patient for the day's levity. She made seven beds and dispensed numerous treatments. She had a "comforting" talk with a patient about her prospective operation. And so forth. Among all her patients, she did all that nurses are supposed to do. Also, she experienced gratitude and witnessed physical improvement. Because of the composite completeness of her nursing day, she was and is less inclined to be moved by the fact that she avoided a frightened and withdrawn patient, that another of her patients had no capacity to converse and that another of her patients was obviously deteriorating.

There are varying degrees of organizational rationalization within hospital nursing staffs. In that licensed practical nurses and aides are barred by law from performing some nursing duties, nursing staffs must entail some division of labor. Most, if not all, hospitals have hierarchic nursing staffs; some are more stratified than others. Hospitals also vary in the lateral diversification of their nurses. In some hospitals individual nurses are assigned on a daily basis to dispense medications as their sole nursing duty for a shift. Some nurses only start intravenous lines on patients. There are even colostomy nurses who deal only with problems related to colostomies and the patients who have colostomies. There are urology nurses who deal with patients who have ileal loops.

In that the nursing "task" is fragmented and the fragments divided among a number of nurses and aides, professional distance and diversion are facilitated since the individual nurse tends to encounter more patients more superficially—especially if she is merely a supervisor, medication nurse or clinical specialist. In that a nurse is reserved for supervisory or medical tasks her position approximates the physician's, and she is protected from substantial contact with individual patients by those staffers who actually provide the patients with bedside care. Dealing with more patients increases the likelihood that some positive experience will be had. Narrowing the nurse's duties restricts the types of encounters she has with patients, and thus fosters task-orientation. The nurse copes with patients in situations that are less variable and thus she has less opportunity for a full view of her patients' individual personalities or lack thereof.

Attraction, "Power" and a Hint of Obscenity

Sickness does for nurses what crime does for police and war for soldiers; sickness provides nurses their reason for being as nurses and their call to heroism. Since caring for debilitated people is their business, any obscene attraction manifest human ambiguity might hold for nurses is masked by their professional standing. Nurses in the course of their work encounter ambiguous men and thus do not have to make an overt move to wallow in their presence. The humanitarian-rehabilitative ideology of Nursing explains the relationship of nurses toward patients and discourages blatant delight at disease. When nurses want "tougher cases," their desire is readily seen as a mundane ambition to excel in their profession or alternatively as an altruistic ambition to further the Nursing cause. The cover and the inhibition are so complete that there is likely no way I could definitively demonstrate an "obscene" fascination with human ambiguity per se, and yet I suspect that this fascination exists more and less among many nurses.

The "power" and the prestige of Nursing are founded upon rationales and rituals that are a reaction to human ambiguity or the threat of human ambiguity. If patients were never ambiguous or never died, most of the heroism would be bleached out of Nursing.

From what I have seen of them, nurses' reactions to the actual presence of death are preplexingly subtle, inextricable unless one sees them as a consequence of ambivalence. In at least 40 occasions, I have seen nurses swathe bodies in plastic shrouds. Almost without exception, the nurses were hushed and grave as they prepared the bodies. Pleasure played on no one's visage, and yet signs of disgust or horror were rare. Death is the nemesis of medicine and secular humanitarianism, and yet few of the nurses seemed to loath the presence of death. The occasions seemed suspended and surrealistic, a strange overlay that appeared to be one thing and another at once, dirty work and yet solemn rights over sacrificial animals. Like an embarassment and a taboo-mystery, the preparations of bodies were not mentioned afterward. What in a sense is undoubtedly an unpleasant duty for nurses seemed to leave them enlarged, infused with a certain dignity—an aura they often maintained for several minutes.

The reason for the nurses' confounded reaction rests in the irony that while death discredits medicine and humanitarianism, it confirms the significance of Nursing. The nurse who solemnly bundles a body in plastic wrap is presented with the "life and death" nature of her work and also with her competence to confront death "professionally." The attendant who wheels a corpse past a bevy of gasping visitors is impressed with his own sophistication. If the greater likelihood of death did not hang upon the critical care units, the elite status of their nurses would be diminished.

I saw little craving for opportunities for humanitarian heroism in General Hospital. Some nurses claimed to opt for work in the coronary care unit for humanitarian opportunities in that they claimed to want to provide intensive tender loving care to patients. Only in the critical care units at General Hospital are nurses restricted to two patients; however, although cardiac patients are an anxious lot, they rarely are ambiguous at General Hospital unless they are arresting. Interestingly, the intensive care unit nurses, who do confront ambiguous men regularly, did not stress a humanitarian motive for working in their unit. Actually, the greatest humanitarian rewards seem to accrue from work with patients with personalities—patients whose humanity is thus not so problematic. Thus, opportunities for humanitarian heroism are so prevalent that a strong desire for them would not be evident.

Some nurses do evidently desire to practice more technically demanding medicine and some of these anticipate codes and other emergencies. Occasions for the heightened medical heroism, associated with demanding medical procedures and medical emergencies, are not so prevalent. I have known nurses who chafed under the "base oppression" of standard nursing routine and who aspired to critical care nursing. I have known other nurses in critical care units who would be loath to join the bedpan brigade on the general floors.

I asked: "Do you ever feel any pleasure or satisfaction when a medical emergency occurs—such as a code? Do you ever look forward to such an emergency?" Most respondents, 61 percent (70), answered negatively, adamantly:

No! No! No! Do you think nurses are sadistic?

No. I find it a disgusting and a rather foolish question. Do you think nurses are sadistic or what?

Are you for real!

Are you insane!

Are you nuts!

You got to be kidding—NO!

Are you kidding?

No. It is a frightening experience and no matter how many I've been involved with, I'm a nervous wreck. I once used to be the observer, but now find myself an active participant if emergency occurs. I attribute this to experience, and secondly my desire to see the patient pull through. I will admit, though, that the sudden flurry of activity makes it seem exciting.

Seventeen percent (19) find some satisfaction when the code is successful. These examples demonstrate ambivalence via an inconsistency of tone or content:

There is a satisfaction in a successful code, and even pleasure when all the people present "do their thing" smoothly and as a team—that feels good. It's stimulating to exercise judgment. But I dread codes and such experiences.

Yes. Particularly if it is successful. The main ego trip of nursing is saving lives and making people better than they were prior to our intervention. I have noticed an excitement when we have advance notice of a code coming but I don't think of it as looking forward to it.

—Emergency dept. nurse

I admit that I enjoy the excitement of my job or else I would never be working in such a critical area. However, I cannot say that I would look forward to a code, etc . . . . That would be a little sadistic for my taste.

Nineteen percent (22) of the respondents, without substantial reservations, claimed to feel some special pleasure or satisfaction when a medical emergency or code occurs:

Yes. Very much—I have no idea why—but I do look forward to them.

Yes—I like codes. Certainly break up the monotony. Of course, they should all be successful and come not at meal time, visiting or change of shift.

Yes, particularly if efforts are successful and I learn something new from the experience—it breaks up the "routineness" of the day.

Nineteen percent is not an overwhelming portion of the respondents; yet it is significant considering that such a view is hardly humanitarian and that many nurses have confided in me that they fear they are not competent to cope with codes or may fail in some way. However, from watching nurses I have long suspected that some nurses find their heroism more in the humanitarian aspects of their jobs, while other nurses find their heroism more in the medical aspects. Therefore, I am not suggesting that all nurses would admit some pleasure in codes if all nurses were confident and honest with themselves, yet I do believe that more nurses would.

I now attempt to place in context and to expand on nurses' typical reactions to medical emergencies by describing an event that transpired in the emergency department one summer evening. At the time, I was working with another attendant who was a new summer employee, a sophomore and a premed. In the several days we had worked together, cases in ED had been on the order of cut fingers, and the new attendant confided in me that he was impatient for "something to happen." "Something" finally happened; a 26-year-old man of rugged, tanned physique and dark wavy hair sped his car off the local superhighway and into a tree. His large body was hardly marked, but he was unconscious, breathing rapidly, shallowly, and almost everything within him would prove to be crushed. He arrived bloody from small cuts and covered with sugared windshield glass. Two nurses, the other attendant and myself pulled and tugged at him to remove his clothes and the glass. The physicians on hand made a quick evaluation and within minutes a crowd had formed in the patient's cubicle: x-ray technicians, laboratory technicians, respiratory technicians, nurses and a variety of physicians representing various specialties. The wounds were bathed; the body surveyed; an intravenous line started; a foley catheter inserted; and an airway put down—virtually simultaneously. From then on, the work performed on the patient (while he was in ED) was diagnostic since the doctors needed to know which of the patient's many injuries were most threatening to his life, so that these could be treated first. A confusion swirled over the unnatural presence of a body that looked like it belonged on a beach, but which twitched and breathed unnaturally.

How did the principals seem to react? The new attendant mentioned seemed delighted. He grinned from ear to ear, literally jumping up and down with excitement. He enthusiastically participated in any way that seemed possible, and when asked to run an errand would hurriedly scurry out and back lest he miss the action. His reaction impressed me so much that this incident stands out in my mind.

The technicians, all of whom were young, seemed excited too, but deported themselves more "professionally." The X-ray technicians had trouble positioning their plates and the patient to catch steady shots of the desired part of his anatomy. The first echo scan was unclear, much to the consternation of the physicians. They pressed the technicians to hurry and to be careful, flustering the technicians further.

The physicians' reactions varied somewhat. One doctor bellowed orders and his displeasure at nurses and technicians. Another doctor stood aside from the cubicle and nonchalantly munched crackers. A middle-aged surgeon was attracted by the commotion as he was passing through the unit and stood in the doorway for a minute. He gazed on the scene, shook his head, smiled wanly, chuckled to himself and left. The rest of the physicians seemed like calm generals. When the X-rays came back, all the attending doctors gathered around a screen and discussed the films as if they were generals considering battle maps.

The reaction of the three nurses seemed uniform—the most inscrutable. Their expressions were grim and yet their movements were electric. More than anyone present, they seemed charged with their duty and burdened with the chore of this duty. In the turmoil, one nurse paused outside the door and murmured, "I don't believe this." It was a nurse who first noticed that the parents and the wife of the patient had arrived, and with a look of "Oh my God, what am I going to do with them?" ushered them into the cramped, stark, windowless room for the bereaved. It was the nurses also who had to mollify the other patients and their companions who were compelled to wait out "the event." At such times, almost all nurses seem to become "long sufferers," and these certainly did. One gets the impression that nurses hostess such emergencies, which they do, in a sense. When the shift was nearly over and "the event" long past, the three nurses lolled at the nurses' station, looking knowingly at one another, recanting the litany of "the event" and the shift, and commenting on how tired they were. They looked as if they had borne a (the) burden, and I wondered, as I have wondered at other times about other nurses, whether these nurses seemed proud of their tough experience and whether they would relish telling their husbands of the burden of it.

The relatives of the patient were stricken, tearful and trembling without having seen the patient. They were isolated from the patient until he was wheeled from his cubicle, headed for the operating room. Even when the health team became mostly spectators, the event remained their private showing. Whatever reason the doctors or the nurses might have had in mind for not inviting the relatives, the incongruence of these visitors was likely a factor. No team member reacted approximately as did the relatives, and the relatives could not be expected to view the event in the cubicle in a manner in keeping with a "professional" ambience.

The nurses were not unaware of the reactions of the other participants. They realized and were disturbed by the anguish of the family; summoned a priest, and prompted various doctors to speak to the family. At least one nurse noted the exuberance of the "happy attendant," and spoke disapprovingly of it to the other nurses after the event. Also, the nurses did not wholly approve of the doctors, especially the bellowing doctor and the cracker-munching doctor, but this disapproval was softened by an acknowledgement of the responsibility these men bore.

The various reactions of the nurses to the other participants, and the solemnity of the nurses' own reaction can be explained as the result of the humanitarian aspect of Nursing. Their professional humanitarianism separated the nurses from the other participants and chastened any satisfaction the nurses might have drawn from the event.

The nurses were (and generally are) female, and the physicians were (and generally are) male, but I do not believe that sex accounts for the differing perspectives. Most of the X-ray technicians are women who do not act with the bearing of nurses. On the other hand, the one male nurse whom I have had occasion to watch did, as did most of the male attendants who at General Hospital work virtually as nurses' aides.

In their own subtle way nurses do relish the "power" that attends medical drama and some nurses anticipate medical emergencies; however, they do so only in cases in which medical drama can be convincingly staged. Nurses do not like futile codes. Also, medical heroism for nurses is an elaborately structured experience with a clinical setting: technicians, physicians, and patients whose maladies most often are familiar sights.

There are occasions in which the appearances of patients are so horrific that medical drama is subverted, and the nurses' defenses are breached. Emergency department nurses encounter such occasions most often since they see patients before they are cleaned up. The physical integrity of the patient of "the event" was virtually intact. Extremely gross injuries provide more trying experiences. A young man who had been struck by and eviscerated by a car greatly upset all the emergency department personnel, both nurses and doctors.

Burns seem to be the greatest crusher of nursing competence. A gas line blew up where men were working on it, burning them severely and spraying their wounds with sand. The victims arrived at the hospital, the remnants of their outer skin a grey, peeling crust, the rest raw pink and sanded. Their hair was singed so that it disintegrated when touched. They were in agony. The stench was horrible. The nurses were upset for several days, as were the nurses who cared for a man who burned himself to death via a bathtub filled with lighter fluid. He came in charred yet miraculously still alive. His body was so desiccated and thus shrunk that the nurses thought he was a small child and were amazed to learn that he was a grown man.

"Prejudiced Reaction" and Deficient Personalities

I saw no evidence at General Hospital that nurses and aides as a group use "prejudiced reaction" toward patients with deformities or debilities unrelated to personality. However, nursing personnel did specially regard and treat patients with apparent personality deficiencies in a manner that disassociated these patients from humanity. No formal ideology governed this separation; such would not be in keeping with a humanitarian-rehabilitative ethos. A barely veiled and yet unscrutinized prejudice operated that was not clearly "aversion" or "taboo," but which had, at times, the flavor of these. To the extent that a nurse perceived a patient to be unaware, to that extent she tended to deny his humanity through her behavior and attitude.

There are several possible reasons why there is "prejudiced reaction" regarding patients with personality debilities, but not regarding patients with deformities and physical debilities. The hospital establishment has a much greater capacity to mask and to correct the latter. Bandages, soap, bedrest, surgery, clothing and so forth, can be cosmetic. A dearth of coherent personality cannot be dressed up. An incoherent personality draws attention to itself and impedes the ministrations of nurses. Most significantly, an absence of personality is an absence of apparent soul.

In that a patient does not manifest a personality for whatever reason, even weakness, nurses tend to disregard his social sensibilities. They talk as if they were alone or he were inhuman. They talk to one another without inhibition. They talk about him. They talk to him in the manner that people talk to portraits, Raggedy Anns, gravestones or cats.

I once listened to a tale of woe from a man whose cardiac insufficiency had precipitated a loss of control over his behavior but not over his consciousness. During a spell of several days, he made the most contorted facial expressions and stiff aimless movements. In no way did he seem coherent, but he was, and he looked out from his physical prison upon nurses and me who were inconsiderate of his presence.

When patients seem confused, nurses treat them like babies, but often without the maternal warmth. In conversational tones, the nurses chat among themselves as if the patient were not there or as if he were an uncomprehending child, and then they often turn to the patient and address him in loud, deliberate tones, again as if he were a baby who can understand only baby talk. Nurses coerce confused patients to a far greater extent than they would dare coerce patients perceived to be coherent. I have already described the humor that nurses employ to cover the awkwardness of physically forcing or restraining "confused" patients.

I asked: "Do you think that patients who are unaware or incoherent receive less sensitive or less gentle treatment from the nursing staff?" The respondents were divided almost down the middle on this question. Forty-eight percent (55) answered negatively. Thirty-six percent (41) claimed that such patients generally do receive less sensitive or gentle treatment. Ten percent (11) maintained that the care is sometimes less sensitive or gentle. Six percent (7) did not answer.

The negative answers were rarely more elaborate than "No," but I suspect that many of the respondents who answered negatively were thinking in terms of the extensive tactile bedside care that they must provide such patients. The tender loving care of the touch is the flip side of the coin, so to speak. It binds the patient to humanity while social disregard keeps him away. I also suspect some of the negative answers were inspired by a perception of my question as an attack on the humanitarian ideals of nurses. I quote this negative answer, one of the few elaborated ones, as I would like to respond to it specifically:

> No, because we are all aware of the fact that even though people cannot respond does not mean that they cannot hear. It is not uncommon on my floor to hear staff talking to an unconscious patient.

Yes, staffers often talk to unconscious patients, and I have already described the manner in which most staffers do it. However, some nurses make an especially sensitive effort. The nurse who gave the above answer is likely one of the nurses, judging from her questionnaire, which was the most eloquent, lengthy and detailed one I received. From what I have seen of them, the most humanitarianly imbrued talks directed at unconscious and confused patients are highly conscious efforts that represent a cause for the nurses. Such efforts are a steeled rush for humanitarian heroism. Quieter, more sensitive words said over unaware patients do almost dissipate prejudiced reaction, but still these words are soliloquies to a person who was or might be again.

The affirmative answers that were elaborated tend to corroborate my point of view. Here are some representative samples:

> Yes, many times nurses, caring for apparently unconscious or incoherent patients, talk over the patients about others, personal items, etc. They tend to speak more harshly, impatiently, and movements become rougher because the patient does not know the difference.

> Sometimes this is true. For some reason when a patient becomes incoherent, the staff does not explain to the patient what procedure they are about to perform. Also, the patient tends to be avoided.

> I think they might receive less sensitive rather than less gentle care. I've never seen anyone really treated physically roughly, although I have noticed verbal displays of anger towards them. When one is incoherent or unaware, it is almost like a waste of time to talk with them (even though this is not true because their hearing may be intact and mind) because these patients do not respond to you very well. Usually, these patients are given their routine care and treatments, and more or less forgotten about in-between times.

> Probably, without us realizing it we know we can rush through their care because they won't complain.

These "affirmative" nurses and aides suggest also that more is lacking in nurses' relations with patients than sociable contact. There is mention of harshness, impatience and avoidance. From what I have seen, such "aversion" does steel the "prejudiced reaction" of many nurses and aides, though by no means is it apparent in all or most nurses' postures toward confused or unaware patients. Aversion does reduce the humanitarian sensitivity associated with tactile bedside care. Ambiguous men inspire ambivalence. In general, as nurses are less socially inhibited in the presence of patients who are incompetent social actors, so nurses are more likely to express their hostility toward such patients. Nurses sanction their hostility as aggravation arising from nursing routine, and avoidance-hostility as a necessary requisite of nursing routine. Nurses who seem to avoid all repulsion do so at a cost of exhausting repression or a developed sensitivity to human signs, such as tactile signs or feeble indications of personality.

As senility is a common malady of elderly patients, many nurses presume at the slightest sign of feebleness that an elderly person is feebleminded. Unless an elderly patient strongly demonstrates a normative mentality, license will likely be taken. If a nurse joins another nurse in an "unfamiliar" room in which two old patients lie limp on their beds, the first nurse is far more likely to make uninhibited conversation than she would if the limp patients were middle-aged.

Often older patients are not so unaware as they seem; their awareness varies from hour to hour or day to day, and thus nurses often offend them. Conflicts ensue, especially at night when normally coherent oldsters often grow somewhat disoriented. The patients attempt to climb over their rails, often to find the bathroom, only to be confronted with nurses who impertinently jostle them back to bed: "Come on, Mr . . .Let's go." I have heard patients complain: "And she wasn't the least bit nice about it either!"

Nurses do vary considerably in the manner they humor, coerce and condescend to old people. Some nurses, such as this one, are gentle and sensitive, appreciate older patients and like working with them: "Older persons—well, that is my bag. I love geriatrics and I am not alone. I was brought up with grandparents in our home and this is where I fell in love with older people, and I am old enough to see my own end." That nurses like oldsters does not mean that these nurses do not use the standard prejudiced reaction toward them, but it does mean that they are more discerning and gentle in applying it. However, there are nurses whose prejudice is steeled with aversion—sarcastic and rough. One nurse put her views about the senile elderly succinctly: "I hate them—it bores me to take care of these patients."

I have four examples to illustrate the points I have been making.

1. One day while working on a large medical unit, I was attracted by a screaming protest: "Aeee! No! No! No! No!" I followed the noise to a patients' room wherein a husky nurse was force-feeding an old lady who was tied to a chair. The nurse mimed the patient's expressions and gestures, laughing as she did so. "Come on, Mamma, you haven't eaten all day!" The patient screamed and the nurse scooted a spoonful of food into her mouth. The medication nurse came in behind me; we both surveyed the scene. The attending nurse warned, "Look out, you must stay out of range. She will spit her food

out at you." The medication nurse circumspectly popped a pill into the patient's mouth and then added, "She's looking for someplace to spit that pill out—there . . ." The pill and the food splattered on the floor. "I can't stand patients like that. She knows what she's doing." The two nurses continued to discuss the doctors' orders concerning the patient. Occasionally, the attending nurse cast a loud aside to the patient, accompanied by exaggerated gestures, "How's it going, Mamma?"

2. A nurse and I were making beds for two old men who were passive and seemed a bit slow, but not unaware. The nurse initiated and kept up an animated dialogue concerning birth control and a woman's right to have an abortion. I took part but I tried not to be the moving force. When necessary, she would cock her head toward one of the men, "OK. Move over on your side. That's right. . . ." I must say the men seemed little perturbed with our conversation.

3. A young student nurse working for the summer as an aide was assigned a man who had had a severe stroke, and whose expressions were restricted to moaning, drooling and groggy motions. Ever so gently, this aide bathed him, labored to feed him, made his bed, fluffed his pillow and all the while addressed him soothingly. I was assigned to the other patient in the room, and therefore was present through much of her ideal tender loving care. I was musing on the idealism of youth when she straightened up, gazed across at me. She said, "You know, I just hate the way nurses treat old people. . . ." She continued with a lengthy diatribe.

4. I happened to walk in on an aide who had floated to my floor and therefore was a stranger to me. She was caring for an elderly man, speaking to him earnestly. She did not cease and shift her attention to me. I was so astonished by her breach of standard procedure that I caught myself and played along, turned my attention toward the patient. The aide did not talk to me until we left the room; then when she learned I was the man behind the questionnaire, volunteered that her biggest gripe is with people who carry on as if senile old patients were not there or did not matter.

In a sense, "prejudiced reaction" toward patients who might have deficient or unapparent personalities is a form of diversion. By shunning efforts at normal social interaction with such patients and by focusing sociability, when possible, on normative

co-workers, nursing personnel avoid confronting damning per- 177
formances. By expecting less from old people, nurses are less
likely to be disappointed.

In another sense, prejudice toward patients with deficient
personalities defines them as separate beings. The nurses, especially the young nurses, can thus attenuate identification with
them. This prejudice is very much like a common social prejudice
based on class or ethnicity, only "prejudiced reaction" serves to
defend the generic identity of the nurses.

The degree to which a sorely afflicted patient develops positive
social interaction with nurses is a significant factor in how they
treat and regard him. A patient must reach out to achieve
positive personal contact with nurses. In that he does so, and is
successful, the nurses' "prejudice" and their "diversionary" defenses are less effective. The nurses care more. If the patient is
also courageous, he may become a hero.

A patient who fails or does poorly on the personality test is a
far less poignant presence. This man is a case in point. He was
a "cute" elderly man whose hearing was poor and whose mind
was foggy, though functional. A cancer budded on his lip and
blossomed like a scarlet cauliflower across his face. Much of his
day he sat propped up in his bed or tied in his chair. He rolled
or moved in the right direction if one spoke to his ear. Due to
his hearing debility, he made humorous statements that were
incongruent with the question put to him or with the conversation around him. "I said, are you through going to the bathroom?" "Ah, no sonny, I've been a Catholic all my life." His
eyes shot around in perpetual wonderment. Eating became increasingly painful for him; yet, he fed himself the baby food
which we set out for him in cups, and in the process he did no
more than cringe and hiss quietly. His face became increasingly
grotesque. Some mention was made of this fact by several staff
members; yet putting aside this mention, nothing unusual
marked the reactions of nurses to his presence. He was treated
like any other senile old man. That he was dying horribly had no
impact on his treatment. He was attended to, jostled around and
talked about. While in the room, no one seemed to notice the
mushrooming scarlet cauliflower.

If this man had looked straight into the nurses' eyes, quoted
Mark Twain, and queried the nurses about their children, things
would have been much different. Some distance would have been
maintained, as it is with all patients, but the nurses would have
been more concerned about this man. He would not have shared

a room with a teeth-grinding, bed-fouling, Mongoloid idiot. Nurses would have displayed more emotion and would have made more mention of the cauliflower in the nurses' lounge.

Nurses noticed this man's cancer—and shrank from the thought of it. Two respondents mentioned it in their questionnaires. The cancer had an impact, but almost a disembodied, conceptual impact far more readily put out of mind than a cancer grown out of a living man uncompromised by "prejudiced reaction."

MASH

Counting on the educational popularity of the television program, $M^*A^*S^*H^*$, I decided to ask straight out about MASH in General Hospital. I asked: "What do you think about the irreverent MASH-type humor that sometimes breaks out in nursing units regarding the behavior or conditions of certain patients?" A whopping 81 percent (93) of the respondents claimed that they basically approve of this humor. Two percent more (2) qualified their approval with strong reservations. Eight percent (9) had no opinion. Only nine percent (10) totally disapproved. The negative responses are epitomized by simply declaring that the program is disgusting—"There is a time and a place."

However, the positive and mixed responses were in this vein:

It's not right, it is irreverent, rude and unprofessional, but serves as comic relief because nursing can at times be downright depressing.

If I don't laugh, I'll probably cry.

It is a defense mechanism against depression and frustration in that sense can be considered necessary but it *should never* get out of control so that alert, oriented patients are exposed to it.

I don't particularly think humor, MASH-type or not, is irreverent. Some humor is necessary to maintain well-balanced state of mind when dealing with elderly and dying patients daily.

It keeps us sane.

I think it is the nurses' way of relieving their own tension or frustration over some of the conditions they are dealing with. Unfortunately, this behavior is misinterpreted sometimes by the public so personnel (myself included) should be more aware of this aspect of it.

Normal—it's a great way to divorce yourself from the horrors that
go on in acute medical areas.

I believe it a form or release, some work can dishearten the
strongest; it is not meant as cruelly as it sounds.

I love it.

Fantastic! It is a normal release of energy to reduce tensions that
build up as a result of workload and aggravation by staff members.
I can't be sympathetic gung-ho all the time.

After I asked this question I realized it did not include all that I
place under the rubric, MASH. Left out were mentions of exotic
individual diversions and horseplay among personnel, horseplay
which is not directly related to patients. Also, I have no way of
knowing whether my respondents interpret patient-related
MASH as do I. I believe the responses show that nurses generally
believe in the importance of some comic relief, and in that they
are concerned about reactions to it, they are concerned about
the reactions of *aware* patients and the public.

Actually, only in the intensive care unit did I see any substantial MASH among nursing personnel; I saw little more than mild
MASH in the rest of the hospital. There, horseplay is limited,
and that which nurses suspect will offend certain patients,
visitors, supervisors or doctors is usually carefully kept from
their sight. Nurses sometimes, as I have said, laugh at confused
patients whom the nurses dress up to look "cute," or whose
abnormal behavior strikes their fancy.

Some scenes are funny. A middle-aged man who had dimmed
his brain with alcohol was regularly (against his uncoordinated
will) tied into a chair from which he never ceased attempting to
escape. One day he pushed his chair along with his feet, out his
door, down the corridor, through the double doors, and completely off the unit. The nurses received a call that one of their
patients was trying to push his chair and himself onto an
elevator. The rescue party laughed all the way out to get him
and all the way back with him. Another example involved two
96-year-old Italian women who were located in the same unit.
The nurses discovered that these ladies had been friends for 70
years. So, the nurses brought them together. Even though the
patients could not hear well, they jabbered at one another,
nonetheless. Every nurse and aide on the floor came by for a
peek and a laugh. Another example might be cited. A young man
came into the emergency department with a particular problem.

180 He had placed his penis through a large nut (as in nut and bolt). The nut had constricted circulation and his penis had blown into a small balloon. The nut had to be sawed off. The ED staff laughed plenty but not to the patient's face.

These examples epitomize mild MASH as it is derived from patients. Never is it directed at physical deformities or debilities per se. No one is amused at an amputation or at cancer. When nurses are openly bemused by patients, the nurses are bemused at appearance as it is qualified by behavior. Much of the time the humorous behavior is not a direct result of a debility, but is merely some quirk that one might expect from any heterogeneous group of normal individuals.

The mild horseplay and the mild fun at the expense of patients provide a mild release of tensions, a diversion, and a lightening of mood that greases the nurses' routine. The hospital, by and large, is no fun house, at least as far nursing personnel are concerned. However, the air does not hang with tragedy. The ambience is mundane, and mild MASH sustains and is part of the mundane.

MASH comes in degrees; with certain qualifications, the more ambiguous the patients seem the greater the MASH. I decided this is the precipitating factor in this case rather than time-task pressure. Time-task pressure makes some nurses giddy, but also tends to keep nurses apart from one another, occupied with their various duties, thus vitiating the shared joke that MASH so often is. MASH tends to occur on moderately busy days, or in quieter interludes when standard diversion slackens and there is time for skits and shared humor.

The evidence to support my conviction that ambiguity fosters MASH is not compelling. It is mostly comprised of vague impressions. There seems to be more MASH on regular floors when the patients there seem more vegetative. The coronary care unit and the intensive care unit are similar in terms of size, visiting hours and criticalness of care, and yet CCU is rather staid whereas ICU exhibits more MASH than anywhere else I have been in the hospital. The CCU's patients are generally normative, while the ICU's patients are rarely normative. However, quiet is a special injunction around coronary patients. Like the ICU, the emergency department encounters many startlingly ambiguous men. The ED comes next to the ICU in the degree of MASH, and I think there would be more MASH in ED if the staff were not under the watchful eyes of normative patients and multitudes of normative visitors.

I have in part described MASH on the intensive care unit elsewhere. Since I do not wish to repeat myself, I shall merely complete the picture here.

Not all nurses participated in MASH to the same degree. Two did not participate at all. Individual disposition and inhibitions seemed to be important factors. One of the no-MASH nurses was so placcid that a joke circulated on the unit that if she saw a patient arrest, she would calmly approach the head nurse, wait for her to finish whatever she was doing, and then quietly say, "I think that patient over there isn't breathing." The other no-MASH nurse was especially high-strung and compulsively conscientious. She had a nervous laugh, and one had to be most careful not to startle her by approaching unseen. The rest of the nurses indulged in MASH. The ringleaders were not so much clowns as screamers—yelling at patients, yelling at other nurses across the unit, yelling taunts and banter.

The MASH was rarely subtle—almost always broad and frenzied. Sometimes it broke out spontaneously among a group of nurses. The taped morning report for fewer than ten patients was about a half hour long, so long were the lists of pertinent facts regarding each patient. When a new patient arrived, a list of his ailments and the procedures administered to him would be included in the report, a list which sometimes seemed incredibly lengthy. Several times the nurses who huddled around the recorder would begin to laugh as the roll went on, and then to laugh uncontrollably for some seconds perhaps saying, "The poor bastard!"

As with mild MASH on the regular floors, the greater MASH in ICU served as a diversion, release and a denial. Reality on ICU was grimmer than on other units and thus the need for release was greater. One ICU nurse said the following about MASH and ICU:

MASH-type behavior is a necessary release on an ICU. One laughs in preference over other emotional reactions. If I did not laugh, I am afraid what I might do. However, this humor can get out of hand. Aware patients may be somewhat afraid of it. "If the nurses carry on so over that patient, how would they treat me?" Visitors would not be expected to understand at all. Also, for nurses themselves, too much hysteria can lead to general loss of control—to insensitive callousness in regard to patients. Keeping a lid on the "fun" is an on-going problem. . . . Today I unwrapped a head bandage to reveal dried brain tissue, and dry heaved for the next few minutes. . . . Working on ICU does adversely affect a nurse, and perhaps an individual can tolerate working on ICU for only a few years. I find myself wondering as I drive on the highway, who is going to pull out in front of me, what motorcycle might run up over my roof. I see myself in a stryker frame, sandwiched between two pieces of steel with tongs in my head. There is also insomnia. Working here does strange things to one's head.

An event that included some more subtle MASH occurred while I was observing in the intensive care unit—an event which was so obscure as it unfolded I did not realize what was going on until it was virtually over. This event demonstrates the surrealistic detachment and the corresponding almost antithetical, surreptitious awareness that operate in the ICU for at least most of its participants. Some days before, a teenage boy had been admitted. He had been driving when his car was struck head on by another car with three drunk young men. The men survived with moderate injuries. Our lad had multiple fractures and a severe head injury. His chances were poor. In a day or so, his skin chilled while his innards spiked an incredible temperature. The doctors decided he had no hope—mentally. He was put in traction and sustained on a respirator. That morning the anesthesiologist arrived, adjusted the respirator, and then went over and sat down behind the glass partition of the nurses' station opposite the boy. I thought nothing of it. It was a normal morning. Everyone was going about her business. The curtain was drawn around the boy; I peeked through it to see if I might help whoever was working behind it. She was one of the no-MASH nurses; she barked at me, "Get out! Just get out!" I had no idea why. She apologized later; by then I understood. She finished, drew back the curtain, and retired to the far end of the unit where she worked with a patient until the event was past. A ruddy-faced internist, who had no professional connection with the boy, entered the unit and sat down beside the anesthesiologist. They were joined by two nurses and an amiable chat ensued. I removed myself to a corner of the nurses' station. The internist had a joke to tell. I knew because the day before I had heard him tell it in the coronary care unit. He told the joke: "The Pope dies and goes to heaven. When he gets there, he finds a long line waiting to see St. Peter, but the Pope figures, 'Hell, I'm the Pope,' and so he goes to the head of the line, but St. Peter tells him that all souls are equal in heaven and he'll just have to wait his turn. So the Pope goes to the end of the line. He isn't there long when this character shows up, dressed in a green scrub gown, with a green cap, green covers for his shoes, a surgical mask, a stethoscope, the whole bit. His head bent down, he trudges along right up through the whole line and right in through the gates of heaven. The Pope is incensed, goes to St. Peter and says, 'Look here, I thought you said all souls are equal. What about that guy?' St. Peter goes 'Shshshsh!' bends over and whispers in the Pope's ear, 'That's God, He thinks He's a doctor.'" Everyone laughed naturally, I thought. In five minutes the anesthesiologist asked for the time and jotted it down in the chart before him. I looked up and saw that the boy's monitor line was flat; only then did I begin to realize what had been going on: passive euthanasia. The respirator had not been switched off. The volume or the mixture of its output had been changed.

No one showed any surprise, including me, and I was surprised; therefore, I do not know how many persons present were aware of what was going on. None of the other patients was, I am sure. The anesthesiologist knew. At least one nurse knew. The rest took the news easily, apparently. I have since been told by an ICU nurse from a large teaching hospital that humor, a strange humor, often accompanies the performance of passive euthanasia. Peculiar jokes are told when respirators are "turned off."

Induration and Living with Inconsistency

On some level, nursing personnel are aware of the disease they witness. Many of the incidences I have cited indicate this awareness. Knowing the conditions of patients is a nursing responsibility. When I asked nurses about the condition of certain patients, the nurses have given me unhesitant and succinct replies, and when prompted (and sometimes voluntarily), nurses describe vividly the horrors of certain diseases and injuries. In these descriptions, one hears "terrible," "horrible" and "hideous." Nurses often refer to the patients as "that poor patient."

On some level, also, many and perhaps nearly all nurses and aides are aware that medical heroism per se is sometimes incongruent with Nursing, that actual nursing practice falls short of Nursing ideals, and that a desire for "heroism" is a motivation for them. Almost all the nurses of my acquaintance believe that an unrestricted use of medical heroics is unhumanitarian and would have these heroics restricted. Responses to my questionnaire show that many nurses perceive that diversions, prejudices and MASH impede Nursing. At least some see these impediments

184 are resultant in part from the strain of close contact with sorely afflicted people. Nurses do not admit enjoying human agony as an opportunity for humanitarianism, but they are generally proud of their humanitarian heroism. Some nurses admit to anticipating opportunities for medical heroism.

On some level, for many nurses, this general awareness exists, and yet it does not apparently much burden them when they perform their nursing duties, or when they are away from these duties. From what I have heard of them, the rationales nurses construct concerning horrors and the shortcomings of nursing practice do not seem much developed. A fatalism seems to prevail; horrors and failures are considered to be unpleasant realities over which one should not brood. As many as 12 nurses volunteered that my questionnaire made them think about issues they have never much considered. From what I have seen, except in certain cases, these realities are not much pondered. When nurses think about what bothers them, they think in terms of mundane, social grievances. In the nursing units, the work is to be done and nurses dwell on the navigational, sociability concerns of this work. Thus, though nurses perceive disease and the failures of "competence," the implications of these are not fully "felt." The logical and the affective ramifications of the awareness are repressed. Induration sustains the competence of nurses.

Induration is an aspect of competence. Equanimity and "power" are the chief ends of competence that is a combination of methods that effectively assuages manifest human ambiguity such that the competent individual can seem unperturbed to himself and to others in the presence of manifest human ambiguity and can continue to endure its presence comfortably. In that other means of assuagement do not resolve human ambiguity, and in that they express the inconsistencies (ambivalences) of the Gregor Effect, induration is necessary to forge a competence from these methods. Since nurses' other methods do not resolve ambiguity and are not consistent, induration is necessary for nursing competence and for a faith in Nursing "competence." Almost all nurses are apparently competent almost all of the time. What is at issue is how inwardly competent they are. In a given class of confrontations with ambiguous men, those nurses who feel more comfortable are more indurate than those nurses who feel less comfortable.

Individual nurses display varying degrees of induration. The least "hardened" are the most troubled by disease and the detached treatment of sorely afflicted patients. They are the most fatigued by encounters with ambiguous men. The most indurate "fetishize" their nursing such that their power-generating war against mortality is transposed to an administrative, technical or task arena. Such nurses believe that they are Nursing in that they overcome obstacles to administrative, technical or task proficiency.

Intelligence per se has no bearing on induration. Sensitive nursing personnel are sometimes stupid, and some of the most indurate nurses are also some of the most intelligent. This latter group contains nurses who associate Nursing solely with elegant, topical organizational schemes or with the latest in cardiology. Such nurses are similar to nurses who think of their work solely in terms of "doing up" patients.

Education is also an insignificant factor. Whether one is an aide, a licensed practical nurse, registered nurse or registered nurse with a university degree, seems to have no bearing on one's induration, though it may have some bearing on the specific form of one's competence.

I have said that induration takes time to develop, but some nursing competence is quickly achieved for a variety of reasons. Since the confusion of the beginner may impede an awareness of ambiguity and inconsistencies in the adjustments of nurses, it is questionable how much true induration aids the adjustments of neophytes. Perhaps the question is moot. People who come to nursing come with a desire for competence and come with a familiarity with the medical and humanitarian ideology of Nursing. Nursing competence is so institutionalized within a hospital that if neophytes do their prescribed duties, they go through the motions of rehabilitative and humanitarian rituals—and diversion. They are placed in a society of nurses that defines their professional identify and distance. Experienced personnel, through example, quickly educate neophytes in prejudiced reaction and MASH, although some time must generally elapse before they use these. Beginners are kept preoccupied with learning their complicated roles, appearing right and doing right, and thus they are provided a diversionary boost. Also, the hope exists for beginners that there is more to this nursing competence than meets the eye, and that the calm of the experienced denotes some wisdom. Thus, one shuns the shock one feels, taking it to be a sign of immaturity, and thus conscious effort aids the development of induration.

Less experienced nursing personnel as a whole are less indurate than more experienced nurses and aides. Induration and maturity appear much the same. More mature nurses may or may not be more "mature" in an ideal sense, but they have greater ease with and perhaps more modest expectations concerning their competence. They are more phlegmatic, more likely to be "long suffering." Numerous exceptions exist. Some nurses will never be moderately complacent with their nursing. However, the less experienced as a group are more excitable and more hopeful. They are more likely to anticipate emergencies. They are more likely to practice "taboo reaction," such voyeurism as making special efforts to peek at horrible wounds, injuries and deformities—and to attend codes. They are more likely to seem upset over patients' conditions. They are more likely to attempt an idealized humanitarian treatment of confused and unaware patients. The least experienced nurses and aides are the most likely to provide patient care that is good by the humanitarian standards of Nursing; although I firmly believe that the very best humanitarian care is provided by very special nurses of long experience in nursing and in living.

Most nurses do not stay in hospital nursing long enough to accrue decades of experience, and many of those who do move on to supervisory, administrative or educational positions; thus those nurses who remain for many years as bedside nurses may be a select group. Be this as it may, older staff nurses do often seem to be "harder" in the classic sense. Some seem almost bitter. Others complement their hardness with a softer side—a gentle, patient, almost tactile dedication to the welfare of their patients. From what I have seen of it, this humanitarian "competence" is not achieved through elaborate conceptualization, although it may be related to a more sanguine religious belief. I suspect that developed sensitivities to the feel of a man, and to the more subtle signs of personality in illness are vital factors in this humanitarianism that is somehow more genuine than the exuberant humanitarianism of the young which seems akin to the love children lavish on dolls. Both the crones and the saints of long bedside experience exhibit a developed induration.

Strictly speaking, induration may not be a means of assuagement, since repression is a nebulous quality that cannot be summoned directly. Induration may be merely a measure of competence since induration is evidenced indirectly by a dearth of anxiety or apparent strain concerning ambivalences of which men are at least marginally aware. The indurate man is a man whose adjustment to manifest human ambiguity is apparently working well. If induration is an active force, it likely has a cost in terms of energy. If it has a cost, there is a question as to whether induration is more costly than a lack of induration which sets the person scurrying for orientation. I suspect that a lack of induration costs more since the "softer" nurses definitely wear thinner than the "harder" ones. However, I also suspect that there are limits to both induration and competence, and that the presence of manifest human ambiguity continues to pose a threat. Also, adjustment itself requires elaborate, consuming performance.

The prize of competence is heroism and self-certainty. For this prize and for their general orientation, nurses do believe in Nursing and hope in Nursing, even while they know and fear its inadequacies. With a slight of hand and a partial eye, nurses conjure certainty out of ambivalence. Uncertainty characterizes nurses' regard for ambiguous men, and ambivalence the reaction; but ambivalence is disorienting to admit unless one's perspective encompasses both tendencies and one is relatively free from contact with ambiguous men.

One of the greatest difficulties in gathering substantive data on nurses' reactions to patients is that answers given are often contradictory in themselves and contradictory with observed behavior. For example, I asked: "Do you think the nursing staff treats dying patients differently because they are dying? If so how?" Twenty percent (23) of the respondents admitted that the nursing staff treats dying patients differently without specifying how. Twenty-two percent (25) maintained that dying patients receive better care because they are dying. Nineteen percent (22) claimed that dying patients receive poorer nursing care because they are dying. Thirty-one percent (35) denied that dying patients are treated any differently. Eight percent (9) did not answer this question. To confuse matters more, I put my question to many nurses verbally and found that the "better" nurses may avoid the apparently dying; while the "worse" nurses may and often do attempt to give the dying special care.

The Success of Nursing Competence

Before one can determine how successful nursing competence is, one must consider whether there is one competence for staff nurses and aides. I believe such a competence exists. The social structure, the ethos and the ecology associated with hospital nursing virtually choreograph nurses' adaptations to manifest human ambiguity. The competence is complex, and thus there is much opportunity for idiosyncratic emphasis that renders some impression of variations; yet if one scrutinizes a given staff nurse's adjustment, one will most likely find that all of nursing competence is being employed. Saintly nurses keep their distance, and apparently incompassionate nurses feel some humanitarian swell. The nurses who would stick to tender loving care, and who shun the responsibility of more technical medicine, still participate in medical heroism vicariously and directly; they are part of the rehabilitative team, and in their own way they see themselves as serving rehabilitative ends. Nurses do not evade identification with Nursing or with other nurses. They rarely transcend their secondary relationships with patients. Routine diversions are used by all, and few nurses bear a constant air of pathos or gravity. Few withstand the temptation to dabble in at least mild MASH. Some prejudiced reaction to confused and unaware patients is all but universal.

If there is a wild card in individual nurses' adjustments, it is most likely religion. Eighty-five percent of my questionnaire respondents claimed some religious affiliation. Twenty-seven percent claimed to attend religious services at least twice a month, and only twenty-nine percent maintained that they never attend religious services. To various questions, several nurses volunteered that religion influences their adjustments to disease and to patients. I do not doubt that religious faith or lack thereof has some bearing on a nurse's competence. Since I did not investigate this probability, there is not much to say about it. I suggest that in General Hospital and perhaps even in modern hospitals with religious affiliations, the impact of religion is minimized due to an absence of external supports for a religious view. General Hospital's ambience is starkly secular. The meditation chapel was torn out to make room for the electroencaphalograph. Religion is rarely mentioned; patients are discussed in terms of nursing and medicine. I speculate that despite the uneven impact of individual faith, nursing competence is virtually the adaptation of nursing personnel to ambiguous men.

The success of nursing competence depends partly on how one defines "success." If success is considered to be the extent to which idealized rehabilitative-humanitarian Nursing defines what nurses do for and how they feel about patients, actual nursing is less than ideal. Patients tend to be regarded less in a rehabilitative-humanitarian light and to be treated less in a rehabilitative-humanitarian way as they appear more irremeably ambiguous. The human ideal type does not allow for much evident variation. The hospital establishment has a limited potential for rehabilitative, cosmetic, and situational normalization. The establishment conjures up an illusion of power, but the smell of defeat is too strong for this illusion to be thoroughly convincing for the persons who arrange props. In that men seem hopelessly ambiguous, nurses manifest the ambivalences of the Gregor Effect. Also, as some distance and diversion are built into the nurses' role and status, all patients are subject to them. However, for most patients most of the time a semblance of Nursing is maintained.

If "success" is considered to be the success that nurses as "competence" professionals have in helping the public (as patients and visitors) cope with human ambiguity, then success is again limited. When hope of recovery can be nurtured, nurses can be seen as agents of that recovery. When patients manifest viable personalities, nurses can address the humanity of these patients. However, when there is no apparent worldly hope for a patient, nurses cannot pose as agents of his recovery. When a patient's personality fails, nurses cannot offer visitors much in the way of professional comfort. Nurses do spare friends and relatives confrontations by caring for such patients. Nurses ease visitors' confrontations by cleaning, neatening and medicating patients. Faith in the power of medicine does foster vain hope at times, but this hope is a questionable service. In that patients and visitors are aware of the imperfections of actual nursing performance, they are not comforted by Nursing. Nurses often avoid or ignore the visitors of senile old patients; but when nurses do greet such visitors, what the nurses can offer is limited. They may say, "He had a good night" or "He is stable," but there are many times when even these tepid statements are incredible. On several occasions I have heard nurses say regarding terminal patients, "Well, he's had a good long life." Visitors can make such statements to one another. Only when mortality and human ambiguity can be plausibly denied can Nursing as medicine and charity provide much professional service in the area of competence. Nursing is a secular "competence."

When "success" is deemed to be the effectiveness of actual nursing practice as a comfortable and heroic adjustment to human ambiguity, success is substantial but not complete. In that nurses usually calmly ply their trade and take pride in the medical and the humanitarian heroism of their work, they would seem to be well-adjusted. The stark fear, uncertainty, repulsion and bald obscenity that signal a poor adjustment are rare among nurses. However, milder signs of inefficacy such as fatigue, irritability and despair intermittently plague many if not all nurses. These signs, however, do not prove that nursing competence is somehow inefficient since so many other factors related to nurses and nursing could cause them, and undoubtedly do at least contribute to them. Nonetheless, I believe that nurses, especially the more humanitarian nurses, possess competences that are flawed and taxing. But, I have no substantive data to support my contention, and I suspect that such data might be impossible to collect. I can only speculate.

I have noted a phenomenon I term *nurses' malaise* that plagues many nurses. Like other ailments, it comes in degrees. I shall describe its more pronounced symptoms. The foremost symptom is fatigue, a weariness that hangs over a nurse so that she stumbles through the motions of her work and peers at patients through a fog. Fatigue is a common topic of conversation among nurses when they loll in the nurses' lounge before and after shift, during coffee breaks, during lunch and at the nurses' station. Then, also, days are not infrequent when nurses on their lunch break eat silently, staring blankly at one another. Even effervescent nurses often look tired—around the eyes. Nurses have frequently told me that they collapse for an hour or so when they get home. Others have lamented that they could not collapse because of children or other reasons. What is more, I was myself plagued by fatigue, as is my wife who is a nurse, as is my mother who is a nurse, as are all their and my nurse friends. From what I have seen of it, hospital nursing is exhausting.

Nurses' malaise is more than fatigue; it is a dispirit, which when it is not gripping a nurse, is poised to grip her; it is a dark aura that perpetually threatens to suffocate. Nurses are not walking zombies. They are generally active, often frenetically active; yet there is often a sense of "the show must go on" about this activity, and a sense that the Nursing which deals face-to-face with patients and visitors is something of an empty play. I do not wish my point to seem exaggerated. This malaise is a counterpoint to the more positive aspects of nursing that I have already recounted; yet the counterpoint is real and significant.

I have been haunted by the thought that *nurses' malaise* may be a common condition of life either for all people or for all modern Americans. Certainly, people in other occupations unconcerned with ambiguous men are tired and dispirited now and again. Some of what nurses feel comes undoubtedly from common causes; yet there is something more to *nurses' malaise.*

Nurses of my acquaintance have been almost exclusively women; thus, their tendency toward fatigue might be a natural result of the added pressures of their roles as wives and mothers. I do not think so though, since single nurses and male attendants seem no less fatigued.

As varied and as challenging as nursing would seem to be, some nurses do get bored with nursing and their boredom becomes intertwined with their fatigue. When I have been bored in the hospital, I have not been able to make easy social contact with my patients due to their disinterest or inability, or circularly, due to my malaise. In claiming that some people live beyond their time, one of my respondents made a comment on boredom:

> "Yes—for example, some people we keep on respirators who cannot ever survive without the machine have lived beyond their time. You become bored with the person because there isn't really anything you can do to *really help*—you may even be adding to his suffering and you insulate your frustration by being bored.

A number of my respondents in answer to various questions volunteered that they grow bored with caring for the same "total care," "nursing home" patients day in and day out.

The greatest contender with resistant human ambiguity as a source of *nurses' malaise* is the operational nature of nursing itself. Nurses suffer multifarious pressures: task-time pressures, considerable responsibilities and the necessity of coping with numerous supervisors, colleagues and patients who confront nurses with navigational problems as well as manifest human ambiguity. Staff nurses have prodigious leg work. Head nurses are nerve centers for their units. Of course, these pressures as diversion are a part of nurses' competence, but since causality cannot be drawn directly between ambiguity and these pressures, that part of the malaise which the pressures generate cannot be considered to be a failure of competence per se.

The impacts of ambiguity and "work" are likely confounded. Nurses do seem to be just as tired (if not more tired) on quiet days as on normal days. Nurses claim to like moderately busy days and to dislike days that drag. I suspect that if the pressures were stripped away and the nurses were left to cope with their patients alone, they would still be threatened with fatigue. But, multiple pressures without ambiguous men are also fatiguing, a fact to which waitresses would attest. I suspect a complicated chemistry operates between the impact of ambiguity and the impact of the navigational exigencies of nursing. Multiple pressures as diversion diminish the impact of ambiguity, but what is left of that impact augments the strain that the pressures themselves cause. When nurses think of strain, they usually think of some aspect of the operational, multifarious pressure they endure. This focus of lamentation is in itself a diversion; yet mortality and ambiguity aggravate the dissembling of nurses.

By and large, nursing is a young woman's profession at General Hospital, a fact that suggests the possibility that the debits of staff nursing are greater than the glory and the remuneration. Though my respondents were a self-selecting sample, I believe they fairly represent the age distribution in the nursing staff. Sixty-seven percent (77) of my respondents were less than 30 years old. The average age of the respondents was 32, 27 for those who work the 7–3 shift, and 34 for those who work 3–11 and for those who work 11–7.

The turnover rate at General Hospital is quite high. Although I do not know what it is exactly, I know that nurses and aides come and go so frequently that in a couple of years most of a unit's staff often changes. Very few of the nurses and none of the aides with whom I worked in 1970 were still at General Hospital in 1976.

Again, the youth and the turnover at General Hospital are likely attributable to a number of factors. I suggest only that a deficiency in nursing competence might well be one of these factors.

The foremost problem with nursing competence is that it charges with a humanitarian injunction persons who must sustain extensive contact with ambiguous men. Although the relationships between staff nurses and patients are structured, they, nonetheless, entail nitty-gritty contact. Generally, more than other health workers, staff nurses and aides see individual patients under the more informal circumstances of daily living. Thus, nurses and aides are most likely to be pressed with human ambiguity. Their heightened perception makes a humanitarian view and effort difficult to achieve in extreme cases (although easier to achieve in less extreme cases). The effort required to be humanitarian impresses nurses further with their own inadequacy and with the ambiguity of the patients. Failure to achieve the ideal is bound to generate some cognitive dissonance, especially when the failure is manifest in "prejudiced reaction" that cannot be readily covered by nursing routine.

Nurses depend on medicine to buttress their humanitarianism, but close contact with patients vitiates the more fantastic medical pretensions, thus in some cases, bereaving nurses of the hope that humanitarianism requires regarding acutely ambiguous men. In the quest for hope, the secularity of nursing is a major drawback. Nurses must look for a corporeal humanity and hope which become more problematic as patients degenerate and die.

However, in that nurses maintain extensive contact with patients, no easy or entirely successful humanitarianism is possible, indeed no easy or complete certainty is possible. Spiritual transcendence is entirely intangible, and thus it also cannot erase the uncertainty which ambiguous men pose. An approximately complete competence is perhaps only possible for those nurses who climb up the social ladder and away from sorely debilitated patients.

If humanitarianism were jettisoned, and prejudiced reaction were given free sway, perhaps nurses in a base sense would find their work more rewarding. They could vent their anxiety as hostility, their fascination as obscene cruelty. Neglect would be easier. Yet, such an approach also has costs. Since identification with ambiguous men cannot be completely stemmed, fear must be a product of a hate approach.

Nurses look much like Kierkegaard's Philistines since nurses are dependent on the "power of doing" entailed in nursing routine, on the diversions of that routine, on the temporal heroism of medicine, on prejudices, on levity, on social honor and on an avoidance of profound introspection. However, the appearance is somewhat deceptive. Considering the ultimate inexorability of human ambiguity and thus the Gregor Effect, nurses must use some evasion and deceit to fabricate certainty. Their use of such means does not prove that nurses are thoroughly unaware of the underlying truth, the uncertainty. I suspect they are. That nurses do not make odesseys through their uncertainty does not debase them. After all, those persons who do undertake such odesseys live in misery, or find the ways of their people or the future ways of their people. Who is to say that orientation in the form of social play, social doing is ultimately less profound than a search for paradigms?

Summary

In a world which is ever problematic, abnormal men confront their normative brethren with the transience and the uncertainty of human identity, the positive definitiveness of which is the keystone of orientation. In that other men are manifestly inconsistent with the ideal type that governs an individual's perception of "man" as a social actor, these men challenge that ideal type and are thus ambiguous men for that individual. The individual regards ambiguous men ambivalently. He is both fascinated by their mystery and fearful of their implications for him. He both accepts and rejects them as men. In that he is confronted with manifest human ambiguity, the individual works to protect his certainty by denying this ambiguity by working to exclude ambiguous men from or to include them in humanity, or by disdaining or avoiding their significance. However, as long as the individual confronts manifest human ambiguity, absolute denial is impossible, ambivalence remains. The individual can assuage human ambiguity via certain means of assuagement or combinations of them that play out the individual's ambivalence such that an overt posture is defined and opposing tendencies are concealed.

The individual may be drawn to ambiguous

9

men for purposes of heroism. By building and using a "competence," the individual can build and demonstrate a "power" over human ambiguity and thus over his own self-certainty. A "competence" is a combination of means that enables the individual to seemingly, comfortably maintain a posture toward substantially ambiguous men, in substantial encounters with them.

The most powerful and thus heroic competences are sustained by "competence" institutions that establish contextual supports and impressive drama, and structure encounters with ambiguous men such that they can be thought of and treated as men. "Competence" institutions create a heroism that is sustained by a hypocrisy in a denial of countertendencies and by an illusion of power sufficient to stem manifest human ambiguity corporeally or to transcend it spiritually.

As central figures in a "competence" institution, nurses are "competence" professionals. They possess a humanitarian perspective that is buttressed, albeit imperfectly, by a medical perspective. Through humanitarian rituals, nurses affirm the humanity of patients who are ambiguous or potentially ambiguous. Through performing medical rituals and participating in the heroic dramas of physicians, nurses generate and witness an illusion of rehabilitative power, which fosters a hope vital for the maintenance of a humanitarian perspective in the face of acute manifest human ambiguity.

The hospital as a "competence" institution directly supports the humanitarian and medical perspectives in a number of ways. Humanitarian and medical rituals are institutionalized into nurses' roles. Nurses' status as Nurses is recognized and complemented by other functionaries and by most patients. The hospital context is fraught with the paraphernalia of medicine and with symbols of "institutional" egalitarianism. Medicine entails some real rehabilitative powers and much more cosmetic potential. Patients are so restricted and covered up that their abnormality is made less evident.

Despite the above supports, nurses' substantial contact with patients and nurses' humanitarianism limit their susceptability to an illusion of medical power. Nurses sometimes see medical "heroics" as mutilating and agonizing to no rehabilitative end. In such instances, medicine no longer supports nurses' "competence," and they would have it restrained. To maintain hope when medicine fails, nurses speculate about "death with dignity" and "debility with dignity," reasoning, in many cases erroneously, that sheer humanitarian supports can provide such dignity.

196   As counterpoints to the apparent, altruistic acceptance that characterizes Nursing, nurses practice a number of "antithetical" methods that are masked by the status and the routine of nurses. Nurses' identification with patients is limited by the formal, secondary nature of the nurse–patient relationship. Nurses and patients are substantially strangers to one another, persons whose association is limited to nurse–patient rituals. Identification with other nurses and rapid patient turnover are also factors that restrict identification with patients. Nursing tasks and responsibilities are various and extensive. They, thus, serve to divert nurses' attention from the ambiguity of patients, allowing nurses unobtrusively to avoid certain disturbing patients. The social demands of working in direct association with many co-workers and with many "more normative" patients also pull nurses attention away from ambiguity. On the other hand, since nurses are constrained to be near ambiguous men and to practice nursing, any obscene fascination nurses may have with disease and any attraction they may have to patients as mere objects for self-aggrandizing heroism are unapparent. Yet, nurses desire to be heroic; some engage in voyeurism, and others admit to anticipating medical emergencies.

Rehabilitative-humanitarian methods (Nursing) and hidden countermeasures seem insufficient to assuage the ambiguity of patients whose personalities are apparently deficient. Toward such patients, nurses employ a "prejudiced reaction" by which patients are treated as uncomprehending children or nonentities. To ease the incongruity presented by this approach, nurses tend to subdue any expression of hostility and to couch their actions in a humor meant to imply that apparently disrespectful treatment is not seriously so. In that an unaware patient calls no attention to himself, ignoring his social presence altogether is facilitated.

MASH also is not in keeping with the ethos of Nursing, although in mild form some argument can be made for it as uplifting distraction for patients. MASH is used as catharsis, as diversion, as masked hostility and as disdain for the dilemma of ambiguous men.

Nurses are not unaware of the horrors of disease; neither are they unaware of the inadequacy of medicine, their own inadequacy as humanitarians, the inhumanitarian ploys they use and their quest for heroism. The dilemma of mortality is also generally acknowledged. The awareness exists but is veiled. Nurses maintain some faith and pride in Nursing even while they doubt.

In the hospital, disease is banalized and a posture to it is cast.
Induration keeps the antithetical aspects of the Gregor Effect
from toppling nurses into manifest uncertainty. Nurses remain
certain enough to act and to live. Ultimately, however, an
underlying uncertainty remains, and competence remains
imperfect.

The Moral Development
of Nursing and Medicine

The Gregor Effect is a sober conception, and as such might have sobering effects if recognized; yet, its recognition is problematic in that it is perceived to be repugnant and thus incredible. To the extent that the exigencies and the limitations of human living are grim, the Gregor Effect is grim, as it reflects them. Yet, erroneous impressions of the Gregor Effect's implications may make it seem intolerably heinous. Such erroneous impressions are readily made since the Gregor Effect divulges the naked desires, insecurities and incapacities of men and thus cankers the altruistic and optimistic glosses of humanitarianism and medicine. Wrongly, the motives of all persons who care for the deformed or the disabled may seem impugned. Wrongly, all postures toward ambiguous men may seem equally and totally dissembling and niggardly. Wrongly, all efforts toward a wiser posture may seem futile.

Man is selfish, but this selfishness encompasses both what is "selfish" and "altruistic" in common usage. The individual craves orientation and thus a

10

meaningful definition of himself. Toward this end, he uses other people, both unambiguous and ambiguous men, the former for identification, the latter for plays of ascendency over the uncertainties of human identity. Such usage is not necessarily at odds with doctrinaire altruism. As the great religions have defined it, "altruism" is enlightened self-interest. One gives all to receive all. One loses oneself to find oneself. One does unto others that they may similarly do unto him. One looks beyond his corporeal, temporal self that he may be "saved," that he may be wise, and that he may ultimately be secure. One works to affirm a meaningful human identity for ambiguous men that one can feel more secure in one's own identity. Humanitarianism, medicine and spiritual transcendence are all means of this affirmation. Humanitarians attempt to see meaningful humanity in all the permutations of the living human form. Healers attempt to enforce corporeally a meaningful standard of human identity. Spiritualists attempt to see a meaningful continuation despite the deterioration and the dissolution of individuals. All three methods entail a reaching out, a service to others.

What part of his experience an individual incorporates as the self varies in scope from kernel to oceanic. He may view himself as some intangible aura focused in his body, or as his body, or his family, or his nation, or the totality of his experience. The scope of an individual's self varies from situation to situation. Sitting on a cliff, surveying a panorama, the individual may see the entire world as his self. Hanging from that cliff, his imperiled body may seem his self. Watching a parade on Flag Day, he may feel one with his nation.

Without anticipating reciprocity, a man may serve his environment, his nation, his religion, his family, or mankind because he identifies with them. Such acts selfishly serve his personal orientation, and yet, they are commonly considered "selfless" because they do not serve the body or the personality. Serving a greater self may cost the corporeal man much—perhaps even his life.

In any situation, the breadth of an individual's identification is not absolute since any number of self-concepts might be simultaneously operating more and less implicitly or consciously. As long as these perspectives govern different aspects of an individual's behavior, they need not conflict. Just as a man can believe something and not believe it all at the same time, so he can see himself as many things with little sense of incongruity unless a situation manifests a discrepency. A man may identify with his companions even though he also identifies with his bodily self. The distinction may remain mute being unconsciously respected by both the companions and the man. However, if a companion forced some untoward intimacy upon the man, the incongruence would emerge, and the man's identification with the companion would likely wane. On one level, a man may identify with his nation, and assume its causes as his own, and yet a more primordial interest may compel him to shield his body in battle, and thus to shrink from heroic transcendence.

The ambivalence inspired by ambiguous men arises from the fact that men both identify and shrink from identifying with ambiguous men as men, and cannot ignore the incongruence because of its significance. Men are primordially individual animals. They may think of themselves in broader or more rarefied terms, but the requisites of living are constant if sometimes quiet reminders that man is experience in terms of an animal. The ambiguous man, being problematic in his bodily identity, compels attention to man's primordial identity. In his ambivalence, the normative man is not caught on some middle ground, but in two places. He does see his humanity in the ambiguous man, and he does not see it all at the same time. His vision of the ambiguous man's humanity and his effort to augment this vision can be genuinely humanitarian in common usage. That this humanitarianism does not define the entire reaction does not mean that there is no humanitarianism. It means that men are imperfect humanitarians.

The "Gregor Effect" as an idea does not ferret out a deficiency of which men are unaware, nor an evil. Men who maintain that the ethos of humanitarianism or medicine governs their relations with deformed or debilitated patients also admit to imperfection. Practitioners realize that there are flaws in their own and their fellows' humanitarianism and medical professionalism, and attribute these flaws to human weakness. To err is human. Shortfalls in altruism are so accepted as to be expected. Men aspire, but they also sin; they are subject to insecurity and "selfishness."

Those persons who work with patients in hospitals know of the human folly and foibles that abound within. They know that doctors stray from the true spirit of medicine, and that nurses are sometimes wanting in humanitarianism. They know that they are not and cannot be saints. Thus, the inexorability of the Gregor Effect is not an outlandish idea, but a common perception. As an idea, the Gregor Effect does no more than explicate a

phenomenon that has heretofore been relegated to that unenligh-
tening category, "human nature."

As an idea, the Gregor Effect will be resisted because it is an
explanation. The phenomenon has been perceived vaguely for a
reason. A graphic description of human motivation and weakness
vis-à-vis ambiguous men is apparently incompatible with the
mystique necessary for heroic transcendence. The argument
runs: if one is to believe in doctors and nurses, one must not be
shown their feet of clay. As long as the ambivalence toward
ambiguous men can be shrugged off as mere human nature and
weakness, it can be acknowledged in soul-searching moments
but conveniently ignored during the practice of medicine or
nursing.

However, knowledge of the Gregor Effect, even if pervasively
held, would not vitiate heroic rituals. Although an explicit
conception is perhaps harder to ignore than a vague impression,
the Gregor Effect would not be touted during the heroic acts
themselves, and these acts would continue because they are
necessary. Indeed, understanding might better adapt these acts to
human needs.

As has been explained, artifice is a functional imperative of
medicine and nursing in the presence of acute human ambiguity.
In that one insists upon maintaining a medical or humanitarian
posture toward men who are beyond the pale, one must employ
artifice to a degree dependent upon the extent of their ambiguity.
Artifice serves four purposes:

1. Artifice is used to control, awing patients and families into a
   compliance necessary for the performance of a "competence."
2. Artifice is used to ameliorate, making patients and families
   feel better than reality would warrant.
3. Artifice is used to inspire a healing confidence, since hope is
   medicinal.
4. Finally, artifice is used to bolster the confidence of the
   practitioner so that he can continue with what medicine and
   humanitarianism he can provide.

Men find in society amelioration of the terror of existential
confusion and individual transiency. Societies seem permanent,
and through consensus, construction and rites combined into
heroic drama, comforting beliefs are reified and thus realized in
the minds of individuals. Heroic affirmation of preposterous

man-conjured power is essential for the hope essential for substantial individual tranquility. Heroics are a sham, but they foster human aspiration—the aspiration necessary for men to survive and to want to survive.

Being both intelligent and insecure, men do not have a perfect faith in their heroic fabrications, but vary in their adherence and employ backstage subterfuges to the extent that their faith falters. Whatever their faith, on some level men know that their heroics represent aspirations and hope. If the Gregor Effect were proselytized throughout the land, heroic postures toward ambiguous men would remain, as an explanation cannot obviate a need. In a sense, men have always known and yet have continued to pretend and will continue to pretend.

Understanding the Gregor Effect cannot eliminate the phenomenon itself, but it can temper it, and this temperance would better enable nurses and doctors to practice in accordance with humanitarian and medical ideals. A "competence," such as nursing or medicine, requires both a socially structured situation and an individual adaptation within that situation. If an individual is prompted toward or independently undertakes too open an effort to distance himself from ambiguous men, he flouts both humanitarian and medical ideals; on the other hand, if he is not allowed or does not allow himself sufficient occasion for distancing himself from acutely ambiguous men, he will be driven to exhaustion or to an exaggerated aversion that is also subversive to these ideals. To approximate humanitarian and medical ideals, one must suffer uncertainty. Artifice mitigates this uncertainty so that it is bearable, but artifice made intemperate, through either institutional instigation or individual predilection, subverts the ideals, as when the backstage dominates the frontstage, MASH masks cruelty, professionalism covers avoidance and futile medicine tortures. Overblown artifice buttressing an overblown sense of efficacy fosters cynicism and a heavier than necessary reliance on backstage compensations.

Heretofore, in attempting to understand society's relationship with ambiguous men, theorists have stressed the perspective of the ambiguous men themselves. The problems and the adaptations of ambiguous men have received much consideration. Their humanity has been emphasized by reference to their normal aspects, especially to their human efforts at adaptation to their predicaments. Underlying this literature is a premise that commiseration with the plight of the unwhole fosters their acceptance. Ignorance and prejudice are blamed for normative society's notion—a notion that if men were only more sensitive and humane, acceptance of ambiguous men would pose no problem, and their decent treatment would be assured.

Heretofore, training for either humanitarianism or the medical perspective has not been comprehensive. In our increasingly secular society, humanitarian training increasingly consists of consciousness raising. Humanitarianism is averred to be a patent truth and good. Workshops, seminars, lectures and readings all provide anecdotes demonstrating the humanity of (living) ambiguous men, and how a humane touch will coax from them greater human display. Medical neophytes are shown that bodies consist of parts, and are informed that what horror these parts hold is in the minds of the superstitious.

Such training is naive in that it does not account for the true dynamics of the relationship between ambiguous men and normative men. The ideas upon which this training is based entail no comprehensive understanding of the significance of ambiguous men for normative society or of the special ambivalence that they engender. In that covert adjustments are considered in either the do-gooder or the medical approach, they are considered as manifestations of human weakness or ignorance—catchall categories that explain nothing and provide no basis for optimal care for the unwhole or optimal adjustments for the caretakers.

Whether there is an optimal adaptation to prolonged encounters with ambiguous men is questionable. I suspect that adjustments meant to include ambiguous men in humanity are better than those meant to exclude them since fear is a concomitant of rejection; but I can proffer no proof. What is certain is that better adaptations are bearable approximations to institutionalized ideals. To approximate an ideal in spirit and in action is to approach certainty. An ideal that is institutionalized is more readily approximated than one which is not since an institution augments a devotee's effort through its rationales, rituals and orchestrated social support.

Although superior to idiosyncratic methods, "competence" institutions are unlikely to be as conducive as they might be to an idealistic posture toward ambiguous men. Institutions, like men, are fallible, and in the presence of ambiguous men, apparent idealism is extremely hard to stage and cast. Powerful ambivalence is not easily masked. Humility and aspiration are not readily balanced.

For humanitarianism and the medical ethic to be maximized

within hospitals, a careful balance must be maintained between an affirmation of these ideals and the backstage latitude required for the endurance of the practitioners. The ideals will be subverted if their authority is either too small or too great; in one case the practitioners will drift into perversion; in the other, they will be driven into perversion. The MASH in an intensive care unit can progress so far as to become a mania that strongly compromises humanitarianism, or the MASH can be so repressed, say by the head nurse, that tensions in the unit will compromise humanitarianism.

Knowledge of the Gregor Effect would provide a rationale for monitoring and moderating tension in nursing units. Nursing supervisors would be better able to recognize when backstage compensation is getting excessive, and when individual nurses are not coping well with the Gregor Effect. Special consideration might be given to those nurses, such as intensive care nurses, who confront the most acute human ambiguity. These nurses might be given special counseling or be allowed to have time off when they feel the need to get away from their work.

Knowledge of the Gregor Effect would also promote the well-being of nurses and the humanitarian ideal by creating an awareness of the importance of "heroic balance." As a heroic adaptation to human mortality, nursing must be heroically balanced to be wise. This balance is distinct from the balance between frontstage affirmations and backstage support. Heroic balance was described in my discussion of Ernest Becker, and is a contrapunctal combination of heroic humility and heroic aspiration, a combination that presupposes an apt understanding of man's existential predicament.

A comparison of contemporary American nursing with traditional religious "competences" suggests that nursing is lacking in overt ritual humility. This paucity is significant because rites of humility allow expiation and catharsis. Personal responsibility for a mortality, which is substantially beyond the control and understanding of man, is too heavy a burden to be continuously endured. By periodically admitting his dependence on a mysterious fate or God, an individual is relieved of both responsibility and guilt. He also joins himself with an entity or force greater than himself, be it existence itself or a deity. Resignation affords him both respite and some sense of oceanic power. Moreover, as a counterbalance to an aspirational heroism, humility tempers pretension. Some humility is essential for the maintenance of a humanitarian perspective in the chronic presence of incurable and acute human ambiguity. Private rites of humility have some utility, but the authority afforded by institutional rites better enables practitioners to wax oceanic since men are inclined to accept consensus as verification and to define what is socially real as existentially real.

The dearth of overt ritual humility in contemporary nursing is largely attributable to nursing's reliance on medicine. This reliance is inevitable and will likely grow. The virtual elimination of religion from hospitals makes a medical perspective essential for any inclusive adaptation. The increasing complexity of medical technology assures that nurses will make increasingly complex medical judgements and will perform increasingly complex medical techniques. Thus, the question of humility in nursing is intertwined with the question of humility in medicine.

Overt humility has always been difficult for healers since they have difficulty construing it as anything other than an admission of failure and impotence. A priest is not in this position. A priest can pray or conjure for a cure (aspirational heroism), but if there should be no cure, he can render acceptance of this fact an act of piety (humble heroism.) He can rationalize the most patent horror to attribute moral blame or to provide a positive interpretation in terms of a mysterious deity. He may be able to facilitate the deceased's passage into heaven. Before intractable deterioration and ambiguity, the priest remains plainly useful in his own terms, while the doctor does not; the doctor must endeavor not to appear paltry. In that a nurse plays the healer or the minion of a healing institution, she confronts a similar dilemma.

Nursing does have its humanitarian perspective, and its main humanitarian ritual, Tender Loving Care, is a classical rite of humility, but the increasingly medical orientation of nursing has attenuated the humility in this ritual. Over the last century in Western countries, nursing has been moving rapidly from alignment with Christianity to alignment with "scientific" medicine. Tender Loving Care—gentle, tactile, intimate, softspoken, commiserative ministration—in a Christian context denoted both acceptance of ambiguous men as men, and acceptance of manifest mortality (humble heroism). The nurse stoically confronted mucopurulence, stool, blood, stench, gross deformity and debility— on faith. Spiritual transcendence rendered morbidity more palatable and calm acceptance of morbidity denoted faith in spiritual transcendence. Normalization was also desired. Nurses have always worked to cure, but within the Christian context, therapeutic failure was more tolerable. Within the medical context,

Tender Loving Care ceases to be charity and becomes more purely therapy, a tactic in the treatment of disease. In that it is not therapy, TLC becomes "social work" and is used to coax patients into behaving more human.

Whether it be charity or therapy, Tender Loving Care constitutes a diminished role in the "competence" of today's more educated and "professional" nurses. The rationalizing of nursing care via "team nursing" has fragmented the nursing task such that the comprehensiveness of a nurse's contact with any one patient is reduced. Registered nurses are increasingly reserved for medical treatments, supervision and paper work, while patient care is becoming no longer their duty, nor the duty of student nurses, but the primary duty of a caste of subprofessional nurses (licensed practical nurses) and minimally trained auxiliaries. Professional nursing's "advance" from patient care has been a result of the medical and the administrative responsibilities placed upon nursing, and also the ambitions of nursing leaders for the elevation and "professionalization" of nursing.

The modern professional nurse is becoming more self-important. This development is also not conducive to humility. Overt humility before the tragic dimension of human existence comes easier for the poor and the downtrodden than it does for the more affluent and elevated. The former's social deprivation and powerlessness are analagous to their deprivation and powerlessness before a capricious fate, and thus one makes the other seem more inevitable. Humility comes harder to the socially elevated because men persist in confusing social preeminence and power with what might be termed existential preeminence and power. Being socially better is construed as being less mortal. Social elevation combined with some real advantage or efficacy is a barely resistable enticement toward hubris. Better living conditions, better nutrition and better medical care that the affluent can afford are salubrious. Medicine cures many persons and partially normalizes many more. That these advantages and this efficacy are meager in the greater scheme of things does not deter men from playing at omnipotence. Nurses are not so lofty as physicians and therefore nurses are not so subject to inflation, and yet at least the more educated nurses are increasingly sharing a difficulty with humility long encountered by physicians and hierarchs.

Undoubtedly, some people will disagree with this assessment of medicine on the grounds that "objective" realism is the essence of the medical approach to mortality, and that medical education is a lesson in humility if not humiliation. Medical 207 students may be something of an intellectual and social elite, but medical school tempers their self-appraisal by first overwhelming them with the sheer scope of medical knowledge and their inability to master more than a portion of it, and then by impressing them with the meagerness of medical power and knowledge in relation to mortality and the remaining mysteries of the human body. During the first semester, the medical student meets human anatomy in the form of a corpse. Doctors touch mortality and morbidity regularly, and their own limited efficacy. Surely, doctors must practice some humility if only for release from what would otherwise be an unbearable burden of guilt.

Ironically, intimate and graphic contact with reality does not nurture overt humility in physicians, just because this contact dampens rehabilitative optimism. Direct confrontation with the infinite and personal finiteness as a rite of passage for medical neophytes is a momentary unpleasantness that is also electrifying defiance and a consecration by which healers are forever parted from the common man. Men will suffer humiliation as a right of passage, but men will suffer strain on the path to maturity that they will not suffer on reaching that maturity. Most youths do not anticipate an adulthood of fear and trembling and sickness unto death, and the adult more frequently than not settles for a compromised but more comfortable perspective. The education that scales healers small within the universe, scales them large among men. Quickly, medicine becomes substantially a mundane task worked in a world of men in which man's relation to society is of greater moment than his relation to the universe. So supported, the aspirational heroism of modern medicine brooks no defeatism masquerading as virtue. To become Odysseus, the healer becomes a "positive thinker" (euphemistically) or arrogant (prejoratively).

Yet, reality is not to be entirely denied, for such in itself would be an unbearable burden. Some expiation is necessary, and doctors do have rites of humility, though they are not readily recognizable as such. The rites are covert. Doctors do periodically, bluntly assess the incurable and the unviable with other doctors and other hospital personnel behind the scenes of overt medical drama. Futility and impotence are acknowledged, at times, almost crudely as if humility in medicine is so unacceptable that expression of it must be obscene. Covert humility becomes counterpoint cynicism to overt medical positivism.

With a certain rueful hostility, patients and conditions are dismissed with a curt word or phrase, or with sarcastic MASH. As an alternative, deadpan technical description is used. With little apparent provocation, the practitioner makes an expressionless soliloquy recounting a detailed and unfortunate history of a patient's condition, tests, and treatments. The "objectified" description, concealing a sigh or a bite, externalizes the event, placing it in the realm of natural events, and thus the practitioner is purged while his evident esoteric command affirms his esoteric powers. Unless particularly jaded, practitioners usually conceal their expiation from patients and the general public.

The covertness of medicine's humility signifies that it is unheroic—enacted via medicine's backstage, those "medical" means of assuagement that counter the medical ideal. This alignment with the backstage holds portentious implications for medicine. This alignment means that humanitarianism is forgone in favor of diversion and expressive aversion. It means that the "humility" that ballasts the hubris of healers does not temper overt medical practice; cynicism not only permits callous treatments and futile heroics, it fosters them. Covertness perverts humility, transforming it from a strength and a virtue into a weakness and a sin.

This assessment of medicine is of its institutionalization. It is not thereby an assessment of individual healers. No institution can subsume individual adaptation. Each individual bears private beliefs that may bend his adaptation toward humanitarian humility. Such an influence is made more likely by the fact that humanitarianism is mouthed as a medical ideal. Thus, some humanitarian physicians undoubtedly exist, and perhaps most physicians are marginally humanitarian. However, within an institutional setting, the sway of an institution is formidable over those men who willingly identify with it. Institutional change is essential if humanitarian humility is to become the prime counterpoint to medical aspiration.

Humble humanitarian heroism is the optimal ballast for aspirational medical heroism. Both are "inclusive" in that they seek to bind ambiguous men to humanity. Both, being inclusive, can share the frontstage. An overt humanitarianism can temper the excesses of an overt medicine, and vice-versa. Also, humanitarianism is the only ideological means of assuagement that is both "inclusive" and exclusively "humble." Thus, unlike spiritual transcendence, which might pit incantations against therapies, humanitarianism poses no "aspirational" challenge to medicine.

Medicine's conception of ambiguous man as "man-with-a-malady" approximates humanitarianism's conception of ambiguous man as "man-no-matter-what." Except for their heroic polarity, humanitarianism and medicine are compatible.

This compatibility combined with America's cultural definition of good medical practice would seem to assure that actual medical practice combined medicine with humanitarianism. Doctors, after all, are supposed to be humanitarians. Some confusion of terminology is involved in this supposition; yet it is reasonable to assume that cultural wisdom for doctors entails both ambition and humility, just as it does for everyone else. Therefore, the fact that humanitarian humility is not an operational ideal of modern medicine requires some explanation, more than has heretofore been given if the introduction of humanitarianism into medical practice is to be contemplated.

The continued humanitarianism of frontline nursing personnel results from a situation that medical practitioners and administrators do not and could not share. Relative to doctors, frontline nursing personnel are less identified with medical ritual, less elite and in more social contact with individual patients; consequently, these personnel are less able to credit medical pretensions and more likely to have substantial and egalitarian interaction with patients. As the humble complement to normalization, humanitarianism emerges as a logical response to this situation. Therefore, physicians might be moved toward humanitarianism if they were more involved with nutritive care, were less prestigious and were in more contact with fewer patients. Such change might be promoted but could not be sufficiently developed to sustain much humanitarianism since change of this scope would presuppose simple organizational structure and simple medical technology. Institutionalized medicine is on the opposite track. Some of the division of labor in patient treatment and care may be functionally unnecessary, and some of the complexity of modern medical techniques may be overblown, but enough technical complexity exists to assure that physicians will not become bedside nurses and vice-versa. Those persons, doctors and nurses, who orchestrate medical treatment and patient care are not now, nor will they be concurrently subject to the humbling effects of administering direct patient care.

As has been stated, overt humility in any form is difficult for healers since it attenuates the type that is both psychologically essential to them and functionally imperative to their role.

210 Humanitarianism, however, is in itself such a prestigeful persuasion in this society that some measure of humanitarianism would likely be welcomed by the medical profession if objection to humanitarianism were merely a matter of its being a humble heroism.

Medical practitioners eschew humanitarianism because they view it erroneously as both more and less than a humble heroism. In the first case, humanitarianism holds an unwarranted association for modern physicians. Humanitarianism's traditional alignment with spiritual transcendence within Christianity has caused the medical profession to associate humanitarianism with superstitious, ineffective cant that for centuries forestalled scientific, effective medicine. The advent of modern medicine was a revolution against traditional practices concocted of nostrums and incantations, and bearing a resemblance and often a connection to religious practice. Revolutionary ardor broadened intolerance for curative cant into intolerance for all rituals of religious derivation, including humanitarian rituals. This prejudice has been institutionalized in large part because medicine's sometimes heady successes and almost continuous minor innovations have fomented an expectation that ever greater medical power can be had through a singular dedication to medicine.

In light of a radiant hope for what amounts to ultimate curative omnipotence, the acceptance of an ambiguous man as a man hardly seems courageous, and thus humanitarianism's heroic proportions are diminished. The medical profession thinks in these terms:

> To cater to the ambiguous man as a man when medicine is available borders on foolishness or negligence. To stress a humanitarian manner in lieu of a medical one smells of heresy, the supplanting of a potentially effective measure with a definitely ineffective measure which, like religious incantation, is merely expressive of an imagined reality. Sociable acceptance, like incantation, is a palliative for the impotent. If there is to be any real man-bred hope, medicine must be the answer, and if no hope can be conjured for an individual patient, medicine must still be the answer if there is to be hope for similarly afflicted patients in the future.

Humanitarianism is further bereft of its heroic proportions by being confused with a pretender. The medical profession does not consider problematic the perception of ambiguous man as man. For the medically enlightened, all patients are just men who are sick. Humanitarianism in this sense becomes a mundane activity that men practice without much ado; but this mundane activity is pseudohumanitarianism, a pastiche mostly of normalization, diversion and avoidance. Physicians, mistaking the ersatz for the real thing, view themselves as humanitarians by virtue of being doctors.

Medical practitioners must be disabused of misimpressions concerning humanitarianism if there is to be any prospect of its introduction into medical "competence." Doctors must know the following:

1. Overt humanitarianism would not forestall medical progress, but would modulate and refine it such that future medical developments would more certainly serve mankind.
2. Medicine does not nor is it ever likely to surmount mortality, and therefore not only is some humble adaptation not futile, it is perennially essential to the well-being of patients and practitioners.
3. No earthly enlightenment will render perfunctory the acceptance of ambiguous men as men. Such acceptance will always be a heroic challenge.
4. Humanitarianism is not synonymous with normalization. The humanitarian deems the ambiguous man to be an equal in terms of a mutual humanity. During a humanitarian act, the human status is paramount, and thus the humanitarian also deems the ambiguous man to be a social equal due the consideration and the empathy worthy of a friend. Universal love is the ultimate expression of humanitarianism. The healer is bent on rehabilitation. In this task, the healer may serve the ambiguous man, but the healer does not have to consider the ambiguous man to be an equal in any sense. Normalization does not impel the healer to love his patient either in fact or in the abstract.

Even a broad acceptance of the foregoing principles would not be sufficient to institutionalize a heroic humanitarianism in the practice of medicine. Any institutionalization of humanitarianism requires a supportive ideology and affirmative rituals. Humanitarianism in medicine would require a well-developed rational authority to complement in kind and in degree the authority of medical normalization. Nursing's humanitarian ideology would be inadequate since it is truncated, rationalizing its rituals, but neither explaining nor justifying humanitarianism itself. Tradition validates nursing humanitarianism, a tradition derived from religion, but now bereft of religious substance. Humanitarian tradition separated from its roots cannot provide credible rationales for a heroic cast or for innovative rituals suitable for modern medical practitioners.

American humanitarianism has been and still is sanctioned by God, either explicitly or implicitly. A secular philosophical validation has yet to be developed which can compete with this divine validation in directness, simplicity and authority. As a result, secular polemics for humanitarianism are rarely heard in secular America. Instead, humanitarianism is presented as so obvious a truth and good that it requires no verification. It is brandished like a crucifix before which the heartless must shrink. If the situation requires some justification, there is usually a nod toward God. When the Nazis challenged the humanitarian ideal internationally, many secular humanitarians became religious recidivists in their condemnation. The resolutely secular were reduced to muttering about "civilized" behavior or were left aghast.

Despite the dearth of immediate precedents, a supportive, secular philosophy should be developed and promulgated if humanitarianism is to be sustained in medicine, since a significant introduction of religion within hospitals is doubtful. Private religious belief, unritualized within hospitals, does not and could not alter appreciably the hospital milieu. Many doctors and nurses are already privately religious to minimal avail. Many hospitals have nominal ties to religious sects, but these ties become evident only when there is some topical controversy such as abortion or euthanasia, and do not much influence the daily operation of the hospitals. If religion is to stand with medicine, hospitals must have an improbable development of religious rituals and religious consensus.

Religion and modern medicine are not mutually exclusive, but they are not readily compatible. In order for there to be a significant infusion of religious rituals into medical practice, medicine's prejudice against rituals of spiritual transcendence would have to be overcome, but this turnaround is improbable since the prejudice is justifiable. Between prominent religion and prominent medicine, jurisdictional confusion would be a difficult problem. Any medically tolerable division of labor between religion and medicine would consign religion to the comfort of the incurable. Such an assignment would cast religion virtually as a harbinger of evil and demise within the hospital. Unless medicine were subverted, medical tests and treatments would continue to take precedence over religious ceremonies, thereby diminishing to incredibility religious authority that is supposed to be ultimate and absolute. Religious and medical ceremonies might be combined, or individual ceremonies might be imbrued with both religious and medical significance, but such efforts would likely seem contrived. While they perform surgery, doctors may pray aloud, but such practice would seem patently incongruous in contemporary operating rooms. Religious ceremonies are stylized expressions of revealed truth; it would be difficult to conceive of them as medical techniques, and difficult to conceive of medical techniques as religious rituals.

Some inspired combination of religion and medicine is possible, but the requirements are severe. Religious humility (eschewing religious aspiration) might ballast medical aspiration. Prayer might be so combined with medicine that prayer would acknowledge the proportion of man to the universe, and would thereby ease the pain of medical defeat such that doctors would be better able to stop curing and to start alleviating. Such prayers could not be cliches, but would have to represent a religion to which the practitioners genuinely, consensually adhere. Medical pragmatism and a myth of pragmatism foment within hospitals a quotidian bustle most inconducive to spiritual contemplation; to create some spiritual pause in this bustle would require a pervasive and a strong conviction to do so.

The humanitarianizing presence of religion in hospitals requires a religious consensus comparable to the existing medical consensus; but in this polyglot and substantially secular land, such a religious consensus would require a national religious revolution. Contemporary American medical schools could hardly imbue their students with a religious faith. Truly sectarian hospitals would belie the homogeneity of medicine, and would foster a societally unacceptable disparity among hospitals. A national ecumenical religious presence, innocuous to all major persuasions, would be ideologically etiolated and ritually unconvincing. Religions ostensibly derive from divine revelation, but a babel of conflicting revelations and exigeses is certain to obliterate the authority of religion in the prime preserve of a far more monolithic medicine.

Though difficult, a secular approach is more feasible than a religious one to the institutionalization of humanitarian heroism within medical practice. Some faith in spiritual transcendence

214 may be necessary to a medical practitioner if he is to maintain a primarily receptive contact with severely ambiguous men, and yet a ritual affirmation of this faith is not essential to his humanitarian effort in hospitals. The practitioner's faith can remain implicit if his humanitarian heroism is secularly substantiated and ritualized. Since a secular humanitarianism would not be divinely authorized, and since the authority of sheer human will would be incredible to the medically-minded, a secular substantiation of humanitarianism must be rational and empirically premised, and the concomitant ritualization must seem pragmatic. A secular, rational, empirical, pragmatic and inclusive humanitarianism is the most congruent heroic complement to a secular, rational, empirical, pragmatic and inclusive normalization.

The foundations of an appropriate humanitarian ideology are found in this book, in its explanation and elaboration of the Gregor Effect. These expositions contribute to either an understanding of humanitarianism vis-à-vis ambiguous men or to a polemic for its ritualization in medical practice: (1) the inevitability and the nature of normative society's ambivalence toward ambiguous men, (2) the necessity and the nature of heroic confrontation with manifest human ambiguity, (3) the challenge and a description of humanitarian heroism, (4) the necessity of affirmative rituals for the maintenance of any heroic stance, (5) the wisdom of heroic balance between aspiration and humility, (6) an explanation of modern medical practice's heroic imbalance and its need for overt rituals of humility, and (7) reasons why humanitarianism is the best heroic complement to medical positivism.

A humanitarian concept derived from an understanding of the Gregor Effect could be an important factor in a wise resolution of major questions concerning medical practice. Medical practitioners are currently without definitive mores concerning the use of life-support for unviable patients, the propriety of euthanasia, the use of painful and debilitating methods which are of marginal or questionable utility, the development and use of mutagenic techniques, and the development and use of physiological mind control. The medical technology, largely responsible for these uncertainties, will continue to grow, exacerbating them. Medical practitioners cannot cope wisely with the major choices involved unless they understand humanitarianism, balance aspiration with humility, and comprehend the nature of their motivation and its capacity to pervert an ideal.

This book does not elaborate fully a humanitarian ideology for medical practice since an exhaustive empirical verification and demonstration of the concepts presented is beyond the scope of this work; however, such an elaboration is imminently possible. The suppositions that expound the Gregor Effect are testable and demonstrable. A desire for a humanizing of the health care system is growing in this country, and there will likely be many explications of medical and nursing practices that will directly or indirectly demonstrate or refine the Gregor Effect and the conception of humanitarianism presented here.

The affirmation of a "medical" humanitarian ideology would be culturally familiar. This ideology would be no more than a suitable clarification of an ancient wisdom. The medical humanitarian would acknowledge tragedy and pathos. He would consider his work to be more of a calling than a profession. He would consider the welfare of patients in terms of their personalities rather than in terms of their potential for rehabilitation. He would question existing and proposed tools, techniques, policies and facilities to discern whether they serve primarily patients or the self-importance of practitioners and administrators.

The heroic rituals themselves would exhibit humility and the utilitarian pragmatism of modern medicine. They would be neither histrionic nor highly stylized, but would be a studied courtesy combined with a professional openness akin to that which some laymen and practitioners now espouse. The humanitarian-medical practitioner would systematically scrutinize his patients to ascertain their needs and desires both as men and as personalities. The practitioner's careful judgement of his patients' needs and desires would determine his demeanor toward them and his use of available medical procedures. This judgment and the courage to act upon it would be heroic in that they cannot be easy. The humanitarian-medical practitioner must confront his patients as men and in so doing, he must confront the consequences of his work. He must try to share his knowledge and his decisions with his patients, but he must also not harm them. The calculation of benefit and harm is especially complicated for the humanitarian-medical practitioner since he must determine them not merely in terms of normalization, but in terms of his patients' total welfare as men with consideration for their individual personalities and medical prognoses.

Humanitarianism would promote a greater participation of patients in medical practice, but not so much that the heroism of physicians is vitiated. The humanitarian-medical practitioner would tend to explain conditions and procedures, and share decisions with patients, but he would not do so uniformly with all patients, nor would he share all his relevant knowledge or decisions with any patient. The humanitarian healer cannot relinquish his heroic stature either as a humanitarian or as a healer, and his patients cannot comfortably accept this relinquishment. In many instances, deferring decisions to patients or families fosters character among them, absolves the physician of some responsibility, and accommodates cultural relativity. However, in many instances the conditions or the personalities of patients and families render a practitioner's openness futile or irresponsible in terms of rehabilitation and humaneness. Ultimately, the physician's role as priest of a heroic "competence" requires him to interpret the realities he shares with patients. As a hero in the assuagement of manifest human ambiguity, the physician has been and will continue to be sought for his wisdom as well as for his technical expertise.

The institutionalization of humanitarianism into medical practice requires the development of norms to guide and to support practitioners in their expanded role. A philosophy alone can sometimes inspire a man toward commensurate activity, but an institutional ritualization of the philosophy makes this activity less dependent upon individual character by setting a pattern and making it expected behavior. However, if a man is to possess a humanitarian "competence" before manifest human ambiguity, his behavior must be part of a scenario since orchestrated social support is essential to all "competences." Thus, normative humanitarian procedures must be developed. "Professional" procedures may be adopted by which a physician can learn the characters and the desires of his patients. A physician who failed to follow these procedures would be practicing medicine reprehensibly. Norms must also be developed which delineate humanitarian-medical criteria for judgement under an array of circumstances. Individual situations require the judgements of individual practitioners, but major, common questions concerning the relative importance of the quality of life, the rights of patients to self-determination, and physicians' commitment to rehabilitation must be answered consensually because these dilemmas are too great a burden to be borne idealistically by individuals.

Certain conditions may have to be altered. If the typical

workload of physicians is found to be too large for them to be properly humanitarian, the number of physicians may be increased or the increased use of medical auxiliaries may be fostered to reduce the workload of individual physicians. The manner and the amount in which physicians are paid, the settings in which patients are seen, the delineation of responsibility for individual patients and the manner in which patients select physicians may be among the circumstances that are found to be pertinent to physicians' propensity or capacity for humanitarianism.

If humanitarianism is developed in medical practice, this development will arise from the deliberations and the proselytizing of many men. Receptivity to a humanitarian conception will develop out of a growing dissatisfaction nurtured by the heroic imbalance of contemporary medicine. Supportive norms for an accepted humanitarian conception will evolve via a broad effort. Medical educators, theorists and practitioners will consider and debate many specific issues in light of the new humanitarian spirit. These men will promote, try and temper reforms in the mores and the conditions of medical practice. The process will be arduous since the provision of medical care is complex, the requisites of rehabilitative medicine must be accommodated, and traditional adaptations are entrenched.

The education of new doctors and nurses in humanitarian ideology and practice must be commensurate with current rehabilitative education. Small children will not be removed to monasteries for instruction in the fine art of being a humanitarian doctor, however efficacious such a method might be. Student nurses will not return to cloistered three-year training programs. Classroom instruction, seminars, workshops and the examples of established practitioners—the open measures of the time— must be brought to bear on neophytes who are not impressionable children. The scientific and technical training in medical rehabilitation must be matched by a social scientific training in humanitarianism.

Nurses and doctors need a theoretical understanding of their professions, the functions that these professions perform for society and the nature of the relationship between man and ambiguous man. Nurses and doctors do not need "pop" sociology for bleeding-heart humanitarians, but serious sociology that can impress upon the scientifically-minded the importance of understanding the social dynamics of health care to the wise practice of medicine, and the importance of humanitarianism, not as nice behavior, but as an effective method of adaptation to manifest human ambiguity.

The achievement of a heroic balance between humanitarianism and normalization in medicine and in nursing will facilitate "inclusive" adaptations to ambiguous men, and thus will promote closer approximations to both humanitarian and rehabilitative ideals. There is an old saying that power corrupts. In the case of medicine, the self-aggrandizement of physicians combined with the pretensions of medical practice nurture a cynicism and a callousness that are detrimental to health care and to the spiritual well-being of the physicians themselves. Unable to admit their limitations and the awesomeness of fate, physicians dwell too much on status, money and hegemony over the provision of health care. Only humanitarianism can check this destructive hubris that is spreading throughout the hospital from physicians to nurses and technicians.

Humanitarianism cannot cure, but it can mitigate the impersonality of hospitals and the muted horror inherent in this impersonality. Organizationally, hospitals reflect their society. The utilitarian, rational organization of hospitals in which strangers serve strangers via formal roles is unavoidable in an urban and mobile society in which a complex division of labor grows incessantly more complex. Hospitals process patients, just as General Motors processes cars and insurance companies process claims. The impersonal management of patients and the medical manipulation of bodies may be incongruent with the pathos of individual suffering, physical deterioration and death, but humanitarians cannot close this gap short of drastic societal change. They can promote an awareness of this gap, and thereby narrow it. Each patient may be assigned a "primary" physician, a "primary" nurse, a "primary" physical therapist, a "primary" nutritionist and so forth; however, as long as a paucity of true primary relationships exists between patients and their caretakers, some avoidance and alienation will be inherent in the system.

Even if they could be freely applied, institutional reforms can do only so much. They can improve an institution's capacity to support and to enforce wise and idealistic behavior, but only to some indefinite limit. No choreography, no system can expunge or circumvent either ambivalence toward ambiguous men or the horror inherent in mortality. Heroic balance will reduce but not end the need for backstage compensations. The men who care

for ambiguous men will never be able to accept (or to reject)
them fully. Nothing can make confrontations with acute manifest human ambiguity easy. Nothing can make hospitals halcyon; men suffer, rot and die there.

An institution sets the stage and provides the scripts; individuals make the interpretations. Individual interpretations derive from individual personalities that are wild cards in determining adaptations to ambiguous men. At any time, a personality is the product of a development that is substantially indiscernable and idiosyncratic. Standardization in training cannot standardize practitioners since their experiences cannot be standardized from birth to diploma, and since even if such standardization could be achieved, men will differ in strength, abilities and character. Each man is variable and somewhat volatile, having many faces and moods marking his multifarious efforts at orientation, and these aspects of himself variegate his relationship to his world even in his performance of a single role. In a profession, social control circumscribes appearances. These circumscriptions will cull and dissuade from the profession persons who cannot or will not meet them; yet they must be sufficiently broad to accommodate personalities, and thus they will always be sufficiently indefinite to necessitate individual moral struggle.

Ultimately, all adaptations to manifest human ambiguity are individual ones. Medicine, for example, allows many subtle variations of emphasis and would regardless of how it were reformed. Among healers, some are partial to social acclaim and status; others seek gratitude or skill or medical results. Some physicians are more selfish in their quest for heroism, while others are more altruistic. Some physicians use mankind for personal aggrandizement, while others help themselves through serving mankind.

The true humanitarian-medical hero is a person who closely approximates his institution's ideal; a wise hero is one who approximates this ideal without exhaustion and who thus endures as a hero. To be a hero is difficult; to be a wise hero is more difficult. To be a wise hero, a person must understand, explicitly or implicitly, human needs and limitations vis-à-vis manifest human ambiguity. He must be wise enough and strong enough to confront human ambiguity and to suffer the attendant doubt, but he must also be wise enough to accept his limitations even as he strives to transcend them. A hero is a self-creation, a personal work of art. His adaptation is an inspired integration of his personality and his calling, and a careful balance of pride and humility. A hero's achievement is dynamic and athletic. Equanimity toward human ambiguity is not an end that man can achieve, but one toward which he can strive. No living man is ever at peace; living is a continuous challenge, which a man can confront or from which he can shrink, but which he cannot elude. The heroic role requires relentless discipline. A hero does not surmount his doubt and ambivalence; he compresses them into resolve. He keeps to the straight and narrow despite a raft of psychic temptations.

Most people do not have the will or the inspiration for a personal or true heroism, but rely on collective images sustained with unheroic amounts of avoidance and diversion; yet the struggle for the hero and the commoner is the same. Doctors and nurses usually settle for the heroism of being doctors and nurses. Thinking themselves realistic, they tolerate and even expect a degree of hypocrisy in themselves and their fellows. The true hero both inspires and threatens common practitioners since he shows them their potential and their failings. The mediocre value the hero's elevation of their collective image, but the mediocre are also comforted by mediocrity. Yet, even among the medical and the nursing proletariat, there are better and worse doctors and nurses, stronger and weaker ones, wiser and more foolish ones. The moral struggle for them is not qualitatively different than it is for the true hero. Every individual works to be oriented, and heroism comes in degrees.

Between man and ambiguous man the human condition is dramatized. As in a morality play, denouement characterizes society and mortality assumes bodily form as the ambiguous man. In facing manifest human ambiguity, a person acts in a play within a play. His adaptation to ambiguous man models his adaptation to life itself.